This is a philosophical treatment of ı
conceptual and normative aspects
topics which are currently a matter oı
policy debate in education. The authors
have focused on such concepts as
liberty, autonomy, equality and pluralism, and have provided a philosophical
commentary which relates these concepts
both to a background of philosophical
literature, and to the institutional
contexts and policy debates in which
they function. The book will be of
significance not only to the philosophical
specialist, but also to all policy makers
who need to gain an understanding of
the values and concepts involved in
major policy problems.

The Editors
Kenneth A. Strike is Associate Professor
of Education at Cornell University. He
has previously taught at Northwestern
University and the University of
Wisconsin. Kieran Egan is Associate
Professor of Education at Simon Fraser
University, Burnaby, Canada. Both
editors have written widely on the
philosophy of education.

International
Library of the
Philosophy of
Education

**Ethics and
educational
policy**

International Library of the Philosophy of Education

General Editor

R. S. Peters

Professor of Philosophy of Education
University of London
Institute of Education

Ethics and educational policy

Edited by

Kenneth A. Strike

Associate Professor
Department of Education
Cornell University
New York

and

Kieran Egan

Assistant Professor
Faculty of Education
Simon Fraser University
British Columbia

Routledge & Kegan Paul

London, Henley and Boston

First published in 1978
by Routledge & Kegan Paul Ltd
39 Store Street,
London WC1E 7DD,
Broadway House,
Newtown Road,
Henley-on-Thames,
Oxon RG9 1EN and
9 Park Street,
Boston, Mass. 02108, USA
Printed in Great Britain by
Redwood Burn Ltd
Trowbridge and Esher

British Library Cataloguing in Publication Data

    Ethics and educational policy. — (International
    library of the philosophy of education).

    1. Education – Philosophy
    I. Strike, Kenneth A   II. Egan Kieran
    III. Series
    370.1   LB41   77–30516

ISBN 0 7100 8423 4

Contents

vi Contents

General editor's note

There is a growing interest in philosophy of education
amongst students of philosophy as well as amongst those
who are more specifically and practically concerned with
educational problems. Philosophers, of course, from the
time of Plato onwards, have taken an interest in education
and have dealt with education in the context of wider concerns about knowledge and the good life. But it is only
quite recently in this country that philosophy of education has come to be conceived of as a specific branch of
philosophy like the philosophy of science or political
philosophy.

To call philosophy of education a specific branch of
philosophy is not, however, to suggest that it is a distinct branch in the sense that it could exist apart from
established branches of philosophy such as epistemology,
ethics, and philosophy of mind. It would be more appropriate to conceive of it as drawing on established branches of philosophy and bringing them together in ways
which are relevant to educational issues. In this respect
the analogy with political philosophy would be a good one.
Thus, use can often be made of work that already exists in
philosophy. In tackling, for instance, issues such as the
rights of parents and children, punishment in schools, and
the authority of the teacher, it is possible to draw on
and develop work already done by philosophers on 'rights',
'punishment', and 'authority'. In other cases, however,
no systematic work exists in the relevant branches of
philosophy - e.g. on concepts such as 'education',
'teaching', 'learning', 'indoctrination'. So philosophers
of education have had to break new ground - in these cases
in the philosophy of mind. Work on educational issues can
also bring to life and throw new light on long-standing
problems in philosophy. Concentration, for instance, on
the particular predicament of children can throw new light

on problems of punishment and responsibility. G.E.
Moore's old worries about what sorts of things are good
in themselves can be brought to life by urgent questions
about the justification of the curriculum in schools.

There is a danger in philosophy of education, as in any
other applied field, of polarization to one of two
extremes. The work could be practically relevant but
philosophically feeble; or it could be philosophically
sophisticated but remote from practical problems. The
aim of the new International Library of the Philosophy
of Education is to build up a body of fundamental work in
this area which is both practically relevant and philosophically competent. For unless it achieves both types
of objective it will fail to satisfy those for whom it is
intended and fall short of the conception of philosophy
of education which the International Library is meant to
embody.

This collection of papers on 'Ethics and Educational
Policy' continues the policy of the International Library.
It concentrates mainly on topical problems such as liberal
education under current conditions, students' rights and
compulsory education, autonomy as an educational aim and
the 'freedom of free schools', cultural diversity and
equality of educational opportunity, and the connection
between technology and education values. These are dealt
with mainly by well-known figures in American philosophy
of education. But the problems are not local ones, which
should make the collection of interest to readers on both
sides of the Atlantic. It should also contribute to
answering the criticism that philosophers of education,
because of their interest in concepts, ignore or take for
granted major issues of policy.

Introduction

The papers in this book aim to contribute to that still
slight body of literature which uses appropriate philosophical skills towards the clarification and resolution
of practical educational problems. Such an aim has long
been explicit in educational philosophy, but its achievement has been quite rare. The proper balance of focusing
on practical educational issues and effectively using
philosophical skills has been more difficult to achieve
than it seems intuitively it ought. Too frequently either
the educational issue has been clear but philosophical
tools have been employed inappropriately or incompetently,
or methods derived from academic philosophy have so dominated that the educationally crucial, but philosophically
inconvenient, core of the issue has been left untouched.
If our Scylla is philosophical incompetence, our Charybdis
is to be so sucked into philosophical discourse that we
lose our educational goal.

Attempts to apply philosophy to educational problems
in this century may be described as involving two fairly
distinct phases. The distinction is now commonly made
between that style which saw philosophy of education as
developing a systematic and coherent world-view and
deriving from it appropriate recommendations for educational practice, and the more recent application of the
tools of modern philosophical analysis to educational
concepts.

In the former phase debate occurred between advocates
of comprehensive positions wearing labels such as prag-
matism, essentialism, transactionalism, idealism, etc.
The training of novices involved laying out the con-
stituents and implications of each, especially the educational implications, and leaving the novice more or less
free to adhere to the -ism with which he or she had most
sympathy. This conception of philosophy of education was

susceptible to breaking up on the Scylla of inappropriate
or incompetent philosophizing. It involved the largely
abandoned conception of philosophy as a kind of super-
science, incorporating and integrating all human knowledge. Such philosophers of education aimed to produce,
or espouse, a philosophy which provided a grand perspective on education together with an implementing set
of prescriptions. Only the very greatest minds could be
expected to do this with any measure of coherence and
success. For the rest, the gulf between academic philosophy and philosophy of education left them without the
intellectual support of a philosophical training and led
increasingly to philosophical vacuousness.

While perhaps philosophically weak, this older phase of
philosophy of education was in some ways more substantial
than what replaced it. It pronounced on problems which
people who never darkened the door of a philosophy classroom regarded as problems. It was a respected component
of educational policy debates, and as its practitioners
were sometimes opinion leaders, it sometimes produced
consequences in educational practice. Its major practitioners were occasionally people of some cultural
weight, and even if their philosophies and recommendations
seem to reduce to something like the assertion: 'Make
people like me (without the warts)!', it was worth educators listening because the production of such educated
people was clearly a sensible goal.

In the late 1950s and early 1960s the second phase
became prominent. This conception of philosophy of education saw its purpose as nearly as possible to that which
had come to prevail in academic philosophy - most commonly
associated with the emphasis on 'analysis.' Its aim was
clarity, its utility was to be precision of discourse,
and its focus was on the language of education. Philosophers of education thus began analysing concepts such
as knowing, teaching, learning, etc.

This new emphasis seems to have succeeded in improving
the quality of scholarship in educational philosophy, but
at a price, for it has also reduced its relevance to
educational issues of concern to most educators. Clarity
is after all a limited virtue. It might be vital to
phrasing questions in a manner such that they can be
informatively answered, but clarity does not answer substantive questions. Nothing, prescriptively or factually,
follows from the meaning of a term. Anyone who derives
a fact or norm from the analysis of a concept has made
a mistake. Philosophy in this conception is a second
order discipline.

The problem with a second order discipline is that for

it to influence the world of decision-making, it needs
consumers among those who actually make the decisions.
One of the results of being sucked into the Charybdis
of philosophical analysis has been the steady loss of such
consumers for the work of most educational philosophers.
Many educational decision-makers simply lacked the skills
and concepts to be able to deal with philosophical
literature of an analytic kind, and the products of it
that they could make sense of did not convince them it
was worth their while developing such skills.

This disenchantment has been further exacerbated by
the unwillingness of many modern philosophers of education, following academic philosophy, to engage norms or
facts. For example, philosophy of this kind might analyse
ethical discourse but it cannot tell one how to live.
Thus ethics was replaced by meta-ethics and serious
political and social philosophy were almost extinguished.
Analysis of concepts meant attending to the way a term
was employed by the appropriate community. Ordinary
usage thus came to dominate the concern of analysts of
educational discourse. One result of this has been the
avoidance of potentially more fruitful attempts to formulate functional concepts, in favor of examining,
criticizing, and censoring those in current use. Ordinary
language philosophy can be quite as effective in frus-
trating the development of a potentially useful technical
vocabulary as well as in clarifying language. For
example, educators may sensibly be no more concerned with
the ordinary use of 'learning' than physicists should be
concerned with the ordinary use of 'force.' The dominance
of concerns drawn from academic philosophy has generally
tended towards educational vacuousness.

We have dwelt on the weaknesses rather than the
strengths of these modes of educational philosophy because
the weaknesses have combined over the years to deprive
educational thinking and decision-making of what should
have been its most disciplined and trained contribution.
The vacuum has been filled with a slew of mindless
faddism. A more effective role for philosophers of
education may likely come, not as a result of some new
conception of their task, but rather from a synthesis of
the strengths of these past modes, and a conscious avoidance of the tendencies that have made them less benefi-
cially effective than they should have been.

These strengths seem to us, in short, a clear focusing
on educational issues, an ability to deal with them in a
way that makes sense to non-philosophers, and philosophical competence. Other books in this series have
contributed towards a synthesis of these strengths.

This collection began very deliberately with the aim to organize a set of philosophically competent papers about significant and practical educational issues. Such an aim is perhaps to be encouraged in the philosophy of education as academic philosophy too seems to be moving towards a conception of itself which is less afraid of norms and facts, and is more willing to investigate and even construct conceptual systems for use in solving problems which go beyond philosophy.

In addition to providing a useful contribution to educators generally, we hope this book will serve to encourage educational philosophers, who are increasingly being trained to philosophical competence, to get their hands dirty with the messy problems that are raised by trying to educate children better. We hope that, increasingly, respectability will be looked for not in aping academic philosophy but by engaging the attention of and influencing educational administrators, teachers, etc. Education is a practical activity and the success of any aspect of the educational enterprise must ultimately be measured in terms of its effect on practice.

K.A. STRIKE   K. EGAN
Cornell University   Simon Fraser University

Liberality and the university

part I

Ambiguities in liberal education and the problem of its content

1

R. S. Peters

INTRODUCTION

If one was mounting a defence of certain distinctive
values in education nowadays, I doubt whether one would
run up the flag of 'liberal education' in order to mark
what one stood for. The term itself suggests the sweet-
ness and light of the nineteenth century rather than the
'relevance' and 'validity' of the twentieth. Liberal
policies, too, notoriously lack the positive cutting edge
of the radical and the defensive solidarity of the conservative. Nevertheless, in spite of the fact that the
term itself is not particularly in vogue, the ideas
behind it are; for contemporary complaint is against constraints of any sort, and the unifying idea behind liberal
education is that of the unimpeded and unconstrained
development of the mind. The concept, therefore, is of
considerable contemporary relevance whatever one says
about the phrase.

A more fundamental difficulty about the phrase is its
endemic ambiguity. It is endemic because, as I have
argued before, (1) 'liberal' functions like 'free' in
that it suggests the removal of constraints, and there
are different types of constraint. There is also the
necessity, if clear communication is thought desirable,
of stating precisely what it is of value that is being
constrained. There are therefore bound to be ambiguities
inherent in demands for liberal education. In a similar
way, when people make demands for 'free schools', further
questions must be asked about what they think schools are
for and whether it is the curriculum, teaching methods,
the organization of the school or external pressures on
it, which are constraining.

Common to all interpretations of liberal education,
however, is the value placed upon knowledge and under-

standing. The various constraints are seen as impeding
the mind in its quest for it. But it is at this point
that ambiguities are most marked; for there is too little
clairty about the type of knowledge that is to be sought.
Indeed, as I shall argue, this question has been obscured
by the tendency to assimilate the position of those
acquiring knowledge in schools to that of those advancing
knowledge in universities.

1   THREE INTERPRETATIONS OF LIBERAL EDUCATION

The ambiguities of what is meant by a liberal education
are embodied in academic folklore by the story of the
Oxford scholarship entrant who was asked by a tutor why
he wished to come up to Oxford. 'To benefit from a
liberal education, sir', he replied. 'And what, pray,
is that?' asked the tutor. 'That is what I hope to discover by coming here', replied the aspiring scholar. If
he had obtained a scholarship and had studied the Classics
he would soon have gleaned that the notion of a liberal
education was introduced by the Greeks. Education was
conceived of as a process in which the mind's development
towards knowledge and understanding was not to be in-
hibited by being harnessed to vocational or utilitarian
ends. Knowledge must be pursued 'for its own sake', not
viewed as instrumental to some other end. This is the
first interpretation of liberal education. It was
strongly supported by nineteenth century thinkers such as
Matthew Arnold and Cardinal Newman in a context of the
rapid development of technical training and technology.
It is still very influential as a characterization of
university education.
     The second interpretation of liberal education is a
plea against the mind being confined to one discipline or
form of understanding. Newman's conception of all-round
development was, to a large extent, a reaction against
the growing specialization and compartmentalization of
knowledge in the nineteenth century. Nowadays, at any
rate at the school level, liberal education is more or
less identified with this demand for a general education
as distinct from a specialized training. This demand is
well exemplified in Paul Hirst's conception of a liberal
education, which involves initiation into all the distinct
forms of knowledge. (2)
     A third interpretation of liberal education relates
to constrictions on the mind imposed by dogmatic methods
of teaching. An obvious example of this is indoctrination, in which a fixed body of beliefs is implanted in a

manner which discourages criticism or an exploration of
the grounds on which beliefs are based. Authoritarianism
is another example; for the reasoning capacity of the
individual is stunted by arbitrariness and by appeals to
or demonstrations of the status of the teacher.

These three types of demand do not necessarily co-
incide. Mary Warnock, for instance, is a passionate
advocate of studying things for their own sake, which she
sees as one of the hallmarks of quality in education.
But she is against general education which she regards as
counter-productive in the attempt to achieve quality. (3)
Catholic educators, following Newman, often favour the
all-round development of the mind; but they are not
notorious for condemning authoritarian methods of instruction. Some advocates of progressive methods, on the other
hand, such as Dewey, do not espouse the pursuit of knowledge for its own sake; rather they see it as subservient
to practical problem-solving. It is, of course, merely
competing for an honorific title to ask which of these
interpretations of liberal education is the real one.

Having distinguished these three interpretations of
'liberal education', I now propose to examine each in
turn in more detail in order to make explicit the positive values in each which are thought to be subject to
some kind of constraint, and to ask questions about the
type of knowledge which the mind should be free to pursue.

2   LIBERAL EDUCATION AS KNOWLEDGE FOR ITS OWN SAKE

The constraints objected to in the first interpretation
are those of utility and vocational relevance. Geometry,
for instance, was found to be of great use in the development of plans for irrigation; but it was also studied
without such constrictions imposed by practical ends.
Indeed, on Plato's view, an understanding of its principles was essential for the mind's development, and hence
a crucial element in education. The positive idea underlying this classical conception of liberal education was
that the highest form of its exercise is in theoretical
pursuits. Education was viewed by him as a process which
equips and encourages a man to develop into being fully
a man by using his reason to the utmost.

In derivations of this conception of liberal education
the 'natural' development of mind is contrasted with the
pursuit of knowledge for utilitarian or vocational ends
by saying that knowledge is pursued 'for its own sake'.
This suggests that the reasons for study are immanent in
the study itself as distinct from benefits which might

accrue from it. These might be stated in a mundane way
by saying that the person did it out of curiosity or out
of interest, or in a more Platonic way by saying that
the person was led by a passion for grasping principles,
for finding the forms in the facts. Alternatively a more
normative note might be struck by mention of the demand
to eliminate error and find out what is true. Finally
such study might be represented as a form of mastery, as
an enjoyable and challenging type of adventure. All such
reasons for pursuing knowledge have the common feature
that they are intrinsic to the pursuit of it and hence
definitive of the mind's untrammelled development. They
are to be contrasted with practical ends which are thought
to act as constraints or limitations on the mind's
development.

In Greek thought this ideal of pursuing knowledge for
its own sake was extolled because practical knowledge
was thought to involve mingling with the materials of the
earth and thus to debase a man's soul, rendering him
'banautikos'. The type of practical knowledge which was
displayed in morals and politics was not debasing in the
same way, but it lacked the pure unimpeded features of
theoretical knowledge and was thus not so valuable. The
'making' which characterized the fine arts was thought to
be inferior for rather different reasons connected with
the metaphysical status of its products. The net result
was that there has been a continuing and influential
tradition which has upheld the training of people in
theoretical pursuits as the paradigm of liberal education,
with a consequent down-grading of the practical. In
universities, for instance, the faculties of medicine,
engineering and education, are not held in such esteem as
the faculties of arts and science. The reasons for this
are complex, but one reason is still that they are closely
connected with mundane practical problems.

It is not my intention in this paper to extol the virtues of either theoretical or practical knowledge, still
less to discuss the Greek arguments about man's function
or essence from which this emphasis on the theoretical
stems. Concern with practical ends, however, need not be
particularly limiting. Freud's basic concern was to cure
his patients, but his speculations about their minds were
pretty far-ranging. The solution of educational problems
requires excursions into psychology, philosophy and the
social sciences in a way which it is very difficult to
delimit. Enquiries spring from problems. Some types of
practical problems require far-ranging enquiries. Others
do not. The same can be said of theoretical problems.

The important difference, I suppose, is that in

practical enquiries knowledge is not pursued 'for its own
sake'. Interest or curiosity is less likely to draw the
medical student to the study of physiology than his consciousness that this type of knowledge is necessary for
curing people. It is difficult to see, however, why this
makes such enquiries less valuable in the absence of a
special ethical theory such as the Greek doctrine of function. For practical ends such as the elimination of suffering and the maintenance of security are surely valuable. Also the obligatory types of value present in
theoretical enquiries, the demand that error must be
avoided and virtues such as those of consistency, coherence, and clarity which surround this demand, are
present in practical enquiries as well. Indeed they have
additional point if practical consequences depend in part
upon the truth of the supporting beliefs. Incorrect
diagnosis may suggest treatment which leads to the death
of a human being. I am not arguing, of course, that the
justification of such virtues surrounding the attempt to
discover what is true is to be sought in such consequences, only that such consequences give additional
point to them. And it is not obvious why this sobering
aspect under which such enquiries can be viewed makes them
any less valuable than if they are conducted purely out
of interest or curiosity.

However, I must stick to my resolution not to enter
into the debate about the value of liberal education and
to the task of trying to delimit what is included or
excluded by this interpretation of it. This is difficult
to decide; for the dichotomy between 'knowledge for its
own sake' and 'knowledge for practical ends' is too coarse
to throw light on the attitude of the learner towards
knowledge. Indeed, as I shall argue later, it is really a
distinction developed within the context of the advancement of knowledge, which is often transferred to the
situation of the learner.

The first difficulty is with 'knowledge for practical
ends'. For this description conceals a distinction that
it is very important to make when considering the motivational structure of learning in institutions such as
schools and universities. A typical example would be a
boy at school practising on a lathe or a miller because
he wanted to be a toolmaker or a medical student learning
anatomy because he wanted to cure people. In both cases
the knowledge and skill attained is indispensable to the
practical activity, and there might be no further end for
the sake of which the activity was practised. The boy
might just want to make tools; the student might just be
very concerned to relieve suffering. They might be

oblivious to any thoughts of pay-off in terms of financial reward, approval, status, etc. On the other hand these further ends might exert a strong appeal and infect their learning and general conduct in their practical acti- vities. They might equally well infect the activity of a scientist engaged on pure research; for he might become 'double-minded' in valuing his reputation as much as or more than the pursuit of truth, and be driven by this narcissistic ambition in his studies.

In learning at school these further ends are extremely important; for the learning situation is very often geared to obtaining rewards, doing better than others, avoiding punishment, winning status and approval, and passing examinations which are often seen as prerequisites to wealth and status. There are two features of such further ends which provide a contrast to the case of the toolmaker interested just in making tools or the medical student with a concern about human suffering. The first is that motives such as greed, envy, fear of disapproval and ambition, supply ends which exert a variable, extrinsic influence on learning activities. A student may cheat to do better than a rival; he may learn just enough to get by if he wishes to avoid the disapproval of the teacher. His care and effort is not determined by the intrinsic nature of the learning task. By contrast, the medical student with a concern about relieving distress, works at tasks which are all determined by their relevance to this end. Ideally he takes care because he cares about the suffering of the patient. In a similar way the toolmaker may be moved by his love of precision, accuracy and neat- ness which are values instantiated in what he is learning. Thus the motivation to learn is not so dependent on external and variable interpersonal and institutional factors. Second, the knowledge attained in the service of these extrinsic ends is not indispensable to their attainment or in any way constitutive of them. A student can learn geometry to outshine a rival or to please a teacher. But there are other ways of achieving such ends and his knowledge of geometry is not central to the satis- faction obtained. The marks or the smiles are what matter to him, not the knowledge of Euclid. In the other cases, however, the ends cannot be achieved at all without this knowledge or skill. No one can emjoy making tools unless he has mastered a lathe and miller. Also the exercise of the knowledge or skill concerned is central to the satis- faction obtained. For 'ends' like curing a patient or perfecting a tool are unintelligible without reference to the relevant knowledge and skill.

The distinction between 'knowledge for its own sake'

and 'knowledge for practical ends' is too coarse to mark
these different ways in which practical ends can be pursued. It is also inadequate; for both theoretical and
practical activities can be pursued 'for their own sakes'
or they can be infected by the pull of all-pervasive
motives such as ambition, envy, and greed. Now many argue
that the most corrupting influence in life generally, as
well as in learning, is the influence of these very
motives. As they are very influential in our school
system it could be argued that the dichotomy between
'learning for its own sake' and 'learning for practical
ends', which is provided by this interpretation of
'liberal education', is a very unhelpful one because it
is too coarse to make this crucial distinction. Indeed,
because the further ends that go with ambition, greed,
envy, etc., can be thought of as 'practical' in contrast
to ends provided in theoretical activities by curiosity,
concern for truth, etc., it could be argued that the
dichotomy is positively misleading, for it tends to confuse the practical with the purely instrumental.

There is also the point that such 'ends' are often
represented in too rationalistic a way. Much learning
takes place in situations in which there is an implicit
expectation of or association with something that is
desired, but in which the learning is not viewed consciously as a means to attaining it. When children copy
their elders or pick up their opinions or attitudes, they
are not consciously seeking approval or reward. They may
admire the person concerned; there may be warmth in the
situation which favours attention; they may be afraid of
missing something, or of being out of line. But they are
not explicitly learning for the sake of such 'practical
ends'.

There are inadequacies, then, in one alternative
offered by the dichotomy of 'knowledge for its own sake'
and 'knowledge for practical ends' when it is applied to
the situation of the learner; for 'knowledge for practical ends' has been shown to gloss over crucial distinctions. But there are also inadequacies in the alternative
of 'knowledge for its own sake'. This may rule out
various motivations·to learn; but what does it rule in?
Obviously learning from sheer curiosity or learning
because of the interest, novelty, or puzzling features of
the subject-matter. But are these the only alternatives
to learning for the sake of practical ends?

Suppose a man is exercised about why his friend is rude
to him, worried about his own prejudices and uncharitable
feelings, or concerned about whether he should be patri-
otic or feel awe for the sea or at the sight of death.

Suppose that he is led by such uneasiness into studies in psychology, ethics, politics, and religion. Is he in such cases pursuing knowledge for its own sake? Notions like 'knowledge for its own sake', and curiosity suggest a stance that is too detached and disinterested to do justice to his concern about such questions. On the other hand answering them is not obviously connected with any particular course of action or further end to be achieved. For they are applications of the general beliefs and attitudes which are constitutive of his level of under-standing and sensitivity as a human being. What is he to make of objects in the natural world and of phenomena such as the dark, thunder, the tides, time, and the changes of the seasons? What is he to make of other people and of their reactions to him and to each other? What is he to think about himself and about questions of ownership? What attitude is he to take towards the cycle of birth, marriage and death? In what way is he to react to authority, suffering, and violence? These are ques-tions arising from the general conditions of human life. Answers to them provide a general framework of beliefs and attitudes within which particular ends are sought and particular puzzles arise. Such practical and theoretical pursuits often bring about a transformation within the general framework. But the framework itself cannot be regarded purely as a deposit left by the pursuit of know-ledge for its own sake or for the sake of some practical or extrinsic end.

These categories are probably very much the reflection of the situation in civilized societies when special institutions will either be doing this for its own sake or to prepare people for professions or to contribute to the solution of practical problems in the community. They will, therefore, tend to view the situation of people acquiring knowledge when they are being educated as capable of being categorized in the same way as that of those like themselves who are advancing knowledge. They will, therefore, debate about whether students should be encouraged to learn because of the intrinsic interest of the subject, because it will prepare them for a job, or because it will have some other practical use in life. And they will pass on these ways of viewing the acquisi-tion of knowledge to their students from whom teachers are recruited. What will tend to be overlooked is the need to develop beliefs and attitudes which will help a person to make sense of and take up some stance towards the various situations and predicaments that he will inevit-ably encounter as a human being.

When talking about the educational value of a subject,

university teachers such as Mary Warnock (4) stress the
enjoyment of working at something for its own sake and the
wish to go on with it on one's own. But this, surely, is
a delight that can be experienced in a vast range of
activities such as cooking, gardening, and carpentry. It
is not peculiar to working at subjects such as history or
geography. Nor is it possible, as she so rightly points
out, for anyone to work in many fields of study in this
way which is typical of a person who may go on to discover
things for himself. Given, then, that subjects such as
these provide all sorts of answers to questions which a
man may ask about the world, and human life, how is he to
be introduced to this human heritage? Mary Warnock views
subjects rather from the point of view of potential
research workers; but an equally important educational
question is to ask how the products of such work can
become significant to the majority of people who are never
going to transform such products by their own activity.
A person without a consciousness of the historical dimension of current social problems is poorly educated; but
does he have to work systematically as a historian to
develop such a consciousness? The sort of knowledge that
enables a man to understand better the layout of a town,
in which he is spending a holiday, to appreciate features
of the rocks and rivers, or to speculate about the customs
of the local inhabitants, is not the product necessarily
of any specialized study on his part in history, geography, or anthropology. But it is very much the hall-
mark of an educated person. Did he acquire such knowledge
for its own sake? Or to accomplish any practical purpose?
Parts of it perhaps. But it is just as likely that he
picked it up because of his concern to assess the significance of the context in which he has to live his life.
Or perhaps he just picked it up from a talkative friend
over a pint of beer.

   In brief my argument is that there is a body of knowledge, entertained with varying degrees of understanding,
that is extremely significant or 'relevant' to a person in
so far as it determines his general beliefs, attitudes,
and reactions to the general conditions of human life.
This is not necessarily acquired for its own sake, as is a
field that a person studies in depth out of interest or
pure curiosity, or acquired because of its usefulness to
particular ends. Liberal education, in the first interpretation, is too often equated with the stance of a
scholar pursuing a subject that he loves. There is great
value in this type of activity; for it involves not only
the joys of mastery and the adventures of discovery, but
also intellectual virtues such as clarity, humility, and

impartiality of mind. But not all our beliefs are acquired by this sort of activity and many people are not
at all drawn to it. They therefore often complain of the
irrelevance of learning and are only disposed to apply
themselves if they can see the pay-off. Yet if this
knowledge and understanding could be presented to them
more imaginatively in ways which take much more account
of their concerns as human beings, their attitude towards
learning might be different.

There is too much of a tendency to regard motivation
just as a bundle of interests or needs that the individual
brings with him ready made to a learning situation. In
truth it is just as much a product of the situation in
which he finds himself as something which he brings to it.
If an institution is geared towards providing people with
levels of qualifications to determine their point of entry
to the occupational structure, this is the motivational
message which its students will ingest, however hard its
teachers work to present learning in a different light.
Of course gifted teachers may arouse different attitudes
in a few. In others, the desire to pass the required
examinations may be reinforced by interests aroused by
the subject-matter itself once they start to work. But
the majority are likely to remain strangers to such non-
instrumental attitudes to learning. They learn, if they
do, in the way in which the logic of their institutional
situation requires them to learn.

There is a question, though, whether people who talk
about 'liberal education' in this first interpretation
are primarily concerned with the motivation for learning
characterizing the 'process' of education. They might
be more concerned with the state of mind of the 'product'.
A person, for instance, might have learnt mathematics
because he saw it as being of practical use, but might
gradually have become 'hooked' on it, to use a colloquial-
ism. He might end up by being fascinated by it 'for its
own sake'. Alternatively he might have worked at it just
because he enjoyed solving these sorts of abstract problems. But later on he might come to appreciate its practical use. Indeed the concern with motivation might be
only indirect. When, for instance, Whitehead fulminated
against 'inert ideas' he was not directly making a motivational point. He was lamenting the lack of application
to people's experience of so much that was learnt at
school - mere book-learning that did little to transform
a person's understanding of situations which he was likely
to encounter. He then jumped to the other extreme and
argued that knowledge should be 'useful'. Indeed he
claimed that education is the art of the 'utilization'

of knowledge. (5)   But is this really what he meant?   Did
he not really mean that the knowledge and understanding of
an educated person should have application in his life,
should give him concepts and generalizations for understanding better situations in which he was likely to be
placed?   Did he mean 'useful' in the strict sense of
instrumental to the realization of some practical end?

This dichotomy between 'inert' and 'useful', made in
the context of characterizing the type of knowledge that
it is important for an educated person to possess, tends
to reinforce the dichotomy in motivation between 'for
its own sake' and 'for the sake of some practical end'.
It encourages the neglect of that same body of knowledge,
entertained with varying degrees of understanding, that
is extremely significant or 'relevant' to a person in so
far as it determines his general beliefs, attitudes, and
reactions to the universal conditions of human life.   This
is neither 'inert' nor 'useful' in any ordinary sense.

I said that Whitehead, in making this distinction, was
only indirectly concerned with motivation.   By that I mean
that he was concerned with knowledge which seems of
obvious 'relevance' to a person's situation.   Presumably
he assumed, like most people, that learning will be
improved as well because it will be seen to be relevant
by the learner.   But this is not necessarily the case, and
the same point needs to be made about the kind of knowledge concerned with the human condition which I have
assumed to be of some kind of emotional significance to
anyone.   For even though everyone is likely to be confronted at some time by emotional problems to do with
death, personal relationships, authority, violence, etc.,
these may not seem to be of any particular significance
to him while he is at school.   That is why, in talking
about liberal education, it is important to distinguish
the motivational thesis from the sort of thesis developed
by Whitehead about the features of the knowledge or understanding that anyone should be encouraged to develop.

My own view is that the content of education should not
be determined by what, at any particular moment, the
learner finds interesting or important, though obviously
this is something of which any good teacher should be
mindful.   The teacher's task is as much to arouse interest
as it is to build on existing interest.   The same applies
to concern about predicaments like those of death, suffering, and sexual infatuation to which it would be somewhat
inappropriate to apply terms such as 'interest' and
'curiosity'.   These are likely to compel the attention of
students because of the universal emotions which are
aroused by such predicaments.   But even if they do not

immediately do so, something should be done about the development of beliefs and attitudes in this area because of the predictable significance of these predicaments in anyone's life at some time. With the declining influence of the church, which traditionally dealt with issues in this area, so many people encounter such situations with so little preparation for them. I am not saying, of course, that the content of education should be centred entirely in this area. Only that it is an important area that tends to be neglected. This neglect is encouraged by the demand that knowledge should be either for its own sake or for its practical use.

3   LIBERAL EDUCATION AS GENERAL EDUCATION

This sphere of knowledge which seems essential to an educated person, but which proved, in the preceding section, to be very difficult to fit into the categories of acquired for its own sake or for the sake of some further end, seems extremely relevant to the second interpretation of liberal education, as general education. It is relevant because there are three types of problem which any advocate of general education has to face and some kind of answer to them is provided within this sphere of knowledge. There is first of all the problem of avoiding an assemblage of disjointed information; there is second, Herbert Spencer's question 'What knowledge is of most worth?'; third, there is the demand for 'integration' that lurks behind talk of developing 'the whole man'. I will, therefore, on occasions, make reference to this sphere of knowledge which is relevant to any person, in dealing with these three types of problem in relation to which ambiguities arise in the second interpretation of 'liberal education'.

   (i) The demand that people should be allowed to develop in many directions rather than be confined to some particular specialized way of thinking is straightforward in a negative sense, though the constraining enemy appears in many guises ranging from the academic pedant to the demands of government or industry for specialized manpower. But the positive implications are obscure. It is clear that a man should not be, for instance, just a narrowly trained scientist, but should he be philosophically sophisticated as well as aesthetically sensitive and well versed in history? How coarsely or finely are such divisions to be made if illiberal specialization is to be avoided? Does it matter, for instance, if a scientist supplements his outlook by a developed appreciation of

music, but misses out on literature? Or what if the
literary man understands the Second Law of Thermo-dynamics
but misses out on Mendel, Freud, and Durkheim?

To answer this kind of question it must surely be
insisted that this conception of liberal education
suggests only a continuum at one end of which is narrow
specialization. It would be impossible to locate any
particular point on the move away from this towards the
other end of breadth of understanding and sensitivity, at
which a person could be called 'educated'. Also some view
would have to be taken, such as that of Hirst, about the
arbitrariness or non-arbitrariness of divisions within
knowledge. In the history of philosophy there has been a
gradual differentiation. Empirical science was shown not
to be just a branch of mathematics because of the difference in its criterion of truth and testing procedures.
For similar reasons moral experience was shown to be
unassimilable to either mathematics or science, to have
a degree of autonomy. Questions then arose about the
status of religion and about the possibility of regarding
human studies such as psychology and history as similar
to or distinct from the natural sciences. And both
aesthetic appreciation and philosophical understanding
seemed also to have sui generis characteristics.

If such non-arbitrary distinctions could be made in
terms of truth-criteria, testing-procedures and distinctive conceptual schemes, some beginning could be made to
answering questions about the ideal implicit in the continuum. It would be absurd to expect, for instance, that
in all these various disciplines a person should be able
to operate the testing-procedures in the way in which a
trained specialist, who helps to develop understanding,
must operate them. On the other hand it would not seem
desirable for a person to amass a store of disjointed
information from a variety of disciplines. What would
seem desirable and practicable over a long period of time
would be that a person should acquire essential elements
of the different conceptual schemes by means of which
various items of information are given a place and organized. He should also learn to apply this scheme critically, which implies understanding of the different
criteria of truth. Understanding of principles would be
attempted which would increasingly structure a person's
outlook and help him to organize experience in a variety
of ways, and to think critically and imaginatively.

(ii) With the vast development of knowledge in all
these different disciplines questions would obviously
arise, about which branches to single out for study within
them. Within natural science, for instance, should

chemistry be studied rather than astronomy? In other
words the question of what knowledge is of most worth
would have to be faced. If there is any substance in the
points made before about the sort of knowledge which is
relevant to anyone who has to face the general conditions
of human life, some kind of answer could be sketched. In
this sense within philosophy, for instance, ethics would
obviously be more relevant than symbolic logic; within
history social history would be more relevant than
diplomatic history; and so on.

This, of course, is not the only criterion for including studies in a curriculum. There are many others. I
am merely drawing attention to an important criterion of
the 'worth' of knowledge that is too often overlooked by
teachers who see subjects merely as first stages in
specialized study. At universities, too, an important
consideration for any teacher is what there is in his
subject for the majority who have neither the aptitude
nor the inclination to develop it as a research worker
like himself. The neglect, however, of this criterion
both in schools and universities underlies much of the
complaint by students of the lack of 'relevance' in their
studies.

(iii) The third type of problem implicit in general
education is that of how all-round understanding is to be
conceived. One facet of this ideal is the capacity of a
person to view what he is doing or what is going on under
different aspects. A scientist, for instance, should not
be oblivious to the moral dimension of his work; an
engineer should be sensitive to the aesthetic aspect of
his constructions. But more than this is often implied;
for the different ways of organizing experience should not
be compartmentalized and insulated from each other. There
should be some kind of 'integration' between them. This
is not the place to explore the different things which
might be meant by 'integration' in this context, but one
very pertinent meaning is the way in which different types
of understanding interpenetrate in the spheres of knowledge which are relevant to anyone facing the general
conditions of human life. In dealing with death, for
instance, there is empirical knowledge about man's mortal-
ity, but this is inescapably tinged with philosophical
assumptions about the relationship between consciousness
and its bodily conditions. There are also inescapable
ethico-religious questions about what is to be made of
this universal predicament. The same sorts of considerations apply to confrontations with human violence or
deceit. There are first of all straightforward factual
questions about the actions. But these quickly shade into

further questions about the motives of the person or
persons concerned. And it is significant that motives
such as envy, jealousy, and greed do not just explain;
they are also the names of widespread vices. Moral judgment and interpersonal understanding are inextricably
interwoven. And both types of knowledge are exercised
within a context of beliefs of varying levels of sophistication about how society works.

My point is not just that in this sphere problems
seldom turn up that can be neatly labelled 'empirical' or
'ethical' or 'requiring understanding of persons'. It is
also that there is a widespread interpenetration between
the forms of understanding that we employ to sort out
the specific aspects of problems. There are links, though
tenuous ones, between pure mathematics and moral understanding. But pure mathematics has little purchase in
this realm. There are, however, countless links between
moral knowledge and interpersonal understanding, both of
which have ubiquitous application to it. So the sphere
in which it is easy to make some sense of the notion of
the integration of forms of knowledge is the sphere in
which it is possible to give at least one type of answer
to the question 'Which knowledge is of most worth?'.

4   LIBERAL EDUCATION AS THE DEVELOPMENT OF THE FREE MAN

In the classical view of liberal education the assumption
was that movement towards the natural end of rationality
was self-originated, the development of a potentiality
immanent in any individual. Processes of education provided support and encouragement. The 'free man', on the
Platonic view at any rate, was the man whose reason was
properly in control, who was not constrained by unruly
passions. Modern variants of this ideal stress different
aspects of it without its underlying doctrine of function
which assigned a universal end to human development. They
are more individualistic in that they envisage different
ends for different men. But they share the belief that
it is of crucial importance that the individual should
choose what he is to become.

Extreme versions of modern individualism stress the
importance of everyone doing his own thing, of being
'true to himself'. Self-origination is interpreted in
terms of authenticity, of not copying others or conforming
to social roles, whether of being a woman or being a
waiter. Thus any processes of education which involve
being told things by others, being initiated into public
traditions, or being influenced by example, are thought of

as constricting on the individual's development. He must
find his own way by his own experience and discoveries
and eventually learn to be himself, do his own thing,
even, in some versions of this doctrine, construct his
own reality.

Less extreme and more intelligible versions of
individualism, which are usually put forward by people
who would not mind calling themselves liberals, combine
this stress on individual choice with an equal stress on
the role of reason in informing such choices. The
emphasis is on autonomy as well as on authenticity. In
other words the importance of first-hand experience, of
beliefs which are not second-hand, and codes of conduct
that are not accepted just on authority, is granted. But
stress is placed on the role of reason in achieving such
independence of mind. On this view the development of the
free man (6) is not necessarily impeded by instruction
from others. Indeed it would be argued that the development of mind is inexplicable without reference to such
social transactions which the extreme liberal regards as
restrictions. What is crucial is the encouragement of
criticism in the individual so that he can eventually
accept or reject what he hears, sees, or is told, on the
basis of reasons. What is inimical to such development
is any process, such as indoctrination or conditioning,
which inhibits or undermines the capacity to reason.

This third interpretation of liberal education brings
to the fore again the question about the type of knowledge
which is of most worth which was raised in relation to
the two other interpretations; for, if autonomy is to be
anything more than a pious hope, the individual must be
possessed of relevant information to make realistic
choices and have his imagination stimulated so that he can
envisage all sorts of possibilities. In addition to
specialized knowledge necessary for the pursuit of a
particular occupation, the individual will need various
types of general knowledge which are relevant to his
choices as a citizen and as a human being. In such
general education too little attention is given to
political education and what any individual should know
who is to make informed choices as a citizen in a democracy. Too little attention, also, is given to that body
of knowledge that bears directly on the general conditions
of human life which has been referred to previously in
this article. The Schools Council Humanities project is
one of the few attempts to connect the development of
understanding in crucial areas such as those of violence,
law and order, sex and personal relationships, with the
development of autonomy. Many may have doubts about its

emphasis on the 'neutrality' of the teacher, though this
has to be understood against the tendency for teachers
to indoctrinate their pupils on such controversial issues.
But this emphasis of the project on a particular sort of
teaching procedure must be separated from its emphasis on
the importance of understanding in certain areas to the
development of autonomy.

There may seem to be some inconsistency between this
ideal of autonomy and what was said about the unrealistic
tendency to think of pupils as potential research workers
in the context of the first and second interpretations
of liberal education. This is a vast topic about which
it is possible, in the space available, to make only a
few brief points. The first is that autonomy is very much
a matter of degree; it indicates an attitude of mind
rather than an achieved state. Knowledge has developed
to such an extent in so many specialized branches, many
of which impinge on our daily lives, that we have little
alternative but to take a great deal of it on trust.
Also, even in a sphere such as the moral one, the lives
of reasonably autonomous people are governed by all sorts
of rules on which they have reflected little. How many
English people, for instance, have pondered deeply on the
ethics of 'first come, first served' in queues? Most
people are brought up in some established way of behaving
and reflect on various elements of it in the light of
their developing experience. The liberal ideal of autonomy is to be understood in contrast to unthinking con-
formity and rigid adherence to dogma. It does not demand
making explicit everything which has been picked up from
various sources and subjecting it all to constant criticism. What it does require is a willingness to learn and
to revise opinions and assumptions when confronted with
situations that challenge them. Logically speaking, too,
criticism must take certain presuppositions for granted.
Not everything can be questioned at once.

Second, it is important to distinguish approaching
what one is told critically and attempting to organize
and synthesize what one hears or reads in one's own way
from either slavishly reproducing the views of some
authority on the one hand or developing a highly original
thesis on the other. Autonomy is most frequently associated with the moral sphere; but few people who attain a
fair degree of autonomy in their moral life are moral
innovators. This introduces the third point which is that
there are great differences in respect of being able to
manage without authorities in the various ways of thinking
that are relevant to the sphere of knowledge which is of
central importance to any human being. In the natural

sciences, in so far as they impinge on everyday life, most people perforce rely on authorities. They may get as far as understanding some of the underlying theory; they realize that it is subject to error; but very few have the necessary training to locate possible sources of error. Morals are very different; for its underlying principles are not particularly recondite and a highly specialized training is not necessary to be sensitive to them. What is needed is the judgment and imagination to apply them in varying circumstances. There is also the problem of the degree of weight attached to different principles, which is one of the most potent sources of moral controversy. In between fall the various branches of human studies in which the 'common-sense' understanding of others and of ourselves is illuminated by theories supplied by specialized disciplines such as psychology, economics, and sociology. In assessing such theories, or the interpretations of actions and policies which they provide, the knowledge of particular men acting and suffering in particular circumstances is of crucial importance. We all possess such knowledge in various degrees; so we have a shared basis for criticism, judgment and making our own syntheses of what we glean from various 'authorities'. We have, of course, to be sufficiently 'on the inside' of such disciplines to understand the struc-ture of their principles and how to apply them. But we do not have to be specialists in them in order to form some view of our own.

What emerges from this sketchy piece of probing is the need for more careful attention to a group of qualities associated with autonomy such as being critical, being independent, having judgment, being authentic, being imaginative and so on. The application of these in spheres such as those of morals and politics, understand-ing on the one hand and more exalted qualities such as being original, creative, and inventive on the other. In so far as liberal education is concerned with autonomy it obviously aims at getting people beyond the level of just understanding and being well informed. But it does not demand the other extreme of originality and creative-ness. Such qualities are extremely important for uni-versity teachers who are training specialists likely to advance knowledge, but they are an extra bonus for liberal educators concerned with the development of autonomy.

CONCLUSION

This paper really has no conclusions. This is partly
because its intention was not to reach any but to explore
some of the ambiguities inherent in liberal education.
But it is also because, as the exploration proceeded, I
began to feel an increasing dissatisfaction with the
dichotomies in terms of which liberal education is usually
interpreted. In particular I found difficulty with the
dichotomy between 'for its own sake' and for the sake of
some practical end which seems to me to have application
to the advancement of knowledge but to fit very loosely
over its acquisition. It seems to apply hardly at all
to a sphere of knowledge, sometimes referred to loosely
as 'the humanities', which is of central importance in any
attempt to determine the type of knowledge which should
form the content of liberal education. Having come to
the end of this paper, therefore, I really feel that I
should now get down to the very difficult task of trying
to delimit this type of knowledge more precisely, examine
its relationship to traditional disciplines, to vocational studies, and so on. But this might mean that the
paper would become only marginally concerned with 'liberal
education' as it is normally understood, even though it
might be 'liberal' in exemplifying the untrammelled pursuit of knowledge; and it would certainly become too
'liberal' in its length.

NOTES

My thanks are due to Paul Hirst whose constructive criticisms helped me to revise a first version of this paper.
 1 See R.S. Peters, 'Ethics and Education' (London:
    Allen & Unwin, 1966), pp.43-5.
 2 See P.H. Hirst, Liberal Education and the Nature of
    Knowledge, most easily available as reprinted in
    R.S. Peters (ed.), 'The Philosophy of Education'
    (Oxford University Press, 1973), pp.87-111.
 3 See M. Warnock, Towards a Definition of Quality in
    Education, in R.S. Peters (ed.), 'The Philosophy of
    Education' (Oxford University Press, 1973), pp.112-22.
 4 See ibid.
 5 See A.N. Whitehead, 'The Aims of Education' (New York:
    Mentor Books, 1949) p.16.
 6 For detailed development of such a view see R.S.
    Peters, Freedom and the Development of the Free-Man,
    in J. Doyle, 'Educational Judgments' (London:
    Routledge & Kegan Paul, 1973).

2 Liberality, neutrality and the modern university

Kenneth A. Strike

Universities in the Western world are generally held to
ascribe to certain liberal ideals. They conceive of their
basic ends as the pursuit and dissemination of truth,
and they maintain that these ends require a climate of
liberty and tolerance if they are to be successfully
pursued. This commitment to liberality and tolerance
has been held to imply an additional commitment to
neutrality. A university, so the argument goes, cannot
maintain an atmosphere of free and open discussion of
significant issues while at the same time taking an
official stand on such issues. Thus, the liberal university must be neutral.

This position concerning neutrality has been under
strong attack in recent years. Three distinct sets of
issues should be considered.

First, neutrality is sometimes objected to on the
grounds that those who pay for a university have a right
to determine its commitments. One author, for example,
writes:

> To begin with, no institution, based upon the philo-
> sophical presuppositions of its founders and directors,
> can achieve total neutrality. But not only is total
> neutrality unachievable, it is also undesirable,
> especially if the university in question is tax-
> supported. When citizens of the United States have a
> portion of their income confiscated for purposes of
> educating other citizens of the United States, they
> should at least be offered the minimal assurance that
> their tax dollars will be used to train loyal citizens
> and not revolutionaries. (1)

This line of argument, of course, poses the issue in
its traditional form. The university's liberal position
is intended to ward off exactly this sort of encroachment
on its intellectual liberty. This line of objection to

neutrality requires the university to defend its liberal conceptions against the more conservative notion that the university exists to serve some set of vested social interests or to defend some particular social ideology.

A second line of objection to neutrality has been expressed by a more radical group. The claims are typically two. First, it is held that the doctrine of neutrality typically functions to cloak the fact that the university is in actuality a vassal of societies' dominant interests. Second, it is held that the ideal of neutrality is not just objectionable, it is impossible. A university cannot be neutral with respect to dominant social interests or issues. Its only serious choice is to opt for the right sort of social perspective. Robert Paul Wolff provides a quotable version of this orientation:

> As a prescription for institutional behavior, the doctrine of value neutrality suffers from the worst disability which can afflict a norm: what it prescribes is not wrong; it is impossible. A large university in contemporary America simply cannot adopt a value-neutral stance, either externally or internally, no matter how hard it tries.... One of the first truths enunciated in introductory ethics courses is that the failure to do something is as much an act as the doing of it. It is perfectly reasonable to hold a man responsible for not paying his taxes, for not exercising due care and caution in driving, for not helping a fellow man in need. In public life, when a man who has power refrains from using it, we all agree that he has acted politically ... acquiescence in governmental acts, under the guise of impartiality, actually strengthens the established forces and makes successful opposition all the harder. (2)

In this paper I shall deal with the second and the third sets of issues. I will assume for the duration that the battle between liberals and conservatives has been fought and won by the liberals. No doubt there are still occasionally successful purges against ideologically unpopular professors, but the prevailing orientation on campus is liberal and liberals have achieved acquiescence if not enthusiasm from society at large concerning such liberal institutions as academic freedom and tenure.

The second and third sets of issues are, however, newer and as yet not adequately explored. Thus, I shall focus on them. I shall begin with the question of the possibility of neutrality since this will enable me to develop some of the conceptual apparatus necessary to understand the policy questions involved. Initially,

therefore, it will be useful to distinguish two types of
possibility and three types of neutrality.

A state of affairs may be either logically or factually
possible. To say that something is logically possible is
to say that its conception is consistent. To say that
something is factually possible is to say both that its
conception is consistent and that there are no facts which
preclude it. For example, a round square is logically
impossible in that it must both have and not have corners.
It is only factually impossible, however, to cool a substance to absolute zero. The conception of absolute zero
is quite consistent, however; what physics we know,
indicates that the state is unattainable.

Now those who have argued that neutrality is impossible
have argued both claims. Often political and economic
pressure or hidden bias are the sorts of facts appealed
to to show that neutrality is factually impossible. It
has also been claimed that neutrality is logically impossible. Wolff, for example, appears to have this in mind.
To try to be neutral, Wolff claims, is to try to do
neither A, or not-A. Thus, on Wolff's view, the advocate
of university neutrality is not bucking the facts, he
is bucking the Law of Excluded Middle. Neutrality is not
just unattainable, it is inconceivable.

This distinction is of interest, because different
conclusions follow depending on what sort of possibility
one has in mind. What is important is that a situation
which is factually impossible can be approximated whereas
that is not the case for a situation which is logically
impossible. It follows from this that the factual impossibility of a goal is not a fatal objection to the desirability of attempting to achieve it, whereas the logical
impossibility of a goal is fatal.

Perhaps we cannot achieve absolute zero, but we can
get close. And there may be benefits in trying. Thus,
if neutrality is factually impossible it may nevertheless
be desirable to be as neutral as possible. Therefore, it
seems to me that claims as to the factual impossibility of
neutrality are not especially interesting in this context
since nothing much follows concerning whether we should
try to be neutral.

On the other hand, an argument to show that neutrality
is logically impossible would be most interesting. Since
a situation is logically impossible in that it both must
have and not have some property a logically impossible
state of affairs cannot be approximated. Thus, if a goal
can be shown to be logically impossible, this is fatal to
its desirability and to any policy meant to implement it.

Given the above analysis in what follows, I shall be

largely interested in deciding if neutrality is logically impossible. Consider, then, that there are at least three sorts of neutrality.

First, it is necessary to distinguish neutrality of opinion from neutrality of consequence. In one sense of neutral, to be neutral is to not take a stand on an issue or to not have a position about an issue. In a second sense, to be neutral is to act (or not act) such that one's actions do not have consequences for an issue.

These two types of neutrality are logically distinct and may be factually independent. It is quite possible for a person or an institution to have no stand or opinion on an issue, but yet to act so as to effect the issue. Likewise a person or institution can have an opinion on an issue but act in a way which has no effect on the issue.

This distinction is important for understanding the character of certain debates concerning university policy. Let us suppose, for example, that the investment policy of a university is under attack. The university (let's say) has invested its endowment in a given oil company which, it turns out, has substantial interests in South Africa and which contributes substantially to South Africa's economy. This leads to the charge that the university is investing its funds in a way such as to indirectly support South Africa's racial policies and to demands that the university either liquidate its interests in the oil company or use its interests to pressure the oil company concerning its policy toward South Africa.

The university may respond to such charges by maintaining that its investment policy is neutral with respect to such questions. It is neutral in the sense that only financial considerations are considered in determining the investment policy. The university takes no position on other matters. It may perhaps add to this that its liberal ideals preclude it from taking a stand on such issues and require it to develop its investment policy without considering them.

Here the university defends itself against the charge that it is not neutral concerning some issue by claiming that it is in fact neutral. But, of course, the charge and the denial are not a charge and denial of the same thing, nor are the charge and the denial incompatible. The charge is that the university's actions are not neutral in that they have some effect on a given issue. The response is that the university is neutral in that it has not taken a stand on the issue. There are two sorts of neutrality at issue, and there is no logical reason why both the charge and the response cannot be true.

Two conclusions can be drawn. First, it is dangerous
to talk about neutrality as though it were a single thing.
There are different types of neutrality and one can be
neutral concerning some issue in one sense of neutral and
not another. Failure to recognize this is apt to introduce substantial confusion into debate. Second, we have
to ask exactly what sort of neutrality is required by
our liberal ideals. Is the liberal university required
not to take stands on issues or is it required not to
have an effect on issues. Or is there some third, still
to be discovered, sense of neutral in which a liberal
university should be neutral?

I shall develop a third sense of neutrality and try to
sort out the requirements of a liberal ideology vis-à-vis
these three concepts of neutrality shortly. At this
point, we need to turn to the question of whether there
is any logical problem in supposing that an institution
can be neutral in either of the first two senses of
neutral.

This question can be addressed by asking if the argument suggested by Wolff succeeds. Wolff's claim is essentially this. In any case where a university wishes to
be neutral, it will find that it must either do some
action, A, or not. (It is, of course, logically true that
A and not-A exhaust the possibilities.) Moreover, the
university will find that neither A, nor not-A, are
neutral.

I shall attack this argument by claiming that the
options available to an institution are typically not
plausibly expressed as a choice between A and not-A.
Consider, first, neutrality of opinion. What would have
to be shown in order to show that a person could not be
neutral concerning some opinion, O? Presumably it would
have to be shown that it is necessarily the case that one
must either believe O or believe not-O. But, of course,
it is not necessarily the case that one must either
believe O, or believe not-O. What is necessarily the case
is that one must either believe O, or not believe O. The
point here can be put in two ways. First, it seems clear
that when we formulate the issue properly, that is, when
we understand neutrality of opinion as a matter of neither
believing O to be true or believing O to be false, it
turns out that there is a third option. One may not have
an opinion on the matter. Second, if one insists on
forcing the options into Wolff's A, or not-A, schema, then
the options we get concerning O are that one must either
believe O, or not believe O. And, while it is indeed the
case that one must either believe O, or not believe O,
it is also the case that it cannot be inferred from the

fact that one does not believe O that he believes not-O.
Thus, in either case it is clearly possible for a person
to have no opinion about an issue and, thus, to be neutral
about it. And, assuming that we could attach some meaning to the idea of an institution rather than a person
not having an opinion, it seems clear that neutrality of
opinion is possible for a university.

Much the same point can be made concerning neutrality
of consequences. Is it the case that one must do A, or
not do A? Surely. But again it has to be pointed out
that under many conditions A, or not-A, misrepresents
the actual character of the choices available. To be
neutral in some dispute is to act in such a way as to not
have a material effect on the outcome of the dispute.
It is to act in such a way that one's actions do not help
or harm the cause of any of the disputants, and it is
often the case that one does have such a course of action
available.

That one does often have such an option can be shown by
examining what I shall call the zealot's ploy. The
zealot's ploy consists in treating any act other than one
which aids his cause as one which harms his cause or
helps the cause of his opponents. Such slogans as 'He
that is not for me is against me,' or 'If you're not part
of the solution, you're part of the problem' indicate
common instances of the zealot's ploy.

Now at best, the zealot's ploy will make the claim that
one is not neutral about a given dispute trivially true.
It will trivialize the claim in that it will be capable of
showing that acts intended to avoid involvement in a
dispute even when apparently successful in fact fail to
achieve neutrality. But the problem is even worse,
because the zealot's ploy is capable of showing that one
is simultaneously opposing both sides in a dispute of
which he is not aware and which may be far removed from
him. Suppose, for example, that there is a war taking
place between groups A and B on the third planet circling
Alpha Centauri. Well, on the argument of the zealot's
ploy you and I have been actively opposing both sides.
That our failure to remain neutral in the dispute consists
in not doing anything to aid either side is not mitigating
to someone armed with the zealot's ploy. But clearly
this is a reductio ad absurdum and something has gone
wrong. What is wrong is forcing the options into the
A, or not-A, model, but to admit this is also to admit
the possibility of neutrality.

It is important to note here, however, that the fact
that A, or not-A, is often not a rational way to represent
available options does not show that it is not sometimes a

rational way to represent available options. Often a
university may find itself related to an issue in such a
way that the possibility of a neutral course of action
is effectively foreclosed. A useful example here is the
plight of many American universities during the early
days of the Vietnam War. Universities had for years provided the academic records of their male students to the
Selective Service who used the information to determine
draft eligibility. When the war began to be an object
of intense criticism on campuses, the policy of providing
this information became suspect in the eyes of many.
Was the university not implicated in the war by helping
the military select its manpower? Could it justify continuing to assist a process which sent its students off
to fight in a war which many of them regarded as immoral?
On the other hand, a refusal by a university to provide
such information to the Selective Service seems a clear
act of resistance.

The upshod is that the university seems effectively
precluded from adopting a stance of neutrality. Why?
Essentially, because two sets of conditions are fulfilled.
First, it seems plausible to construe the university's
options as A, or not-A. Either the university continues
to provide information to the Selective Service or it does
not. Second, both options require taking a stand on and
having an effect on some issue. Given the circumstances
continued cooperation with the Selective Service can only
be construed as a pro-war stand and lack of cooperation as
an anti-war stand.

What these arguments show is that the claim that a
university cannot be neutral is wrong only if it is understood as showing that it is a priori impossible for a
university to achieve neutrality on any issue. But there
are cases where the argument works, namely cases where
the options are plausibly construed as contradictories
rather than contraries and where the options affect the
matter at issue. Such cases often arise concerning the
relations between the university community and society.
Typical cases involve the management of endowments, the
performance of military research, the treatment of minorities, and the effects of the university as a consumer in
labor disputes as in the California grape boycott. In
areas such as these it is easy for an institution to
become involved in a dispute in such a way that neutrality
is not an alternative.

We are now in a position to try to develop a concept of
neutrality which relfects the requirements of a liberal
ideology. The question may be approached by asking
whether either neutrality of opinion or neutrality of

consequences provides a suitable concept. It should be
clear immediately that neutrality of consequences is not
what we are looking for. Neutrality of consequences concerns the domain of action, but the sort of neutrality
demanded by a liberal ideology is one which pertains
primarily to ideas or opinions. The primary function of
liberal neutrality is, as has been suggested, to promote
tolerance of dissent and diversity.

Perhaps, then, neutrality of opinion is what we are
looking for. At first glance this would require a university to take no stand or adopt no official policy
concerning any idea or opinion in order to give free play
to inquiry and discovery among the members of the university community. This seems close to what is required.

But it is not quite right. It is not quite right
because the university does intervene in intellectual
disputes in certain ways. In essence the university
intervenes by certifying the competence of the participants in its intellectual life. Typically, this function is performed by granting the faculty control over
areas such as the selection of its members and over the
academic life of students on the assumption that the
faculty is the repository of those skills required in
order to judge competence.

When this type of judgment is exercised concerning
the university's intellectual life, it will effectively
exclude some points of view. Astronomy departments will
not hire astrologers or disciples of Ptolemy, and
chemistry departments will not hire alchemists. A university may tolerate such persons on the periphery of
its intellectual life, but they will be denied access to
the center.

Is this role a violation of neutrality? I suspect not,
but it requires a new conception of neutrality. Here
the sort of neutrality appropriate is analogous to the
role of a referee or umpire in a game. The ideal is to be
an impartial enforcer of the rules of the game. Let us
call this sort of neutrality impartial neutrality.
Impartial neutrality like neutrality of opinion requires
the university not to opt for one party or another in a
given intellectual dispute, but unlike neutrality of
opinion, impartial neutrality assigns to the university
(or to other university-based communities of scholars)
the active role of enforcing the intellectual standards
of the debate.

This role of referee of the intellectual life of the
community is exercised in a variety of ways. I have
already mentioned the selection and retention of faculty.
But editors of refereed journals (note the word 'referee')

and an extensive, if sometimes subtle, system of rewards
and punishments also function (sometimes) to maintain
standards of competence in intellectual life.

Thus, it seems to me that the main difference between
the liberal's conception of a free and open marketplace
of ideas as it applies to a university as opposed to
society generally is that the university's marketplace
is refereed, its ideological venders are policed, so to
speak, but for competence not orthodoxy.

Is this kind of neutrality possible? There are at
least three assumptions required. First, this concept of
neutrality assumes that there is a recognizable difference
between a discipline's content and its standards of
judgment. Impartial neutrality requires that rewards and
sanctions be applied solely on grounds of competence and
never on grounds of opinions held. That assumes a
systematic ability to distinguish the quality of an
argument in a discipline, but not simply because one dis-
agrees with the conclusions reached. It is my impression
that in most disciplines this distinction is well understood and applied. It does, of course, become problematic to the degree that a discipline's standards of judgment are themselves at issue among the discipline's
competent practitioners.

Second, this concept of neutrality assumes that the
standards of judgment in a discipline are reasonably
objective. The decisions as to who is intellectually
competent can only be as objective as a discipline's
methods. Thus, the 'softer' a discipline, the harder it
is to identify rationally its competent practitioners.

These two conditions are logical ones. The third is
a psychological one. If impartial neutrality is to be
possible, human beings must be capable of applying appropriate standards of judgment in a reasonably fair and
objective way. This requires both that they understand
these standards and that they be capable of overcoming
bias and prejudice.

Concerning the two logical conditions, I shall assume
that in most academic endeavors they are adequately met.
The third condition is, perhaps, most problematic. Here
it will be useful to note that even if bias and prejudice
are inevitable to some degree, they can be lessened.
This suggests that even if impartial neutrality is unlikely to be completely attained, it can nevertheless
be coherently aimed at. Thus, at this point, two conclusions are warranted concerning impartial neutrality.
First, impartial neutrality is the sort of neutrality
which is required by a liberal conception of the university. Second, impartial neutrality is possible and is,
thus, coherently aimed at.

At this point, I shall discuss some different problem
areas concerning university neutrality, and we shall see
if the distinctions I have developed are capable of
shedding any light on questions of policy.

Initially, there are areas in which the requirements
of impartial neutrality are obvious. Impartial neutrality
precludes the university from linking rewards or sanctions
to a person's opinions or from making access to facilities
contingent on any orthodoxy. But this is clear enough.
We need, I think, to focus on some of the more interesting
grey areas. The most fruitful area for inquiry here is
the ways in which the university relates to the larger
society. For purposes of convenience I shall divide the
university's external relations into two classes. First,
there are those activities of a university which are
unrelated to its central functions. Universities spend
and invest money, consume resources, hire employees, and
even affect traffic patterns. All of these activities
have effects on the lives of those outside of the university community. Second, there are those activities
of a university which involve its central purposes, but
which direct them at an audience external to the university. Modern universities generate knowledge for
business or industrial consumers and train manpower for
various job markets. Thus, they provide educational
services for an external clientele.

Concerning the first group, there is that interesting
class of events where the university is involved in such
a way as to render neutrality of consequence impossible.
What are the university's obligations here? I wish to
argue that other things being equal the university has an
obligation to take sides in any such dispute. The university may truthfully claim to be neutral in such cases
in that it has no official policy concerning such a
dispute and that what effects its actions have on the
dispute are accidental consequences of its policies concerning other matters. But such a response merely shows
that in such cases neutrality of opinion is possible.
It does not show it to be desirable. And it is difficult
to see what merit there is in refusing to take a stand
on an issue on which one's actions are bound to have an
effect. Such a ploy seems to amount to nothing more than
a refusal to consider and take responsibility for the
consequences of one's acts. Insofar as an appeal to
neutrality merely serves to enable an institution to
ignore some of the consequences of its actions in its
deliberation concerning its external affairs, it is
objectionable.

Nor is impartial neutrality really at issue in such

cases. This is the case because when issues concern those
external relations accidental to the university's purposes, the university can usually take a stand without
being required to enforce sanctions against students and
faculty who wish to dissent and without restricting the
free flow of information and ideas. Thus, it seems both
that the university has a moral obligation to take a stand
in cases where its actions inevitably produce consequences
and that taking such a stand need not be in violation of
the requirements of its liberal ideas.

The most troublesome cases concern those contacts
between the university and society which can be seen as
extensions of the university's purposes. We need to note
initially that the modern university has undergone considerable evolution concerning the conception of its
central functions. The ideal university to which liberal
conceptions of tolerance and neutrality linked has as its
central values the pursuit and dissemination of truth or
less archaically research and teaching. The goals of the
modern university have evolved into the triumvirate of
teaching, research and service.

This evolution has not, however, amounted to simply
the addition of a third function. It has altered the
conception of the first two as well. In the liberal conception of the university the pursuit and dissemination
of truth are treated as intrinsic goods and do not require
justification in terms of some social agenda. The university is held to be a socially useful institution, but
in a rather indirect way. Knowledge produced for its own
sake nevertheless may have social utility. Educated men,
while not trained for a specific job, nevertheless, prove
adaptable, capable and do their jobs well. Social utility
was something that the liberal university accomplished,
but did not aim at.

In the modern university, however, much research and
teaching is targeted to specific needs external to the
university. Research is supposed to generate solutions
to particular antecedently identified problems, and teaching is supposed to train people to perform specific tasks.
Thus, the service ideal of the university infects its
other goals as well.

How does this newer conception of the university affect
the nature and application of the university's liberal
ideals and its view of neutrality? First, it seems
obvious that if the university is to provide direct solutions to social problems, it must take a stand on these
problems and try to have consequences for them. Any
attempt to serve society assumes some views about what
is good for society. Thus, for example, if a university

develops a program in criminology and fails to make its expertise similarly available to the Mafia it is not being neutral. It seems both to be taking a stand and trying to have consequences.

Perhaps, however, the university can enter into such commitments without sacrificing impartial neutrality. It is plausible to maintain, for example, that such commitments to serving society need not be translated into rewards or sanctions in such a way as to restrict free inquiry or establish any official ideology. The members of the university community will retain their freedom to dissent to their hearts' content. Thus, impartial neutrality is not violated.

This argument seems naive, however, for at least three reasons. First, commitments to provide research or teaching services to society will obviously translate themselves into demands for staffing in such a way that agreement with the particular commitment to service will turn out to be a condition of employment. Second, even for those whose jobs are secure a commitment to the prevailing social service agenda is often required in order to secure institutional rewards and avoid sanction. Thus, a faculty member who dissents on a program to which his colleagues have made a commitment will find himself isolated and his position and salary affected. Institutional incentives thus get linked to a point of view. Finally, a university geared to providing social services will find that the nature of its commitments will be significantly influenced by a kind of service market. The university after all can be expected to provide services to clients who are capable of expressing and funding their needs. This means that universities will not serve any needs, but only those needs which have some access to wealth or power. In short, the conceptions of society which the university will serve will be those held by industry or government. Socially disenfranchised groups are unlikely to find a champion in the modern university until they first can express their needs through political power.

The conclusion here is that the social service university is likely to create mechanisms whereby its systems of incentives become linked to points of view held by external agencies and that this would seem a clear violation of impartial neutrality. It is also worth mentioning here that the consequences of this trend are likely to be a subtle and gradual erosion of the university's tolerance and neutrality. And since this process will manifest itself more via incentives rather than coercion, it is apt to be fairly inconspicuous and not energetically protested. Dissenters will not be coerced. They will be coopted or isolated.

This institutional erosion of impartial neutrality is I suspect merely the embodiment of a kind of conceptual displacement of the ideal of impartial neutrality. I have suggested that the shift from a liberal to a social service conception of the university can be conceptualized in part as a change in the conceptual status of the goals of teaching and research. In the liberal university, teaching and research are intrinsic goods, whereas in the social service university they are instrumental goods. Two things follow concerning liberal ideals such as impartial neutrality. First, it follows that insofar as research and teaching continue to be central activities of the university, liberal ideals will continue to have a place in the university. Second, it follows that these ideals will be evaluated and understood in a different framework.

This second point can be explicated by the following model. Let us imagine a situation where a university's programs are geared to some social goal, SG. Teaching and research will be instrumental to SG and liberal ideals will be likewise instrumental to SG. Now what follows is that criticism, debate and tolerance will be valued so long as they are perceived as part of the process whereby SG is developed and implemented, but not when they begin to be perceived as in opposition to SG. Thus, in the social service university liberal ideals like impartial neutrality will be valued, but they will lead a more circumscribed existence and may be rejected when they seem to conflict with service goals.

These conceptual points suggest part of the explanation of the increasing resistance to liberal institutions such as academic freedom and tenure, institutions designed to implement impartial neutrality in that they prevent linking rewards or punishment to opinions. Such institutions are perceived from a liberal point of view as essential features of an institution whose purposes are the pursuit and dissemination of truth. But in the social service university they are easily perceived as obstacles to achieving service objectives. Individuals who have substantial freedom are not easily gotten to harness themselves to legislative directives or administrative programs. Thus, it seems inevitable that legislators and administrators who feel an obligation to harness the university to public service will come to perceive liberal institutions as hinderances to the flexibility and responsiveness of the university to social goals. Indeed, they are quite right. Liberal institutions which guarantee substantial independence to their individual members will be less responsive than they might to social goals.

It is, thus, reasonable to suppose that as modern universities move from a liberal toward a social service conception that liberal institutions such as academic freedom and tenure will undergo substantial erosion or modification.

What follows from this analysis is that since the modern university is conceptually eclectic combining both liberal and social service perspectives in the same institution coherent solutions concerning neutrality and liberality are not going to be forthcoming. Consistent policies are not likely to be derived from conflicting values. While this state of affairs offends my philosophical sensitivities considerably, I am not convinced that such eclectic institutions are objectionable. Indeed, there are substantial benefits to be derived from the juxtaposition of liberal and social service conceptions. Such institutions may be an effective way to render knowledge useful while avoiding the trap of uncritical subservience to socially dominant interests. My basic recommendation here is for a policy which permits incentives, but not sanctions to be linked to opinion. Such a policy provides leverage by means of which resources can be harnessed to service objectives while at the same time minimizing the penalties to a dedicated critic.

Perhaps two general conclusions can be drawn from this paper. First, neutrality is not easily generalized about. My argument should at least suggest that issues concerning neutrality need to be handled by means of close analysis of particular contexts rather than by means of conceptual broadsides. Second, the analysis indicates that the most interesting problems concerning neutrality and other liberal ideals arise from basic changes in institutional values. This is the area in which further inquiry would be most useful.

NOTES

1 Douglas Peterson, The American Cause and the American University, reprinted in Immanuel Wallerstein and Paul Slar, 'The University Crisis Reader' (New York: Random House, 1971), vol.1, pp.72-3.
2 Robert Paul Wolff, 'The Ideal of the University' (Boston: Beacon Press, 1969), pp.70-1.

3

Student academic freedom and the changing student/university relationships

Romulo F. Magsino

I INTRODUCTION

Somewhere in his 'Adventure of Ideas,' Alfred North
Whitehead observes that 'Great ideas often enter reality
in strange guises and with disgusting alliances.' This
observation might be made, perhaps without much hesita-
tion, by one who has studied the contemporary development
of the idea of student academic freedom. If one grants
that this idea - at least in the field of education -
approximates the significance of the essential equality
of men which Whitehead was alluding to, student academic
freedom might indeed be shown to have entered the world
of the university in 'strange guises and with disgusting
alliances.' It came with ragged clothes and long hair,
rough manners and coarse language, open six, and defiance
of authority. But further, it came initially not as a
moral cause under which student rebels rallied. Rather,
it appeared, in the words of Sidney Hook, 'adventitiously
in the wake of other student demands that required an ex
post facto rationale.' (1)
    The active, sometimes violent, energy that forced the
idea of student academic freedom into our consciousness
seems to have petered out. If recent accounts of student
mood on campuses are not mistaken, we have now the 'self-
centered generation' concerned mainly with preparing
themselves for lucrative and satisfying jobs and divorced
from the political activism and revolutionary fervor of
the not too distant past. (2)
    Nevertheless, student academic freedom has arrived.
As is true of powerful ideas, it will very likely continue
to influence developments in the university. In England,
the Commission on Academic Freedom and the Law, formed by
the National Union of Students and the National Council
for Civil Liberties (NUS-NCCL) and charged with consider-

ing all aspects of academic freedom and the law as they
affect students, has suggested radical changes in the
student-university relationships. (3)   In Canada, the
report of the Commission on the Government of the University of Toronto came out as an affirmation of the
principles called for by the current conceptions of
student academic freedom.   Thus the report, entitled
'Toward Community in University Government,' endorses
the principle of staff-student parity at all levels of
university government and the principle of student participation in matters of faculty appointment, promotion,
tenure, dismissal and in matters of research policy.
The idea of student academic freedom seems to require
all these, as former University of Toronto President
Claude Bissell himself professes:

> Increasingly freedom for the student ... means his
> power to make decisions about his environment and to
> be protected against institutional coercion and
> injustice. He repudiates the in loco parentis theory
> of the function of the institution. In disciplinary
> matters he is concerned about proper legal procedures,
> and about drawing a distinction between offenses as a
> citizen and as a student. All this is defensive.
> But the committed student seeks to give a more positive
> content to freedom. Freedom is the right and power to
> make decisions that shape one's environment. (4)

Unfortunately, the students' claim to academic freedom
sounds perplexing, if not disturbing. Nowhere in federal
or state constitutions, statutes or legal cases do we find
provisions for student academic freedom. University
bylaws or charters, if they say anything at all, confirm
the broad powers of the institution over students. (5)
Educational tradition in most countries, moreover, does
not indicate any student entitlement to academic freedom.
Thus, in the USA, for example, it is only during the
1960s that educators seriously considered extending
academic freedom to students. (6)   The historical fact
seems to be that in the latter part of the nineteenth
century, American educators trained in Germany brought
with them to North America a rich German concept of
student academic freedom. This concept embraced specific
freedoms relating to students' determination of the course
of their study and of their personal and social lives
within the university. Unfortunately these educators
failed to transform the concept into reality. (7)   Con-
sequently, a student claiming academic freedom in the
present time cannot assert that there is a presumption in
favor of his enjoying this freedom - a presumption which,
incidentally, his faculty counterpart seems to enjoy

despite recent blows on the idea of tenure in the university. (8)

That in most places today we do not find educational
tradition granting students academic freedom that could
protect them from arbitrary university action is indeed
to be regretted. However, from another perspective - that
of the university educators - it is also a matter of
serious concern that the claim to an amorphous, vaguely-
defined principle is presented to justify a reversal of
roles within the university community, specifically those
of the student. Naturally we can listen with empathic
understanding to insistent student demands. Wisdom, not
only prudence, would enjoin us to consider such demands,
a typical example of which runs as follows:

> Contemporary issues have come to define student aca-
> demic freedom as student freedom in the academic com-
> munity - not just freedom to explore ideas and express
> them within that academic community....
>
> [Student academic freedom] entails real responsi-
> bility in students - participation, not just consult-
> ation; functionally, not just formally.
>
> Genuine responsibility ... must include a decision-
> ary voice in all elements having an effect on students,
> including academics. (9)

Carried out consistently, such demands could result in
profound changes within the university, particularly in
relation to the roles of the students and the faculty.
As Dewey pointed out about thirty years ago, liberty or
freedom is power - effective power to do specific things.
Now the possession of such power is always a matter of
the distribution of power that exists at the time. Demand
for increased power at one point means demands for change
in the distribution of powers, that is for less power
somewhere else. (10) Thus to grant students the academic
freedom they demand is to diminish the university (faculty
and administrative) power to determine much of what is
being done in the institution, including, of course, the
conduct of academic affairs. Surely, such a serious com-
plication as this requires our close scrutiny. We would
need to ask the question: Does student academic freedom
justify the wide-ranging, specific freedoms demanded by
students?

This paper is an attempt to take the initial steps that
might lead to a suitable answer to our question. However,
before we undertake these steps, two points need to be
emphasized. First, there is, at present, no one formulation that every advocate of student academic freedom
agrees on. Several competing formulations have been presented, (11) and this makes it difficult for us to say

that their formulators are referring to the same thing or idea. The lack of established linguistic usage and educational arrangements embodying the idea of student academic freedom renders it nothing less than an elusive concept. However, we cannot afford to have it elude us here, otherwise we cannot determine whether it does or does not allow the specific freedoms claimed by students under the rubric of student academic freedom. Thus one of the central tasks in this paper is to indicate at least its basic nature.

Second, while formulations differ, nevertheless it is clear that their formulators aim at convincing us to accept their formulations by presenting their justifications for them. Hence, when a formulator explicates his formulation in terms of specific freedoms that make up student academic freedom (this freedom being taken to be nothing much more or much less than its constituent specific freedoms), the specific freedoms are seen to follow from some considered justification. Thus the formulation - and necessarily the idea of student academic freedom it incorpoates - becomes acceptable only to the degree that the justification offered is itself acceptable.

In this paper, I shall elaborate on and assess the justifications offered for student academic freedom. It will be noted that these justifications have not given rise to viable formulations that reflect the true nature of student academic freedom. Having done this, I shall try to make explicit what I take to be its true nature. Finally, I shall indicate, at least tentatively, the specific freedoms that may be justifiably claimed as constituent elements of the student academic freedom being advocated here.

II THE JUSTIFICATION OF STUDENT ACADEMIC FREEDOM

Student academic freedom, in whatever form it has been presented, is generally not thought of as an end in itself. Rather, just like the faculty academic freedom, (12) it is understood to be a means to certain ends. The opening sentences of the 1967 Joint Statement on Rights and Freedoms of Students, by the American Association of University Professors (AAUP), typify the conception of student academic freedom as means:

Academic institutions exist for the transmission of knowledge, the pursuit of truth, the development of students, and the general well-being of society. Free inquiry and free expression are indispensable to the attainment of these goals.

Minimal standards of academic freedom of students
... are essential to any community of scholars. (13)

If, indeed, student academic freedom is a means, it
would seem that its justification would involve its
meeting at least two requirements: (a) Insofar as a means
arises in relation to an end, the acceptance of a means
would require the prior acceptance of its end; and (b)
insofar as a means is resorted to in order to achieve an
end, this means must be the sort of thing that could
achieve the end, and further, achieve it in the most
effective manner consistent with the nature of an end. (14)

Now those who have espoused the idea of student academic freedom see good reason for advocating that students
should enjoy it within the university. They believe that
its desirability can be amply justified, and accordingly,
they have offered justifications. These justifications
fall roughly under two categories. (15) One category,
which we might refer to as 'legal justification,' takes
the students' claim to student freedom as being justified
by their membership in a democratic society that ensures
certain rights and freedoms for its members. Thus
student academic freedom is viewed as a sub-species of an
individual's political, legal, and egalitarian freedoms.
The American Civil Liberties Union (ACLU), John Searle,
William Van Alstyne, and William Birenbaum, among others,
have adopted this standpoint. (16) The other justification appeals to the nature of the university as a
unique, specialized institution charged with some particular task. The pursuit of this task is seen to require
certain freedoms not only for the faculty but also for
students. This 'institutional justification' has been
advocated by, among others, the AAUP, R.M. MacIver,
Philip Monypenny, and E.G. Williamson. (17)

(Parenthetically, it must be noted that in the final
analysis, both justifications are anchored on the ideal
of liberal democracy which stresses knowledge and rationality in human institutions and arrangements. Thus the
two categories of justification for student academic
freedom differ not so much in regard to its ultimate end
as in regard to the manner by which the ultimate end is
to be achieved. One emphasizes the need to establish
uniform standards or modes of relationships for all social
institutions in order to attain the ideal; the other
insists on maintaining unique standards or modes of
relationships within each social institution. (18))

(a) The legal justification

In a recent definitive statement, the ACLU declares as
follows:
> Academic freedom is analogous to civil liberties in the
> community at large, including not only the right to
> free inquiry, expression and dissent, but the right to
> due process and equal treatment, assuring for teachers
> and students the full enjoyment of their constitutional
> liberties. (19)

As civil liberties, they override educational considerations. Thus, Birenbaum states:
> Educational policy ... is not the only nor the con-
> trolling factor in determining what recommendations
> should be made with regard to freedom of expression,
> assembly, press, and association. Ultimately, these
> are questions of constitutional law. We must look to
> Supreme Court decisions for the only reliable guidance
> on these points. (20)

The implications of the acceptance of this position
are fairly discernible. Given that university students
are mostly of the majority age, and given the present
concern for guaranteeing civil liberties in the USA, the
traditional university/student relationship faces upheaval.
Not only are the theories (21) supporting university
authority over students being laid down in the final
resting place, also, as court decisions affecting students
are spelled out, and as legislatures consider enactments
guaranteeing student freedoms, (22) student freedom gains
more and more content. In the USA, court activism in the
1960s produced a plethora of decisions negating the doctrines of in loco parentis and the waiver of student
rights in a contractual relationship. The consequence is
that the university/student relationship has irreversibly
changed. Not only that; more disturbingly, the long-
standing, sacred university autonomy has been effectively
challenged by the judiciary. University presidents or
their representatives have had, on occasion, to encounter
the courts' summons servers. This has led a victim of
student unrest, former President Perkins of Cornell
University to express this fear:
> We do view with alarm the specter that seems to be
> rising out of its ashes and taking the form of a rash
> of court cases challenging decisions in areas that were
> once considered the educational world's peculiar pro-
> vince. The filing of these cases seems to suggest that
> judicial processes can be substituted for academic
> processes. (23)

The alarm is understandable. However, if it is granted

that broad university power over students is founded on
doctrines that are morally and legally suspect; if it is
agreed that it is about time students are given more protection by courts and legislatures from the arbitrary
exercise of university authority, (24) then alarm must
give way to a realistic assessment of the situation.   The
view taken by Professor Sibley of the University of
Manitoba seems to be a sensible one.   Though addressed to
the matter of university autonomy in Canada, his comment
could easily apply to the American or the British situation

> I am willing to postulate that if we do commit our-
> selves to resolute action, we shall eventually be met
> half-way by society and government.   The present surge
> of hostility toward the university may be checked, and
> sensible accommodations arrived at.   Much of our
> former autonomy will vanish: our decision boundaries
> are going to be severely constricted.   Of this develop-
> ment I think there can be no doubt.   In the fact of
> these changes our task is to define and to preserve
> at all cost our inner core of values while surrendering
> much that is peripheral and accidental. (25)

Whether we like it or not, it seems that specific
freedoms will accrue to students through judicial and
legislative action.   The question that concerns us,
however, is this: Could we take the accumulation of these
specific freedoms as student academic freedom?

In response to this question, at least two points can
be raised.   First, it must be admitted that the legal
justification could sufficiently demolish the theories
underlying the overarching authority the university
possesses vis-à-vis students.   Also, it must be conceded
that this justification can serve as a principle which can
determine the contents of student freedom in the university.   Nevertheless, this is not to say that the freedoms attributed to students who are also citizens comprise
student academic freedom.   What we have here, simply and
more accurately, is a set of civil freedoms enjoyed by
any other member of society, whether a doctor, a salesman,
or a garbage collector.   We surely sacrifice clarity - we
can even mislead - if we call these freedoms 'student
academic freedom' merely because they are exercised by
students within the confines of an academic institution.

Second, it is rather obvious that if student academic
freedom is made to represent those specific freedoms
accruing to students from legal considerations, we would
in effect eliminate from the conception those freedoms
for students that arise in the course of the university's
pursuit of its unique task.   These, unfortunately, are the

freedoms we cannot afford to set aside from our conception
if only because they are the ones that appear particularly
associated with the operation of the university as an
educational or academic institution. Take, for example,
the freedom a professor gives his students to devise, by
themselves, the contents of his course, subject to his
supervision. Here we have a freedom that may be educationally desirable but which cannot be regarded legal or
civil in origin by any stretch of imagination. The same
may be said about student freedom to choose elective
courses, to select their professors or course sections,
and to go about researching on an assigned topic the way
they think fit, subject to professorial supervision.
These freedoms do not seem legally justifiable at all,
yet these are precisely the kind of freedoms we would
think students could be given in the academic enterprise.

These points are related to the ambivalence with which
formulators of legally based conceptions of student academic freedom view it. On the one hand they begrudge the
university for its arbitrary and authoritarian treatment
of students, and accordingly aim at establishing student
academic freedom so that students could enjoy liberties
available to every member of society. But to approach
student academic freedom in this manner is to assert in
fact that this freedom is a means not so much to the
attainment of the university's ends as to the achievement
of a desired social arrangement. To say, for example,
that as part of their academic freedom, students are
entitled to demonstrate or picket against the university
is to take the university as nothing different from any
other institution of society that can be subjected to
these activities. It is to say, further, that this has to
be so, because the social good demands arrangements
whereby every social group, whether minority or majority,
can express its interests. Surely there is nothing wrong
about students being able to do so, except that the university is supposed to be doing certain things that do not
lend to a compromise of clashing interests. If we may use
Green's metaphor, the university can be viewed as a
'market' where relationships result from the test of
strength and desire. In the market model, what is tested
is not reason: 'It is power and wants; not the common good
good, but my good. The mechanisms of the market provide
not a test of thinking but a test of bargaining power....'
(26) The present-day university is so complex - with its
dormitories, cafeterias, and contractual relationships
with students - that a substantial portion of its
relationships can be resolved based on the market model.

But, to use Green's metaphor once more, the university

also operates under the 'tribunal' model because of its
organic link with knowledge. It is, so to say, a deliber-
ating tribunal, employing the light of reason, which
determines what is reasonable to believe and do. (27) If
students are to develop competencies in activities distinctive in the 'tribunal' model, and if freedoms are
instrumental in the development of these competencies,
then it is hardly appropriate to give them freedoms the
exercise of which trains them for the 'market' activities.
What we need to provide them, needless to say, are those
freedoms that contribute to student competencies fitted
for the 'tribunal' activities. To do otherwise - to conceive of student academic freedom as if it were made up
of specific freedoms relevant to the 'market' activities
- is to go counter to the very end for which the idea of
academic freedom as means was conceived.

On the other hand, formulators of legally based student
academic freedom might take cognizance of the academic
activities of the university. They might then suggest
that there is every possibility of incorporating into
the formulation distinctively academic freedoms. It would
be fascinating, although perhaps alarming, to hear the
strategy by which this is to be done. At the moment, the
odds are that it won't be done. The United States courts,
notable (or notorious!) for their intervention in university affairs, have by and large refrained from making
pronouncements on matters that are primarily academic. (28)
Of course, they can define, by the process of inclusion,
student academic freedom if they wished to do so. It
would certainly be effectively binding on the university.
(29) (And, surely, courts have conjured up stranger
things before.) The question really is: Ought the courts
to do so?

No doubt, this question is quite involved, and no
answer will be attempted in this article. (30) Nevertheless, for the courts to do so is to upset radically the
traditionally respected (by courts and legislatures)
autonomy of the university on academic matters.
Obviously, the burden of proof lies with the judiciary to
show that stripping the university of this autonomy is
necessary. It has to answer satisfactorily, among others,
the following questions:
 1 Has the university failed in the discharge of its
 responsibilities in connection with its academic
 relationships with students?
 2 Is the court competent in dealing with academic
 matters?
 3 How will judicial intervention on academic matters
 affect the attainment of the university's ends?

4 What effects will judicial intervention in one social
institution produce in relation to society as a whole as
well as its other institutions?
If no acceptable response to these questions is forthcoming, then the judicial formulation of student academic
freedom will have to wait. Meanwhile, it is about time
that we examined the alternative justification.

(b) The institutional justification

Many educators sympathetic to the student claim attempt
to justify wide-ranging freedoms for students in terms of
the function or nature of the university as a unique
societal institution. The real issue, one vocal educator
puts it, is the educational one: 'It is on educational,
not political, grounds that a valid case can be made for
permitting recognized student organizations to invite
speakers of their choice to the campus to discuss any
topic, no matter how controversial.' (31) The same
could be said, presumably, for the freedom of expression:
"On educational grounds, students should be encouraged to
publish their own newspapers, periodicals and pamphlets,
exchanging ideas, commenting on great issues, testing
and challenging their teachers' views.' (32)
    In contrast to the legal justification, the institu-
tional justification adopts a clear-cut position with
reference to the status of student academic freedom as
means to an end - the end being the achievement of the
particular task of the university. Nevertheless, this
justification does not seem to have given rise to an
acceptable formulation of student academic freedom. Two
reasons may account for this.
    The first is that we are not exactly sure where the
institutional uniqueness of the university lies. No doubt
the public on the one hand and educators on the other have
viewed the institutions of higher learning from different
perspectives. They have been seen, using Robert Paul
Wolff's metaphors, as a sanctuary of scholarship, as a
training camp for the profession, as a social service
station, and as an assembly line for establishment man.
(33) At the height of student unrest, the university
was also called upon to provide the testing ground for
the critical citizen. (34) The problem here is that
unless we agree on the precise end student academic freedom is to serve, we cannot assess the efficacy of proposed
component freedoms of the institutionally justified formulations.
    We shall suggest later that the matter is not so much

a dead end as we might be led to think. But for now let
us make believe that we agreed on the unique end for the
university. How would the formulation based on this end
look? An answer to this would suggest the second reason.

What is rather unexpected about the formulations justified institutionally (e.g. by the AAUP, Williamson, and
Miller and Pilkey) is that they include some specific
freedoms that are also found in the legally justified
formulations (e.g. by the ACLU and Birenbaum). And just
like the latter, they appear only a little less extensive.
Could the institutional justification actually justify
the inclusion of all these specific freedoms? Take, for
instance, some of the freedoms enumerated by Miller and
Pilkey:

1. Students should be free to organize and associate
to promote their common interests, whether it be to
establish a student government to regulate campus
activities or to promote common educational, social,
or political goals - even though some of these goals
may be of a controversial nature;
2. Freedom of expression on the part of students
individually or collectively; and
3. They should be free to participate in off-campus
activities, as others do, without institutional
restrictions. (35)

These freedoms, according to Miller and Pilkey, are
intended to ensure an objective search for knowledge and
truth - a function which uniquely characterizes the university. Yet freedom 1 would sanction the promotion of
groups that would actively seek the attainment of social
and political goals. Assuredly, however, there is a
distinction between an open-minded search for the truth on
the one hand, and the persistent attempt to secure by
pressure or lobby a group's interests on the other hand.
One is a scholarly, dispassionate endeavor, the other is
a socio-political action, less concerned with the truth
than with the acceptance of a group's point of view. A
similar comment may be made about freedom 2, frequently
extended (by Williamson, for example) to include the freedom to demonstrate, picket, petition, or sit-in. Such
processes are, familiarly enough, power tactics designed
to force one's viewpoint on another without the benefit
of rational inquiry. In principle, they are opposed to
the objective search for truth. Finally, freedom 3 is
obviously redundant in the formulation because institutions of higher learning have no business meddling with
the activities of students outside of the university.

However, the search for truth may be denied as the only
function of the university. It can be argued that other

functions could justify the formulation of extensive
freedoms for students. Recently, the role of the university in the development of critical citizens has been
strongly suggested. As Broek et al. put it, 'it is no
less true of freedom in the academy than of freedom in
society that it requires regular and vigorous exercise if
it is to survive and serve its ends.' (36) If students
are to grow as responsible, critical citizens would they
need extensive freedoms? In answer to this, two considerations may be taken up.

First, it is not obvious at all that social criticism
or moral citizenship requires involvement on the part of
students in interest groups or in demonstrations, picket-
ing, and the like. Those who advocate the development
of critical citizens do not envision anarchists. Rather,
they envision individuals capable of engaging in serious
moral discourse and moral action. Now engaging in moral
discourse and action requires at least two things. For
one, it demands the participant's possession of knowledge
relevant to the particular problem or issue at hand, or if
he does not have the relevant knowledge on the matter, the
skill needed in seeking out such knowledge. For another,
it demands the participant's understanding of and adherence to certain principles or values that underlie moral
discourse, such as consideration of the viewpoint of
others, respect for persons, impartiality, honesty, and
the like. There is no reason to believe that the two
things we have cited are promoted when students lobby,
demonstrate, picket or sit-in.

Second, even if it is granted that to become critical
citizens, students need to experience such activities as
demonstrating or whatever, nevertheless university consent and supervision on these activities are in order.
If responsibility is placed in the university to develop
the desired citizens, it stands to reason that it should
have the corresponding authority to determine the activities students should engage in. Otherwise, there is no
reason why the university should accept the responsibility. Thus, if the freedoms to demonstrate and the like
are thought to be necessary for critical citizenship,
granting these freedoms to students would still be contingent on the judgment and supervision of the university
or its faculty. As such, these freedoms can not be
equated with students' legal freedoms, the exercise of
which entirely depends on themselves.

The point in all this is that at present, those who
have attempted to specify the constituent elements of
student academic freedom by appealing to the educational
nature of the university have not been able to present any

convincing formulation. This failure is unfortunate
because, as I shall suggest later, the educational nature
of the university indeed points to the appropriate formulation of student academic freedom.

In retrospect, we can observe that the claim to
student academic freedom has not been presented with
either clarity, consistency or adequacy. On the one hand,
advocates of the legal justification arrive at justifications that are decidedly legal or civil, not academic.
Granted that students in the university are entitled to
civil freedoms, the justification still has to account
for some other freedoms students claim not so much as
citizens but as students. Otherwise, it cannot give rise
to a comprehensive student academic freedom which it is
intended to do. Yet the legal justification would seem
unable to do so. Even if it is able to do so, it would
draw the objection from educators who believe, very
reasonably, that in the university they should have a
determining voice in deciding on matters that affect the
conduct of the educational enterprise. The objection,
assuredly, is in order. For to subsume all student freedoms under the civil entitlements of students is in effect
to destroy university autonomy in the academic area.

On the other hand, advocates of the institutional
justification frequently formulate conceptions that are
considerably broader than the justification allows. The
net consequence of this state of affairs is that student
claim to freedoms within the university becomes enfeebled.
This is most unfortunate because arguably, a case for it
may be a meritorious one.

This much, however, is clear from the preceding
discussion. Students in the university may stake claims
to at least two kinds of freedom, and it would not do
students any good to subsume their claimed freedoms simply
under the rubric of student academic freedom. Their case
may be more intelligently and effectively pursued if it
is waged along two fronts: the legal and the academic.
Advocates on either front will have to argue for the
relevant freedoms that their ends require. We shall,
necessarily, leave it to others to argue on the legal
front. In the succeeding section, we shall attempt to
deal with the initial stage in pressing the case for
student freedoms on the academic front by suggesting a
tentative but perhaps a more viable conception of student
academic freedom.

III   TOWARD AN ACCEPTABLE CONCEPTION

Clearly, the first step involves the need to pin down the
end for which student academic freedom acts as means.
The difficulty in making this first step is that we are
here faced with questions about value - questions which
do not frequently lend to easy resolution, as the history
of moral philosophy attests to. Frequently, such questions are settled by force, or, if not settled, are
allowed to remain unresolved and sacrosanct under the
democratic ideal of social pluralism.

Nevertheless, whatever is the case, there is no reason
to believe that the university cannot meet these values
simultaneously. The faculties in a university are varied,
and their activities diversified. It is not altogether
implausible to suggest that in the modern university, one
can pursue his own end, be it preparation for the profession, for social service, for the industry, or for
critical citizenship. But what is crucial in this respect
is that the university can make provision for all of these
only because it has established bodies of knowledge which
it makes available for varied purposes. Further, it is
also crucial that we can hope to facilitate better the
attainment of our purposes only because the university is
able to pursue further knowledge. Thus, whatever task we
attribute to the university, we find a common denominator,
and that is the university's concern for knowledge. Whatever else the university is thought to be or do, its
unique role in the search for and transmission of knowledge is undeniable.

Some features related to the university's concern for
knowledge should now be stated. First, where the concern
is knowledge, the position of the faculty is crucial. It
is not inappropriate to say that knowledge does not exist
independently of the community of scholars who must constantly work to refine and expand it. Since they are
immediately and directly involved in the search for and
transmission of knowledge, the faculty are in the best
position to determine the knowledge activities in the
university.

Second, if the preceding point is valid, then the
university (the faculty, with the assistance of the
administrative staff who facilitate the knowledge activities therein, vis-à-vis the courts, the legislatures, and
the general society. Of course, this is not to say that
the independence of the university is complete. As
Crittenden has noted, academic freedom is a special freedom that depends on 'whether the members of the society
were convinced that the advancement of knowledge, at

least in some fields, was crucial for the attainment of other ends that they valued highly.' (37) Nevertheless, given the pervasive social valuation of knowledge and the competence of scholars engaged in it, the case for their academic autonomy is manifest.

Third, the special position of the faculty in relation to the knowledge enterprise makes it apparent that in determining activities by which students are initiated into and guided through knowledge, the latter take a subordinate status. This does not imply that thereby, students' views should not be considered at all. A perfectly good case can be made for having these views presented and represented in deciding on knowledge activities affecting students. However, clearly the final word must lie with the faculty.

What, then, might be the activities the performance of which must involve autonomy on the part of the university? Tentatively, a list of such activities might include the following:

1 Determining the conduct of teaching, learning, and research;
2 Specifying the academic qualifications of those who will engage in the teaching-learning and research process processes;
3 Fixing the criteria for the award of prizes, degrees, grades, scholarships, and the like;
4 Setting down the minimum academic standards to be met for continuation of one's participation in the university community;
5 Determining the university calendar as well as the course offerings;
6 Formulating the rules and procedures for undertaking any of the above activities, and the sanctions on the violation of the rules and procedures so formulated.

It is in connection with these activities that the university should be fully autonomous without having to fear the creeping legalism that characterizes the contemporary social life. At the same time, it is also in relation to these activities that the university, particularly the faculty, should feel competent in determining what freedoms may be given to students in their pursuit of knowledge. And the principle they might employ in determining such freedoms might be stated as follows: Will this particular freedom promote the students' search for and understanding of knowledge or truth? Using this principle, what specific freedoms will our conception of student academic freedom consist of?

To answer this question satisfactorily, we need to examine rather closely the processes directly related to transmitting and searching knowledge in the university, and then determine whether student freedom in such processes is desirable. Needless to say, this is a difficult task, beyond the intention of this paper. Nevertheless, we can envision what, roughly, such freedoms might be like. They might very well fall under either of two categories: (a) freedoms that are academic because of their intent and the academic nature of their content; and (b) freedoms that are academic largely because of the intent of the activities involved.

(a) Such freedoms as the freedom to choose courses, to select one's professors, to determine the content of one's courses, and the like, can be seen as academic because of their intent and nature. When these freedoms are given to students, the hope is that such freedoms will encourage students to seek actively the knowledge they are interested in, and thus contribute to the universities' task of promoting knowledge. At the same time, these freedoms are of such nature that they can only be found in academic institutions.

(b) On the other hand, students may be given freedoms in engaging in certain activities that might also be found in the wider society. When a student questions and objects to the claims being made by his professor, the latter lets him do so because it furthers the student's knowledge about the subject matter the professor is presenting to him. Note, however, that questioning and objecting are common occurrences in ordinary discourse outside of the university, and are fully protected by law. The difference lies in the intent of the participants in the university enterprise of questioning and objecting - an intent inherent in their roles as scholars and students in search of knowledge. But the tempting question to ask then is: What difference does it make to have freedoms under this category set off as part of student academic freedom? The answer, hopefully, is that it should make a difference.

Thus, for an example, we may conceive of some professors, teaching a course on pornography and its effects on individuals and society, who allow their students to scrutinize and pass around among students of the course what could concededly be classified as pornographic materials. Surely, passing around and scrutinizing such materials are not uncommon in many communities, and are frequently subject to legal penalties. Yet done in the university for the express purpose of furthering our understanding of a pesky social problem, such activities may well be beyond the power of the courts to proscribe.

There might be other protected freedoms in the uni-

versity that students may participate in. For example,
professors and students alike might engage in a frank,
full exploration of the advocacy of rebellion or revolution against the government. Conceivably such an activity
in the wider society could be construed as an incitement
to rebellion, and courts could possibly declare it illegal
and punishable under the law. Yet we would think that
such an activity, carried on in the university, should
not carry any penalty. Similarly, students of a given
course on modern ideologies might invite a known anarchist
who never fails to harangue his hearers and enjoin them
to a revolution. There is reason to believe that in such
a case, both the speaker and the students could be exempt
from legal prosecution. Thus, just like the legally
justifièd freedoms, student academic freedom could provide
students some measure of protection.

Protection for students, however, is not the only or
even the main rationale for student academic freedom.
Ultimately, this freedom arises from the need to have the
students meet the twofold task of understanding the heritage of human ingenuity, and at least for some of them,
of extending further the frontiers of human knowledge.
In the words of Michael Oakeshott,

'Academic freedom' has become a cant phrase in the
mouths of well-meaning but muddled advocates. But, in
fact, it can sustain only one meaning: the freedom to
be academic, the freedom of a university to pursue its
explorations of the enterprises of human understanding
and to initiate successive generations of students into
this intellectual inheritance. (38)

Analogously, we might say that student academic freedom
can sustain only one meaning: the freedom to be a participant in an academic endeavor, to partake of the freedom
of the university in the pursuit of human understandings.
Students are entitled to some other freedoms, namely the
legal ones, and we are bound to observe them in the university. But as initiators of the successive generations
of students into the human intellectual inheritance, the
faculty has one pressing concern: to extend to students
whatever freedom can contribute to their greatest achievement in the knowledge enterprise.

NOTES

1 Sidney Hook, 'Academic Freedom and Academic Anarchy'
   (New York: Dell, 1969), p.35.
2 See, for example, Now, the Self-Centered Generation,
   'Time' (Canada), September 23, 1974, pp. 58-9.

3 The National Union of Students and the National
   Council for Civil Liberties, 'Academic Freedom and
   the Law' (London: Goodwin Press, 1970).
4 Claude Bissell, The Student Version, in 'Student Power
   and the Canadian Campus,' ed. Tim Reid and Julyan Reid
   (Toronto: Peter Martin Associates, 1969), p.128.
5 The bill passed by the provincial legislature of
   Newfoundland, Canada, called The Memorial University
   (Amendment) Act 1974, is as explicit as any act
   relating to the power of the university in disciplin-
   ing and penalizing students. It gives the university
   Board of Regents the full disciplinary jurisdiction
   over students, and provides nothing whatsoever about
   appeal or conviction procedures, leaving the university the chance to suit itself.
6 The American Association of University Professors, for
   example, came out for student academic freedom only
   in 1964 when it formed its Committee S on Faculty
   Responsibility for Academic Freedom of Students. The
   American Civil Liberties Union (ACLU) has of course
   called for it as early as 1925, but the Union worked
   largely outside the university and was not listened
   to favorably until lately.
7 Attempts to make the conception a reality in the
   American colleges and universities were, however,
   made. See Romulo F. Magsino, 'The Courts, the
   University, and the Determination of Student Academic
   Freedom, Ph.D. dissertation, University of Wisconsin-
   Madison, 1973, ch.II, pp.9-47.
8 The reasons for this have not been thoroughly ascer-
   tained. For brief but suggestive comments on the
   matter, see Walter P. Metzger, Essay II, in 'Freedom
   and Order in the University,' ed. Samuel Gorovitx
   (Ohio: The Press of Western Reserve University, 1967),
   pp.63-8.
9 Greg Lipscomb, A Student Looks at Academic Freedom, in
   'The College and the Student,' ed. Lawrence E. Dennis
   and Joseph F. Kauffman (Washington, DC: American
   Council on Education, 1966), pp.289-90.
10 John Dewey, 'Problems of Men' (New York: Greenwood
   Press, 1946, 1968),   p.112.
11 Among the formulations available are the following:
   American Association of University Professors, 1967
   Joint Statement on Rights and Freedoms of Students,
   in 'Academic Freedom and Tenure,' ed. Louis Joughin
   (Madison: University of Wisconsin Press, 1969),
   pp.66-74; American Civil Liberties Union, Academic
   Freedom and Academic Responsibility, 'AAUP Bulletin'
   42 (1956), pp.517-23; American Civil Liberties Union,

'Academic Freedom and Civil Liberties of Students in
Colleges and Universities' (New York: ACLU, 1970);
William Birenbaum, in 'The Campus Crisis: Legal
Problems of University Discipline, Administration and
Expansion' ed. Barbara Flicker (New York: Practising
Law Institute, 1969), pp. 19-51; Rubin Gotesky,
Charter of Academic Rights and Governance, 'Educa-
tional Forum,' 32 (November 1967), pp.9-18; Robert
M. MacIver, 'Academic Freedom in Our Time' (New York:
University of Columbia Press, 1955), pp.205-22;
Theodore K. Miller and George P. Pilkey, College
Student Personnel and Academic Freedom for Students,
'Personnel and Guidance Journal,' 46 (June 1968),
pp.954-60; Student Bill of Rights of the United
States National Student Organization, 'School and
Society,' 68 (August 1948), pp.97-101; E.G.
Williamson, Students' Academic Freedom, 'Educational
Record,' 44 (July 1963), pp.214-22; and Do Students
have Academic Freedom? 'College and University,' 39
(Summer 1964) pp.466-87.

12   This point is clear in the documents of the American
Association of University Professors. The following
statement is representative of the AAUP position since
its inception:

> It is clear ... that the university cannot perform
> its threefold function without accepting and en-
> forcing to the fullest extent the principle of
> academic freedom. The responsibility of the uni-
> versity as a whole is to the community at large,
> and any restriction upon the freedom of the
> instructor is bound to react injuriously upon the
> efficiency and the morale of the institution, and
> therefore ultimately upon the interests of the
> community.

See the American Association of University Professors,
The 1915 Declaration of Principles, in 'Academic
Freedom and Tenure,' ed. Louis Joughin (Madison:
University of Wisconsin Press, 1967), p.165. Also,
see Brian Crittenden, 'Education and Social Ideals'
(Don Mills, Ontario: Longman Canada, 1973), pp.62-6.

13   American Association of University Professors, 1967
Joint Statement on Rights and Freedoms of Students, in
'Academic Freedom and Tenure,' ed. Louis Joughin
(Madison: University of Wisconsin Press, 1967), p.66.

14   In relation to the two requirements, two points may
be mentioned. First, these requirements, it will turn
out, suggest the principle we are looking for. Second,
by 'consistent with the nature of an end,' I mean
simply that if we are concerned with a moral end (as

is true of the end we are concerned with here) and if
we are engaged in a moral discourse in search for
means to our end, only moral means deserve consideration or qualify.

15   I am using 'categories' advisedly to indicate that
each of the two justifications may be subdivided
further. Thus, the legal justification may be either
one that emphasizes the principle of due process, or
one that stresses substantive freedoms. The same may
be said of the institutional justification. For an
extended discussion of these further justifications,
see Magsino, op.cit., chs III, IV, and V.

16   American Civil Liberties Union, 'Academic Freedom and
Civil Liberties of Students in Colleges and Univer-
sities,' (New York: ACLU, 1970); John Searle, 'The
Campus War' (New York: The World Publishing Co.,
1971), pp.184-97; William Van Alstyne, Student
Academic Freedom and the Rule-Making Power of Public
Universities: Some Constitutional Consideration, 'Law
in Transition Quarterly, 2 (1965), pp.1-34; William
Birenbaum, in Flicker (ed.), op.cit.

17   American Association of University Professors,
'Academic Freedom and Tenure;' MacIver, op.cit.;
Philip Monypenny, Toward a Standard for Student
Academic Freedom, in 'Academic Freedom: The Scholar's
Place in Modern Society,' ed. Hans W. Baade (New York:
Oceana Publications, 1964); E.G. Williamson, Do
Students Have Academic Freedom?, 'College and Uni-
versity,' 37 (Summer 1964), pp.466-87.

18   Surely one objection to judicial activism, by which
courts impose uniform standards (for example, of
procedural due process) on social institutions is that
it endangers the nature and contributions of such
institutions. See Lon Fuller, Two Principles of Human
Association, in 'Voluntary Association,' Nomos XI,
ed. J. Roland Pennock and John W. Chapman (New York:
Atherton Press, 1969), pp.3-21.

19   American Civil Liberties Union, 'Academic Freedom and
Civil Liberties of Students in Colleges and Universities' (New York: ACLU, 1970), p.4. This is no different from Searle's statement:
    The basic principle is that professors and students
    have the same rights of free expression, freedom of
    inquiry, freedom of association and freedom of
    publication in their roles as professors and
    students that they have as citizens in a free
    society, except insofar as the mode of exercise of
    these freedoms needs to be restricted to preserve
    the academic and subsidiary functions of the

university.
See Searle, op.cit., p.191. Searle's formulation is
more sophisticated than the ACLU's, though no less
questionable as student academic freedom.
20 Birenbaum, op.cit., p.31. The supremacy of the
Supreme Court in this statement reflects the American
tradition in which the power of judicial review by
the courts is amply recognized, especially concerning
the interpretation and implementation of the Bill of
Rights.
21 The theories or doctrines are 1 in loco parentis,
2 university attendance as privilege, and 3 the waiver
of student rights in a contractual relationship. For
a brief evaluation of each of these doctrines, see
Developments in the Law - Academic Freedom, in 81
'Harvard Law Review', 1144 (1968).
22 As of winter 1973, the Wisconsin (US) legislature was,
for example, conducting hearings in connection with a
proposed Student Bill of Rights.
23 James A. Perkins, The University and Due Process, in
'American Library Association Bulletin'(September
1968), pp.977.
24 These points are, I take it, undebatable. See Roy
Lucas, Student Rights within the Institutional Framework, in Flicker (ed.), op.cit., pp.30-86. For a
more extensive treatment, see 45 'Denver Law Journal,'
502-678 (1968).
25 William M. Sibley, Accountability and the University:
Is Whirl to be King?, in Proceedings of the Third
Annual Meeting (1972) of the Canadian Society for the
Study of Higher Education, no paging.
26 Thomas F. Green, 'The Activities of Teaching' (New
York: McGraw-Hill, 1971), p.223.
27 Ibid.
28 For instance, in Mustell v. Rose, 211 So. 2d. 489
(1968), the court refused to interfere with the
suspension of a medical student based on assigned
grades which the student challenged. See D. Parker
Young, 'The Legal Aspects of Student Dissent and
Discipline in Higher Education' (Athens: University of
Georgia Press, 1970).
29 The law is, presumably, what the courts say it is. In
the language of Mr Justice Holmes, 'The prophecies of
what the courts will do in fact, and nothing more
pretentious, are what I mean by the law.' Quoted by
Clark Byse, Procedure in Student Dismissal Proceedings: Law and Policy, in 'Student Rights and Responsibilities,' ed. J.W. Blair (Ohio: S. Rosenthal,
1969), p.135.

30 The question of judicial intervention in university affairs is evaluated in Magsino, op.cit., ch.V, pp.173-214, and ch.VI, pp.215-29.

31 Sidney Hook, Freedom to Learn but not to Riot, 'New York Times,' 3 January 1965, p.16. Later in his 'Academic Freedom and Academic Anarchy' (New York: Dell Publishing Co., 1969) he uses 'freedom to learn' interchangeably with 'academic freedom for students.'

32 Hook, Freedom to Learn but not to Riot, p.18

33 Robert Paul Wolff, 'The Ideal of the University' (Boston: Lincoln Press, 1969), pp.1-57.

34 See, for example, Richard Lichtman, The University: Mask for Privilege? in 'The University Crisis Reader,' 2 vols, ed. Immanuel Wallerstein and Paul Starr (New York: Vintage Books, 1971), vol.1, pp.101-20; and Theodore Roszak, On Academic Delinquency, in 'The Dissenting Academy,' ed. Theodore Roszak (New York: Vintage Books, 1968), po.3-42.

35 Theodore K. Miller and George P. Pilkey. College Student Personnel and Academic Freedom for Students, in 'Personnel and Guidance Journal', 46 (June 1968), pp.956-8.

36 Jacobus Ten Broek, Norman Jacobson and Sheldon Wolin, Academic Freedom and Student Political Activity, in 'The Berkeley Student Revolt,' ed. Seymour Martin Lipset and Sheldon Wolin (New York: Doubleday, Anchor Books, 1965), p.447.

37 Crittenden, op.cit., p.64.

38 Michael J. Oakeshott, The Definition of a University, 'The Journal of Educational Thought,' 1 (December 1967), p.142.

Students' rights   part II

From childhood to adulthood: 4
assigning rights and responsibilities

Francis Schrag

In 1965 three students were suspended from the Des Moines,
Iowa public schools (two were in high school, one in
junior high) for wearing black armbands to protest the
Vietnam War. When their parents challenged the legality
of the suspension they posed a question the courts had not
heretofore confronted: does the First Amendment guarantee
of freedom of speech apply to students in school? (1)
This is but one facet of a larger issue, the legal status
of young people, particularly adolescents, an issue which
has been the source of continuing dispute both in and out
of court since the mid-1960s. (2) As one commentator
notes, referring to recent Supreme Court decisions, 'the
Court has continued to hear children's rights cases with
mixed and at times incongruous results.' (3)

The question to be discussed here is when does a child
become adult or more precisely, how shall we determine
when a child should be accorded adult status? Such a
question presupposes that the distinction between adult
and child is legitimate, that children should not be
accorded the same rights and responsibilities as adults.
It is precisely this presupposition that has recently
been challenged by various self-styled child advocates,
and before proceeding to the main discussion it is crucial
to confront their point of view. The popular author, John
Holt, for example, in his book 'Escape From Childhood'
takes the following position:

> By now I have come to feel that the fact of being a
> 'child', of being wholly subservient and dependent, of
> being seen by older people as a mixture of expensive
> nuisance, slave, and super-pet, does most young people
> more harm than good. I propose instead that the
> rights, privileges, duties, responsibilities of adult
> citizens be made available to any young person, of
> whatever age, who wants to make use of them. (4)

61

John Holt is correct in claiming that children do not
enjoy equality before the law with adults. They are not
permitted to work or marry. They may neither make a
binding contract nor purchase liquor or cigarettes. They
may not participate in public affairs by voting, holding
public office or sitting on a jury. Finally, children
are required to live with their parents, receive medical
treatment when sick, and attend school for at least ten
years of their lives. Is Holt also correct in contending
that such unequal status does them more harm than good?
I shall briefly argue that the unequal status accorded
children is desirable and indeed protects their best
interests. In order to make this point as clearly as
possible the following argument is meant to apply only
to the very young, let us say, for convenience, children
below age four.

THE STATUS OF THE VERY YOUNG

Even those of Holt's persuasion must admit that very
young children lack the capacity to understand the consequences of their own actions and failures to act. It
is sometimes said of the immature that they are not fully
aware of the consequences of their actions, that they act
imprudently or improvidently. (5) This is too mild a way
of putting it and understates the nature of young children's disabilities. There is no easy way to draw a line
between the meaning or nature of an action and its consequences. It is not as if young children were simply
shortsighted. In failing to comprehend the consequences
of activity, they remain unaware of the significance of
activity in a fundamental way. The very young cannot
realize that in pushing a button, or touching a wire, or
in refusing to go to the doctor when it hurts, they are
risking their very lives. Nor can they realize that in
sticking a diaper pin into a sibling's tummy or in drop-
ping a screaming bundle onto the floor they may be
seriously injuring a human being. Nor can they realize
that by pronouncing certain words or scratching their
names to a piece of paper they thereby commit themselves
to obligations extending over months and years. The very
young, lacking a developed awareness of time and cause and
effect, that is of the reality beyond themselves, literally do not know what they do. Being thus incapacitated
they require not freedom from adult interference but adult
care and protection. They need to be protected both from
others who would exploit them and from the consequences
of their own behavior. The restraint the law imposes on

them therefore does them no injury in depriving them of
their freedom. On the contrary, it protects their own
interests. (6)

Such reasoning is indeed abhorrent when applied to any
class of adults save perhaps the retarded and the insane.
But we err as much in refusing to make necessary distinctions as in making artificial ones to suit our (adult)
interests. The young child's capacities are dramatically
different from the adult's, so his rights and responsibilities also should differ from ours. As Aristotle
remarked we do as much injustice in treating unequals
equally as in treating equals unequally. (7)

The interests of the young child then require that
children not be accorded the same rights as adults. A
second line of reasoning supports this conclusion as well.
Our fundamental notions of fairness demand a balance
between rights and responsibilities. If children were
granted the right to make contracts we would rightly
insist that they had a duty to keep them. If they had a
right to serve on juries sitting in judgment on others,
we would demand that they themselves be liable to criminal
prosecution for violations of the law. Children's
inability to understand and control their own actions is
the source of our refusal to accord them either adult
rights or adult responsibilities. If we granted them the
former we would need to grant them the latter as well.
This notion of fairness extends to the relationship between them and their guardians as well. Thus parents have
the right to impose their will on their own children, to
make decisions on their behalf. This 'benefit' is offset
by parents' obligation to support their children finan-
cially and psychologically.

The position I am taking here seems to deny children
basic human rights. Are children not to be treated as
human beings then? Have they no rights? What is a right?
Without going too far afield into the rich philosophical
literature on rights, let us borrow a definition from the
British philosopher, John Plamenatz: 'A man (or an animal)
has a right whenever other men ought not to prevent him
from doing what he wants or refuse him some service he
asks for or needs.' (8) When all rights are identified
with protected freedom of action, then indeed children
have very restricted rights. All human beings regardless
of age require food, protection from the elements, human
contact, relief from suffering. We may say that any human
has a right to these. (9) Children do have rights qua
children as well, to the care and nurture without which
normal growth and development will not occur. The duty
correlative with this right of providing such care

normally falls on the parent, but it would be impossible
for them to carry out this duty if they were forbidden
from ever interfering with their offsprings' freedom.
Freedom of action is an unmitigated good for any being
which is able to understand the significance and assess
the consequences of alternative courses of action. Freedom of action is a good for almost all adults (excluding
the severely retarded). But if the freedom of action of
the very young were protected by law, if adults were
liable to arrest for ever forcing children to do anything
against their will, few children would survive infancy.

This much has so far been shown: the rights and responsibilities accorded very young children ought to be
different from those accorded adults. In particular the
denial to children of adult rights and responsibilities
usually serves the child's own interests. It hardly
follows from this, however, that minority should continue
to age eighteen. Why should chronological age be the
criterion? Should there be only two statuses, child and
adult? And should acquisition of the right to vote be
connected in any way with acquisition of the right to
marry? These are the questions which will occupy us in
the remainder of this paper.

THE CONCEPT OF MATURITY

We should begin by pointing to two central facts of human
development: 1, Children do not grow by sudden, dramatic
leaps or transformations but develop gradually over many
years, and 2, Children do not develop at the same rate.
No matter what dimension of growth one selects, children
of the same chronological age will be found at different
points along that dimension. Yet society through its
legal system must fix some point in the life of every
individual at which it publicly announces: now you may
vote, now you may marry, etc. On what basis is such
recognition to be made? One plausible answer is: whenever that person reaches maturity. The intention here is
to take cognizance of fact 2 in such a way that the
transition to legal majority is made to depend on individual attainment rather than on chronological age, which
is a very inexact gauge of development at best. As the
noted psychologist Gordon Allport remarked, 'A well-
balanced lad of eleven, "wise beyond his years," may
have more signs of maturity than many self-centered and
and neurotic adults.' (10) We must recognize that what
motivates an objection to the age-criterion is a concern
for justice. When basic rights are withheld from a

population capable of exercising them, a grave injustice
is done. The arbitrary fixing of eighteen or twenty-one
as the age of majority deprives thousands, perhaps
millions of mature younger people of the rights to which
they seem morally entitled.

It is unfortunately far from clear how one would determine whether an individual had or had not attained maturity. What is meant in the first place by 'maturity'?
We must first of all distinguish between physical and
personal maturity. Almost everyone who lives long enough
becomes physically mature but not everyone who is physically mature is also personally mature. Moreover, personal
maturity is to some extent an achievement whereas physical
maturity is not. That is, a person has control or at
least is perceived as having control over whether he will
act in a mature way but no control over whether he will
grow taller or develop secondary sex characteristics.
Thus to say of someone that he is 'mature' or 'immature'
is to either compliment or voice disapproval of his mode
of behaving. Personal maturity, furthermore, varies from
culture to culture in a way that physical maturity does
not. The traits valued in an adult Hopi are not necessarily the same as those valued in an adult Chinese or
American.

What though do we mean when we speak of a person as
being mature? Adults frequently speak of children being
'mature' meaning that they are physically or psychologically developed beyond most children of the same age.
This is clearly not the sense of 'mature' relevant to
determining the transition to adulthood. We also characterize adults as 'mature' but we seem to refer to different aspects of personality depending on the characteristics and attitudes we most value. A person showing
great fortitude, even resignation, in the face of misfortune may seem particularly mature to someone while
another will characterize him as defeatist or unfeeling.
Someone who takes the ups and downs of life with a good
deal of humor and levity may be considered mature by one
person and frivolous by another. Similarly a person who
tenaciously strives for his chosen goals could be considered mature or pigheaded depending on one's point of
view. Allport reports an experiment in which two groups
of people independently rated university graduate students
on the 'balance and degree of maturity which the individual shows in his relations with other people.' The
correlation between the two sets of ratings was 0.41. (11)
There is, to be sure, a vague, general understanding that
the mature individual has a greater sense of responsibility and a greater autonomy than the immature.

But can we reach consensus on precisely what conduct is to count as mature? Unless such consensus can be found the criterion of maturity is likely in practice to be equivalent to 'those who share the particular values and attitudes of those in authority,' a most dangerous basis for extending or denying individual basic rights.

Let us view the problem of formulating a conception of maturity from the perspective of society rather than that of the individual. We can then reformulate our question. Instead of asking What is a mature individual?, we could ask, What are the minimum requirements for assuming the rights and responsibilities of a full member of society? (12)   This question could in turn be broken down into several component questions such as, What minimum capacities and inclinations should a person exhibit before society accords him the rights and responsibilities of voting, marrying, or making contracts, etc. This approach to determining when people are eligible for full membership in society promises to be less subject to diverse value biases and more suited to determining a basis for awarding majority status than an approach which depends on a subjective assessment of maturity. Consider the problem of establishing minimal criteria for voting or getting married.

What must a person be able to do before he or she is entitled to marry? Let us assume that the right to marry includes the right to procreate. Does this mean that if a person is biologically able to bear or father children, he (she) thereby has the right to marry and become a parent? Few would agree, for they would point out that bringing up and caring for children, not bearing them, is what society is concerned about. But on what basis do we determine whether a person is capable of rearing children? Here we come against the same difficulties we encountered earlier. We do not share the same views about what matters in child rearing. Must a person have an understanding of children and child development? Some would answer in the affirmative; others, not. Must a prospective parent have an ability to love his (her) child? Of course. But what does this mean? Does it mean that a parent must place the child's interest first? Always? Does it mean that a parent would refuse to leave the child in someone else's care for most of the day? Does it mean that the parent would cuddle the child and hold it a great deal? Pick the baby up when it cries? Put money away for its education? Or consider the requirement that a prospective parent be able to support his (her) child. What does 'support' mean? Does it mean meeting the child's minimum nutritional requirements?

Does it mean earning enough so one parent can stay home with the child? Does it mean that the child must be able to have its own room? Does it include the ability to provide baby sitters? Children's books? Vacations? Or consider simply the requisite maturity for making a marriage contract without regard to becoming a parent. Must a person be able to form and maintain an exclusive attachment to a person of the opposite sex? Must he or she contemplate a lifetime commitment? Must he or she be capable of deep emotional attachment? The answers depend on one's conception of the nature of marriage which in turn depends on one's personal and social ideals.

The point I am trying to bring out here is not merely that as a practical matter it would be almost impossible to determine whether a given individual would make a competent parent or spouse, which it would be, but that in trying to define the criteria of minimal competence we run into the very problems of value diversity which we were hoping to avoid.

To take another case, consider the problem of defining minimal qualifications for voting. That task presupposes an understanding of the task of the voter. But what is this task? Is it to push down buttons and move a lever? Surely not. The voter must make an intelligent choice. But what is it that he is to choose? Is his task that of selecting among alternative policies or alternative political parties? Does the voter select men to represent his own interests or the public interest? Different answers to such questions have dramatically different implications for determining criteria of minimal competence for voting. For example less understanding is required for a voter to decide between the Republican and Democratic parties than for him to decide between two policies for controlling inflation. It is likewise easier for a voter to predict which of two candidates will serve his own interest than which will serve the public interest. Once again without achieving consensus on the nature of the voter's task we cannot arrive at minimal criteria for voting. Such consensus is unobtainable, however, because of the diverse conceptions of the role of the citizen in a democracy, conceptions that derive from conflicting ideals concerning the good life and the good society. (13)

I have been arguing that the notion of identifying minimum qualifications for becoming husband, parent or voter is value laden, in a sense in which setting qualifications for becoming driver or infantry soldier or bricklayer is not, for we can obtain consensus on the functions or tasks of the latter which we cannot on the former.

This absence of consensus, I maintain, results not because some people are right while others are in error but because of commitment to diverse but equally legitimate personal and social ideals. A pluralist society has no right, I would further argue, to enforce one particular conception of marriage or parenthood or citizenship at the expense of others. The concept of maturity, no matter how it is formulated, is therefore incapable of serving as a direct basis for according majority status unless we are willing to sacrifice our commitment to diverse personal and social ideals. Yet the conventional use of chronological age as a criterion is, perhaps, unjust as pointed out earlier. Two additional arguments favoring the traditional criterion, however, must also be considered.

1 It does not work to either the advantage or the disadvantage of any self-conscious or recognizable groups or special interests. Any other criterion based on individual maturity is likely to benefit some partisan or class interest. The use of some sort of 'maturity scale,' like the use of intelligence tests, is likely to favor the educated, which is to say the more affluent classes. The age-criterion is non-partisan, however, in that the children of Republicans or the affluent or whites and the children of Democrats, the poor or blacks, are a all equally excluded. 2 One of the defects of any criterion based on individual attainment is that it leaves the question of who shall and who shall not enjoy majority status within the realm of human control. It is true that any minimal age requirement illegitimately deprives a segment of the population of its rights. But every such person may look forward to his eventual enfranchisement. There is very little any person or group could do short of mass murder to prevent millions of people from reaching the age of majority. Where majority status depends on some demonstration of maturity by the candidate, however, the possibility and hence the risk exists of a deliberate effort being made by one section of the population to prevent particular individuals or groups from ever being accorded majority status. Nineteenth- and twentieth-century efforts to prevent blacks from voting in the South attest to the fact that the possibility of abuse is perhaps more accurately labeled a likelihood. It is exceedingly dangerous from the point of view of justice to make the possession of basic rights dependent on the probity, good will and impartiality of any man or group of men.

Despite its attendant injustices, therefore, I believe that the relatively equitable distribution of injustice

among all social groupings and the certainty of everyone's
attaining adult status are persuasive enough reasons to
maintain the traditional criterion.

SETTING THE AGE OF MAJORITY

What, however, ought the age of majority to be? Does not
setting a particular age indirectly invoke conceptions
of maturity? Before answering these questions we need to
consider whether there ought to be a single age for
attaining majority status or rather different ages for
acquiring different rights and responsibilities. (14)
The law does already to some extent recognize different
ages in different spheres of endeavor. For example,
fifteen and sixteen are the minimum ages for obtaining a
driver's license in some states, and the age required for
marrying without parental consent especially for women is
often two or three years below the age required for
voting. It does seem as if a lower level of maturity
were needed to drive a car than to vote although it is
not clear what kind of evidence could substantiate this.
One could as well argue that an immature driver poses a
greater risk than an immature voter. Even if there were
general agreement on these matters, however, there is a
persuasive rationale for retaining the overall status
of major and minor. This rationale invokes the idea of
fairness mentioned earlier. It is unfair, we noted, to
assign responsibilities without corresponding rights and
vice versa. The advocates of the recent constitutional
amendment lowering the voting age from twenty-one to
eighteen relied heavily and justifiably on the argument
that a person liable to conscription and possible loss of
life ought to have a voice in selecting those representatives whose decisions will determine whether there shall
be war or peace. This notion of fairness can be applied
throughout. A person permitted to marry and bring up
children into the world ought to assume the responsibility
of sustaining a family and vice versa. For why should
grandparents be responsible for the care of children when
they were excluded from the decision which brought these
children into the world. A person liable to adult
criminal proceedings and the verdict of adult juries ought
to be permitted to vote for the judges who might sit in
judgment over him, and to sit on juries and grand juries
in judgment on others. A person permitted to make and be
bound by contracts offering payment for goods or services
ought not to be legally dependent on another for his
support. Or to put it from the parents' point of view,

if they are legally required to support their child
because he (she) is not yet capable of self-support, then
they ought to be protected from the financial obligations
he (she) may unwittingly or foolishly incur. Again, when
children legally acquire independence from parents to act
as they wish without parental consent, then they ought
also to bear the responsibility for their own support.
I need not continue. The same points have been made,
convincingly I think, with respect to the status of women.
The notion of a fair balance of rights and responsibilities applies in both contexts.

The problem of setting the age of the transition to
majority status still remains. A consensus could probably
be reached that this age should be set somewhere between
fourteen and twenty-five. Most are agreed that children
prior to the relatively dramatic changes, both physical
and psychological, that occur during puberty are unfit
for adult status. Twenty-one has been the traditional age
of majority in the Anglo-American world for centuries
and not many would favor raising it by more than a couple
of years. The selection of this age range rather than
another certainly involves a conception of human development and maturity. How can we select a specific age from
within this range? Are eighteen-year-olds sufficiently
mature to marry, or should the age be raised (or lowered)?
Are eighteen-year-olds today more (or less) mature than
eighteen-year-olds of ten years ago? If my analysis of
'maturity' is correct, no amount of empirical data will
determine answers to such questions. Take the case of
marriage. There is statistical evidence to show that
marriages of those under twenty-one are more likely to
end in divorce than marriages of those above twenty-one.
But what does this prove? That the younger group is less
mature? Not at all. That conclusion only follows if we
assume that it is a sign of maturity for a couple to sustain an intimate relationship which is unsatisfying or
burdensome to one or both spouses. Why make such an
assumption? Could one not as well say that those unwilling to divorce even though their relationship has become
sterile and destructive are the immature ones? And why
should the ability to make long-term commitments be
equated with maturity in the first place? Possibly the
younger generation's expectations and aspirations concerning marriage exceed those of the older generations.
Seeking more, they are more often disappointed. Does
that make them less mature? Is being satisfied with
little a necessary indication of maturity?

How then should the age be fixed if not on the basis of
evidence concerning the maturity of the young? What is

important, I would argue, is whether the age that is set
is perceived to be reasonable by both majors and minors.
If the age is perceived to be too high by the young, they
will feel justified in disregarding or violating the
decisions of those set in authority over them. If the
age is perceived to be too low, the older public is
going to have less confidence in and feel less bound by
the decisions of the electorate, verdicts of juries,
etc., in which younger people have participated. What
is at stake here is public confidence in public processes and decisions. The young need to feel that as
many as possible of those able to make their own choices
and participate in public decisions are eligible to do
so. The older citizens need to feel that public decisions
which affect them are not made by those too immature to
make them. Parents and children need to feel that legal
rights and responsibilities towards each other are not
terminated too late or too early. What counts, in short,
is congruent perceptions of maturity. These perceptions
are likely to differ among members within each group and
between the two groups. Here compromise is necessary and
appropriate. A compromise must be reached which will
leave neither group with a sense of outrage or indigna-
tion. The age of eighteen may be a satisfactory compromise in our time, but since people's perceptions
change, I would expect the age of majority to fluctuate
from time to time and place to place.

TOWARDS DEFINING A NEW STATUS

We have seen that the very young should not be accorded
the rights and the responsibilities of adulthood. Further
I have maintained that the legal transition to adulthood
should continue to be chronological age and that there
should not be different ages for the assumption of different rights and responsibilities. Nothing in my argument
so far, however, accounts for or defends the present
arrangement whereby a person is and continues to be a
legal minor from birth to his eighteenth birthday. It
seems odd, to say the least, that the law does not recognize any significant development in the first eighteen
years of life, that the sixteen-year-old possesses
virtually the same rights and responsibilities as the
sixteen-month-old. In the final section of this paper,
I would therefore like to argue in favor of creating a
new legal status between minority and majority. (15)
    I begin once again with a fact: there is an increasing
recognition by people of all ages that our society is

failing to provide the conditions which encourage young
people to grow into responsible adulthood. A panel on
youth, appointed by the President's Science Advisory Committee, headed by the eminent sociologist James S. Coleman
states the situation concisely: 'In our view the institutional framework for maturation in the United States is
now in need of serious examination.' (16) Neither the
topic nor the analysis and recommendations of the panel
are new. Much the same point of view was expressed
eloquently for well over a decade by the late Paul Goodman
(whose name and works are ironically omitted from the
numerous sources cited by the panel). Indeed the thrust
of the panel's recommendations can be summarized in one of
Goodman's exhortations: 'Our aim should be to multiply
the paths of growing up, instead of narrowing the one
existing school path.' (17) The problem which Goodman,
the panel and many other scholars and social critics
recognize is that the institutional and legal structures
created to protect the development of youth 'have
uncritically been extended to the point where they deprive
youth of experience important to their growth and development.' (18) These institutional structures, the school in
particular, which segregate youth from the adult community
deny to them both the rights and the obligations which
would encourage them to develop in the directions of
enhanced independence and responsibility. I will not
enumerate all the recommendations of the panel. It is
sufficient to say that they are designed to facilitate
the independence of youth (through, for example, work in
production, in public service and participation in youth
communities). (19) The report does not propose the
abolition of formal secondary schooling but does recommend
that the school exercise far less of a monopoly over the
adolescent's time. One section of recommendations deals
with the legal status of youth. Here the panel recommends
nothing more than the establishment of a separate minimum
wage for youth and the revision of child labor standards
in 'the interest of flexibility, individualization, and
the opening of wider opportunities for work experience
and employment.' (20)

It is clear that the authors of the report are conscious of the deleterious constraints which minority
status places upon youth though they are justifiably
unwilling to accord adolescents full adult status. The
idea of a legally defined status between the two has perhaps not occurred to them. I believe that the establishment of such a status would both facilitate and legitimize
the creation of the kinds of alternative institutions and
environments for youth envisioned by reformers. What will

be needed is recognition by all age groups, children, adolescents and adults, that those between say ages fifteen and eighteen are no longer children nor yet adults. Those within this age group would not bear all the burdens nor enjoy all the benefits of majority status. On the other hand they would not be bound by the very severe constraints placed on children or be freed of all responsibilities for their own lives and those of others.

At this level of abstraction such a proposal may sound attractive but what specific rights and responsibilities would holders of the new status possess? These rights and responsibilities fall into three categories: economics, family life and political participation. To require youth to be economically self-sufficient would not be feasible in a society with millions of unemployed adults. Moreover, it is contrary to young people's interests in discovering their talents, finding meaningful work and fashioning their own identity. The burden of responsibility for their own support would foreclose many opportunities for people of this age group. Yet the sixteen- to eighteen-year-old group needs work and needs partial independence. The recommendations of the President's panel include a direct government subsidy to youth in the form of educational vouchers and a vast expansion of opportunities for public service work such as is provided on a small scale by VISTA. (21) These two recommendations could be tied together in such a way that all youth would receive vouchers but would in turn have the responsibility of devoting a certain minimum number of hours a week or a month to such public service work. A balance between benefits and burdens would then be obtained. A young person could choose from among the many service oriented sectors where the demand for personnel far exceeds the supply, in nursing homes and homes for the aged, orphanages, hospitals, day-care centers, etc. They would gain independence by not being beholden to their parents for funds to pursue their own educational interests. Vouchers could be used for a variety of kinds of training in and out of schools and perhaps for such activities as travel as well. The decisions and the consequences would be the young people's, not their parents'.

Adults are reluctant to sanction marriage among members of this age group because the marriage license is also the license for parenthood and there is widespread feeling that those in the sixteen to eighteen range haven't had sufficient life experience to take on the responsibilities of parenthood. Almost ten years ago Margaret Mead offered an intriguing suggestion that two distinct kinds of marriage be established: (22) 'individual marriage,'

an intimate relation in which each partner has responsibilities to the other alone, and 'parental marriage,'
which would be 'explicitly directed toward the founding of
a family.' (23)   The aim of and requirements for entering
into each of the two forms would differ.   I would suggest
that holders of the new youth status be eligible to enter
into such individual marriage, the purpose of which would
be to 'give two very young people a chance to know each
other with a kind of intimacy that does not usually enter
into a brief love affair, and so it would help them to
grow into each other's life - and allow them to part
without the burden of misunderstood intentions, bitter
recriminations and self-destructive guilt.' (24)

As Mead sees it the obligations of the parties would
be ethical.   No economic commitments would be involved:
'If the marriage broke up, there would be no alimony or
support.' (25)   Such relationships recognized by law, are,
I believe, ideally suited to the transitional period
between childhood and adulthood.   They offer prerogatives
and responsibilities to youth which present challenges to
growth without imposing staggering burdens or excessive
risks to the future of the young people.

In the civic sphere the transition to majority status
is abrupt and unsatisfying in several respects.   Participation as measured by voting is low among the newly
enfranchised.   Lowering the voting age to eighteen did not
alter this phenomenon.   Moreover, having little experience
in civic life, youth often harbor attitudes of indifference or cynicism towards politics and the polity.   Participation in school politics is often seen as a sham
since students have little voice in determining the basic
structure and operation of the institution.   I propose
that youth in the fifteen- to eighteen-year-old status be
accorded the right to participate in public life in the
following ways: 1, that they be eligible to vote for those
elected officials whose decisions have the greatest impact
on their own lives; these would include members of local
boards of education, state superintendents of public
instruction, justices of the juvenile court, and of course
those officials whose task it would be to administer the
new institutions relating to youth; 2, that they be
eligible to serve on boards of education or their ana-
logues at every level of government; 3, that holders of
the new status be elected or appointed to serve as
advisors and consultants to the juvenile court and all
other institutions dealing with juvenile problems.   The
purpose of such augmented rights and responsibilities
would once again be to facilitate the transition to majority status in a gradual way which would encourage participation without jeopardizing the survival of the polity.

The particular rights and responsibilities of the youth status which I have sketched out are intended primarily to enable the reader to visualize the kind of thing I have in mind. The spelling out of specifics will require a great deal of social experimentation and analysis of the kind projected in the report on youth. I do not believe that the establishment of such a new legal status can precede the development of new institutions and environments for youth. If such new institutions can be founded, however, I think the creation of a youth status would protect and strengthen them and bring to all age groups a sense of rationality and coherence in the socialization process which would otherwise be lacking.

I would like briefly to consider two objections which I anticipate being raised to my proposal. I think it will be argued that the creation of a new status will foster the sense of separateness which adolescents already feel, will actually intensify the feelings of alienation and hostility towards adults which members of this age group already harbor. I cannot agree. The adolescents' sense of apartness is the result of the conflicting messages they receive from the adult society. On the one hand they are exhorted to 'grow up' and to act as 'mature and responsible people.' On the other hand, they are denied any real independence or responsibility. Informally they are urged to act as adults while their legal status reflects the fact that society does not distinguish them from infants. My proposal would foster in the fifteen- to eighteen-year-olds the sense of having achieved a status beyond childhood, of beginning to take part in the real world of the workplace and the voting booth, of having the opportunity to make decisions about things that matter to others and to themselves. Moreover, my proposal would require youth to work closely with adults in projects that matter to the entire community. The current pattern whereby members of one age group fraternize with each other almost exclusively would be disrupted.

A second concern is likely to be voiced by those who see the proposal as threatening to the integrity of the family and the beneficial influence which parents can have over their adolescent children. Will not the proposal allow or even encourage the boy or girl of sixteen to leave home in order to marry against parental wishes, to squander his or her vouchers of worthless experiences instead of embarking on a serious education? There is some risk to be sure and one can do little more than speculate about probable responses. But three things need

to be kept in mind. First, the period in which the
parents exert the greatest influence over their children,
shaping their basic values and attitudes, is probably
long over by the time they turn sixteen. Second, it is
doubtful that parental coercion and blackmail are ever
very successful where more benign forms of persuasion have
failed. It is doubtful, for example, that parents are
able to compel their children to benefit from the educational opportunities available in college even when they
are able to compel attendance by threatening withdrawal of
financial support. In fact the source of much of the
adolescent's rebelliousness is to be found, I would argue,
in the resentment engendered by his dependent status.
Third, parents would retain considerable leverage over
their adolescent children inasmuch as the latter, though
not barred from employment, would not usually be economically self-sufficient.

One of the fruits of modern life and thought is the
pervasive awareness that the patterns and categories of
social life are human constructs rather than part of the
natural or divine order. This awareness has caused some
to assume that all existing institutions are barriers to
human liberation. Others have taken this awareness as a
spur to their efforts to shore up the established order
through exhortation if possible, by force if necessary.
Amid such opposing tendencies there is a need for sober,
reflective analysis whose purpose is to discern which
traditional patterns are worthy of preservation, which, of
dissolution. Such an analysis in the limited area of the
rights and responsibilities of children and youth is what
I have tried to provide in this paper.

NOTES

I wish to acknowledge the valuable editorial assistance
I received from my wife, Sally. I have also benefited
from the comments and suggestions of students and colleagues. I would especially like to thank the following:
Alan Lockwood, Gerald C. MacCallum Jr, Fred Newmann,
Marcus Singer and Kenneth Strike.
1 'Tinker v. Des Moines School District,' 393 US
   503,515 (1969).
2 Two other often cited, landmark cases in the area are
   'In re Gault,' 387 US 1 (1967), and 'Wisconsin v.
   Yoder,' 406 US 205 (1972).
3 Hillary Rodham, Children under the Law, 'Harvard
   Educational Review,' XLIII (1973), p.499.

4   John Holt, 'Escape from Childhood: The Needs and
    Rights of Youth' (New York: Dutton, 1974), p.18. See
    also, for example, Shulamith Firestone, 'The Dialectic
    of Sex' (New York: Bantam Books, 1971), ch.IV.
5   See B.C. Gavit (ed.), 'Blackstone's Commentaries on
    the Law' (Washington, DC: Washington Law Book Co.,
    1941), p.204.
6   Ibid.
7   Aristotle, 'Nicomachean Ethics,' 5.2, 1131a, 23-5.
8   John Plamenatz, Rights, 'Aristotelian Society Sup-
    plementary Volume' 24 (1950), p.75. This formulation
    is somewhat too broad and fails to distinguish between
    different degrees of 'ought.' See Joel Feinberg,
    Duties, Rights, and Claims, 'American Philosophical
    Quarterly,' III (1966), 137-44.
9   These rights are presumptive; that is, they may be
    overridden under certain circumstances.
10 Gordon W. Allport, 'Pattern and Growth in Personality'
    (New York: Holt, Rinehart & Winston, 1965), p.277.
11 Allport, op.cit., p.282.
12 See Alex Inkeles, Society, Social Structure, and Child
    Socialization, in John A. Clausen (ed.), 'Socializa-
    tion and Society' (Boston: Little, Brown, 1968),
    pp.73-129.
13 See P.F. Strawson, Social Morality and Individual
    Ideal, 'Philosophy,' XXXVI (1961), pp.1-17. For more
    on the problem of setting qualifications for politi-
    cal participation, see my The Child's Status in the
    Democratic State, 'Political Theory,' 111, 4 (November
    1975), pp.441-57.
14 This suggestion is made by Rodham, op.cit., pp.507-9.
15 This is not a new idea. Indeed, human development has
    long been accorded recognition by the Canon Law which
    identifies three distinct statuses between birth and
    age twenty-one. See John A. Abbo and Jerome D. Hannan
    (eds), 'The Sacred Cannons: A Concise Presentation of
    the Current Disciplinary Norms of the Church,' vol.I
    (St Louis, Missouri: Herder Book Co., 1952), pp.123-30.
16 James S. Coleman (ed.), 'Youth: Transition to Adult-
    hood: Report of the Panel on Youth of the President's
    Science Advisory Committee' (University of Chicago
    Press, 1974), p.1.
17 Paul Goodman, 'New Reformation: Notes of a Neolithic
    Conservative' (New York: Vintage Books, 1971), p.87.
18 Coleman, op.cit., p.130.
19 Ibid., pp.145-75.
20 Ibid., p.167.
21 Ibid., pp.169-73.

22 Margaret Mead, Marriage in Two Steps, 'Redbook' (July
    1966), pp.48-9, 84-5.
23 Ibid., p.84.
24 Ibid.
25 Ibid.

Compulsory education: 5
a moral critique

Leonard I. Krimerman

1 AN INTRODUCTORY ANALOGY

In Clark Stewart's virtually unknown novella, 'Auriana,'
everyone upon reaching 50 is forced to spend much of every
day (except Monday) in recreational games and contests
chosen and organized for them by younger folk. (1) They
are picked up in the morning, taken to playing fields or
gymnasiums, given equipment and instruction, and brought
home by late afternoon. This regimen continues for ten
years, after which there is an option to remain in the
program on a voluntary basis. Jake Justin, the central
character of 'Auriana,' comes to resent and then to rebel
against this system of 'compulsory recreation' (CR).
Jake constantly finds himself at odds with his well-
intentioned 'recreators': when they tell him it is time
for karate, he feels like swimming or reading; he gets
enthusiastic about cross-country running, but it turns
out to be the tri-mester for competitive team sports.
'Reading and cross-country track,' he is told by a District Recreation Supervisor, 'are strictly extra-
curricular.' Eventually, Jake sees himself as 'a part-
time slave,' drafted each morning into athletic training,
compelled by law 'to participate in a ten-year long
circus.' He asks the Supervisor, 'How is this different
from punishing people who haven't committed any crime?'
   The ironies of Jake's position are endless. His
keepers are neither cruel nor despotic: they rarely punish
his rebellions, and attempt to understand them as symptoms
of 'senility' or of 'a disturbed marriage.' He winds up
repelled by sports such as volleyball and tennis that,
prior to CR, were sources of spontaneous pleasure. His
'game-mates' are not concerned by the loss of a decade of
free time. They are puzzled by Jake's opposition to what
they regard as no less natural than 'heat in the summer,

ice in the winter.' They expect to be stronger and
healthier at the end of their induction into CR than when
they turned 50. Jake's conviction that they are all
slaves, strikes everyone else as unintelligible: 'How
can CR be slavery if we all are required to spend the same
amount and period of our lives in it?' 'What promotes
such goods as physical vitality and longer life cannot
be slavery!'

'Auriana,' though a fantasy, strikes very close to
home. It raises fundamental questions as to the legitimacy of CE, which most contemporary societies have come
to treat as a natural and useful custom, very distant from
'part-time slavery.' For though there is vagueness in
what counts as 'compulsory education,' the central cases
of this notion involve the use of force and the threat of
legal sanctions to ensure attendance and participation
for several years in a prescribed and standardized
curriculum. Thus, CE does involve a loss of liberty
throughout a substantial period of one's life, it forces
learners to submit to the prejudices and routines of
others, it refuses to honor the learning objectives of
those compelled to participate. Thus, if we agree with
Jake Justin about CR, must we not also view CE as a form
of slavery, or at least of intolerable injustice?

One way to defend CE against this condemnation by
analogy would be to locate a relevant contrast between
the two practices, one that could establish that the moral
objections to CR are without weight against CE. Thus, CR
is a fictional notion, whereas CE has real instances. But
this disanalogy, though clear, cannot show CE to be any
more defensible than CR. The major differences between
these two compulsory practices are easy to spot; they
concern who and what is compelled. Thus, Section 2 dis-
cusses defenses of CE based on the alleged deficiencies
of children: there I argue that we have reason to doubt
whether children are more defective than adults (at least
those in 'Auriana'), and that, even if they are, this
neither justifies CE nor establishes any moral contrast
between it and CR. Section 3, on the other hand, focuses
on the what of CE and CR, and specifically on the claim
that education can be distinguished from recreation by
virtue of its greater contributions to 'society's interests,' e.g. to a democratic polity, to the development of
productive and medical technology, etc. In view of these
contributions, the argument runs, education is justifiably
made compulsory. My response is that the supposed contributions are conjectural and in any case are no less likely
under voluntarized arrangements than under CE.

Finally, in Section 4, I consider and rebut two common

practical objections to the idea of discarding CE; first, that without this practice, unjust and pernicious conditions, such as racism and inequitable distributions of wealth and opportunities, would be strengthened; and second, that CE is not eliminable, at least not from any industrialized society.

In brief, my aim in what follows is to develop and lend support to Auriana's implicit renunciation of CE by showing that presumed contrasts between CR and CE either do not obtain, rest on ungrounded conjecture, or fail to show any respect in which the two practices are morally distinguishable, and by countering practical objections often raised against the goal of voluntarizing education. The case against CE, I shall argue, is no less strong than that against CR.

2   THE DEFICIENCIES OF CHILDREN

2.1   Children, we may think, are under-developed and immature; they lack foresight, experience, information, and responsibility. In this light, the requirement of compulsory schooling may seem to make sense, for it is designed to offset those deficiencies, and thus in the long run to benefit both the child and the rest of society.

2.11   One difficulty with this defense of CE is immediately apparent, for the fifth-decade citizens of Auriana also have diminished capacities. Their powers of coordination, endurance, physical strength and the like have begun to fade; the aim of CR is to contain or reverse this process, to revitalize abilities and energies. Nonetheless, this appeal to deficiencies and their reduction does not prompt us to alter our attitude towards CR; it remains an unjustifiable invasion of personal freedom. Consider also the case of health services. These are seldom furnished on an involuntary basis, even when it is certain that a person is ailing, that their ailment (e.g. alcoholism or VD) is curable, and that it is causing distress, or even spreading, to others. In short, knowledge of a person's deficiencies and of a remedy for curtailing them and their consequences does not invariably license interference with that person or the coercive imposition of that remedy. Thus, even if we assume that children are under-developed as persons and further assume that CE is a remedy for their defects, this alone cannot justify that practice or distinguish it from CR.

2.2   Here it may be countered that children are incapacitated in a different and more severe way than the

adults in Auriana. The latter have begun to lose their
physical powers, but the former lack something which is
more fundamental: the capacity to make decisions based
on past experience. They lack familiarity with their own
enduring interests, they are ignorant about the consequences of varying options. It is because the 'rational
powers' of 50 year old Aurians are undiminished, because
they can all judge what is optimum recreation for themselves, that CR is antithetical to our moral intuitions.
More precisely, it runs contrary to our notion that, on
this matter - choosing the best form of recreation for
oneself - each of these adults is on the whole the best
possible judge.

CE, on the other hand, does not encounter any such
difficulty. For (it is alleged) children do not know what
is educationally best for themselves. Their powers of
discrimination, prediction, self-awareness, etc., are
embryonic and operate only intermittently. They are
inept at choice-making, they have little or no experience
assessing ranges of options, they are not the best
possible - or even competent - judges when it comes to
deciding what sort of education they should have. When
seen in this light, so the argument goes, CE can be distinguished morally from CR. CE makes choices for those
unable to make them on their own, whereas CR makes choices
for persons who, though physically on the wane, are otherwise intact and more capable than anyone else of making
those choices. What we see as intolerable about CR,
therefore, is absent from, and cannot mar the legitimacy
of, CE.

2.21 This line of defense will not salvage CE. It is
far from true, to begin with, that all children are
deficient at choice-making. The choices of most 10 and
12 year olds, not to mention teenagers, might well compare favorably with those of most adults, regardless of
one's standard for 'rational,' 'sensible,' or 'wise'
choices. Like adults, children are a heterogeneous lot;
why should all of them suffer for the defects of some
(or even most)? Suppose, though, that we concede the
problematic assumption that children, by and large, are
less capable of decision-making than adults. This would
certainly supply a contrast between CR and CE, but from
it we need not conclude that CE is justifiable. We could
instead infer that everyone should be exempt from educational impositions, unless and until they had been shown
to be severely deficient in rationality, or to be substantially below most adults in this respect. Our working
principle would then be 'rationally competent unless
proven otherwise'; the clear burden of evidence would

rest with those alleging severe deficiency. Given this
principle, which is fully compatible with children being
comparatively under-developed, our educational arrangements would operate much as do hospitals today. People
would be committed into them temporarily, under extraordinary circumstances, and for the most part voluntarily.
Those arrangements would aim at eliminating the insuffi-
ciences or incapacities which originally justified their
intervention. Where an educational system did not regard
itself as in this sense self-eliminating, it would forfeit
any rights over the time and energy of children, even
those admittedly deficient. Just as juvenile and mental
institutions have recently been put on judicial notice
to 'treat or release,' so such failing educational
institutions would be required to either 'develop
rational powers or release.'

The point which emerges here is this: even if it is
granted that children on the whole are less decisionally
competent than adults, that some are severely defective
as decision-makers, and that in some cases severe defi-
ciences in rationality can warrant educational intervention, this intervention need not take the form of CE.
Hospitals to which people are sent for diagnosis and
treatment, in some cases against their consent, do not
by themselves add up to a system of 'compulsory health
care.' Where people (including children) are ordinarily
allowed to educate themselves as they prefer, with excep-
tions only in extreme circumstances, what obtains may be
'sporadic educational intervention,' but it is too
occasional and peripheral to be CE.

2.22 That one can grant the sub-rationality of children without embracing CE can be shown in another way: by
examining the general relationship between rights and
'degree of development.' For under-developed capacities,
taken alone, do not provide a reason for reducing someone's rights. In certain cases, differences in capacity,
even when extensive, are morally besides the point:
everyone from the severely retarded to the genius is
thought to have an equal right to vote, ride public transportation, use public parks. Moreover, inferior abilities
sometimes warrant the provision of a greater share of
responsibilities: other people may not need the experience
as much, and more growth may be expected from this type
of allocation than from any other. Thus, in pedagogical
contexts, the least advanced may have the greatest need,
and right, to present their thoughts for criticism, to
use the dark room, etc. ('Let Jerry stretch the canvas;
you already know how to do it.')

If defective powers by themselves do not justify a

contraction of rights or responsibilities, then the green-
ness of children as choice-makers cannot warrant the
reduction of their rights under CE. On the contrary,
those deficiencies might either (i) be irrelevant to
whether children should enjoy educational liberty (as
the failings of mentally retarded persons are irrelevant
to their right to vote) or (ii) provide grounds for
extending full educational choice to children so that
they can begin to grow more directly and completely into
competent choice-makers (as the under-development of the
least capable learner is grounds for ensuring him/her
greater access to resources and responsibilities).

Or consider the 'mentally ill.' A person may suffer
from phobias or paranoid delusions that make him behave
irrationally or, like Mary Barnes, may become totally
absorbed back into his own infancy. (2) We have begun
to see that involuntary institutionalization is rarely
a satisfactory way to cope with such departures from
rationality. A close and voluntary association with
people living ordinary lives, who are caring without
being controlling or invasive, may be more desirable in
two ways: in terms of (a) such short-run considerations as
how a person feels about their experience and their
relations with others and (b) their long-range struggle
for fuller health and development. The same might hold
for children. They might learn and grow more completely,
in addition to having a more satisfying or enjoyable
educational experience, where their learning choices were
unrestricted, where adults had no official or coercive
authority and functioned as co-learners, advisors,
resource coordinators, etc. The benefits for children
of promoting education through voluntarized and non-
institutionalized approaches might far exceed those
achieved through CE.

This was William Godwin's contention, two centuries
before 'Compulsory Mis-Education,' 'Deschooling Society,'
'School is Dead,' etc. In Of the Communication of Knowledge, Godwin maintained that where the learner is guided
by 'a perception of the value of the thing learned,'
rather than by 'constraint and fear' or 'by accidental
attractions' appended by a teacher, we have 'the most
desirable mode of education.' For to study because one
desires to, to 'proceed upon a plan of one's own inven-
tion' is:

the pure and genuine condition of a rational being.
By exercise it strengthens the judgment. It elevates
us with a sense of independence. It causes a man (sic)
to stand alone and is the only method by which he can
be rendered truly an individual, the creature not of
implicit faith but of his own understanding. (3)

Given a position like Godwin's, the deficiencies of childhood rationality, even where severe, cannot establish a
case for CE. For according to his position, CE is not the
only or the best way to reduce those deficiencies. It
seemed plausible to Godwin, and remains plausible, that
independent rational judgment is not strengthened by a
routine of restriction and obedience, but by the exercise
of such judgment even in its earliest stages of maturation. (Just as children learn to speak their native
language without formal or compulsory instruction, but
by actively exchanging and experimenting with sounds.)
If this is so, then the routine of compulsory schooling
would tend to stunt development by giving learners no
incentive to acquire the ability (or integrity) to think
problems through on their own, to reach or even conceive
of conclusions beyond those expected, rewarded or
required.

Recently, Godwin's philosophical reflections have been
confirmed by empirical studies which indicate that using
rewards to 'motivate' learning can backfire. Two psycho-
logists, David Greene and Mark R. Lepper, begin where
Godwin did: by distinguishing between intrinsically motivated learning (a child who reads unassigned books for
enjoyment) and learning done for ulterior or extrinsic
motives (a child who reads because books have been
assigned or to do well on tests). On their view, there
is a

> Danger that extrinsic rewards may undermine intrinsic
> motivation.... If we induce a child to engage in an
> interesting activity by offering a reward, the child
> may come to perceive that activity and his engagement
> in it differently. Rather than being an end in itself,
> the activity may become a means to an end. Because
> of the reward, the child has a different, ulterior
> motive for engaging in the activity. At any other
> time, when the reward is no longer available, the child
> may be less likely to engage in the activity on his
> own. (4)

From these considerations, Greene and Lepper formulated
their 'overjustification' hypothesis; i.e. that inducing
people to engage in an activity to achieve extrinsic
goals (avoid punishment, win prizes) may neutralize their
intrinsic interest in that activity. They then constructed an experiment with pre-schoolers and magic
markers. The authors' hypothesis predicted:

> that children who had expected and received an award
> for their drawing would subsequently play less with
> markers, in the absence of further rewards, than child-
> ren who received an award unexpectedly or not at all.
> The data confirmed our hypothesis. (5)

How does this research bear on CE? Ultimately, CE demands
that children learn what they learn not because they want
to or find it intrinsically interesting, but because they
are told to. The threat of force may be naked or veiled,
but it is always present. In this sort of context, the
overjustification hypothesis predicts that intrinsic
learning will be discouraged. Participants in CE will
tend to regard the whole of education much as the rewarded
pre-schoolers reacted to drawing with magic markers: in
the absence of continual extrinsic incentives, they will
turn away from it. If our aim is to expand learning and
development, reliance on CE would appear self-defeating.

It would seem then that CE cannot be justified by
appealing to substantial deficiencies in childhood rationality. For even if these are conceded and with them a
contrast between CR and CE, there are other, less restrictive ways to develop rationality; moreover, there is some
empirical evidence for thinking that CE compares
unfavorably with educational arrangements which provide
learners with access to resources but do not dictate how
or when or where to use them. Perhaps the most that can
be said for CE is that there are unsettled empirical
issues here: To what extent, if any, does CE contribute
to/work against the development of rational abilities?
Would a voluntarized approach (e.g. Illich's 'learning
networks' or the 'sporadic educational intervention' model
referred to previously) facilitate more or less rational
competence than CE? (6) But if these issues are
unsettled, then the defects of children, no matter how
severe, offer no warrant whatever for CE in preference to
more voluntarized alternatives.

2.23 Up to this point, the argument has been restricted to showing that appeals to the choice-making deficiencies of children are inconclusive as far as morally
distinguishing CE from CR and establishing the former's
moral defensibility. But it is possible to go further
than this: there is a serious moral objection to be raised
against CE's treatment of those it regards as defective
in rationality. Thus, not only does this treatment fail
to gain support from the under-development of children;
in addition, it violates a basic moral imperative, and
thus further strengthens the analogy between CE and CR.

Once again, Godwin's position will be found instructive.
That position should not be reduced to the empirical
hypothesis that self-originated learning will give rise to
critical and independent intelligence more effectively
and fully than systems involving CE. In Godwin's account
of the 'most desirable mode of education,' there is also
included a normative principle, i.e. that self-deter-

mination has intrinsic moral value even for those who are
substantially lacking in rationality. In the passage
quoted above, both empirical and normative contentions
are advanced. Proceeding upon desires andpplans of one's
own devising, he claims, 'Strengthens the judgment' and
'is the only method by which [a person] can be rendered
truly an individual.' But beyond this it constitutes
'the pure and genuine condition of a rational being,' a
condition which 'elevates us with a sense of independence.'
In the latter of these assertions, Godwin is not purport-
ing to describe the long-range consequences of allowing
children to choose what they will learn. On the contrary,
he is contending that whenever we deny them this sort of
choice, we deny them - at that time - access to a fundamental good or right.

In Kantian language, we fail to treat them as end-in-
themselves. For treating people as intrinsically desirable involves honoring (taking as decisive) their own
rankings of their own present and future interests. To
do otherwise, is to regard them as subordinates required
to submit to one's own rankings or priorities. Thus, if
Mary wants to roller skate or share fantasies with
friends, but is compelled to study geography or mathematics, a rationale might be constructed in terms of her
long-range interests. But what if Mary agrees that story-
sharing will not advance her future interests as much as
geography, while adamantly preferring the former? 'I know
that geography will be more useful for me, but I don't
care, I'd rather make up stories.' Here there is no
(empirical) dispute over what will in fact lead to maximum
development or future well being, etc. The dispute is
entirely normative: should Mary's projected concerns outweigh her present desires?

Now if we accept the rationale mentioned as justifying
compulsion, we are thereby enforcing what we think is more
important as between two of the child's own interests over
what that child thinks. We have made her comply with our
standards for evaluating desires as more and less desirable, rather than respecting Mary's autonomy in regards to
her own goals. We have treated her as a means, rather
than an end. Furthermore, under CE the situation is not
reciprocal: Mary has no right to use her notion of what
makes goals worth seeking to prevent her teachers or
administrators from pursuing present rather than future
satisfactions.

The point is not that treating children as ends
requires that they never be interfered with to advance
their own long-range interests. This is not true of
adults, and we should not expect it to be true of children.

The point, rather, is that there is a prima facie obligation to respect the goals of children and how they rank
those goals, an obligation which is systematically
violated by CE.   Conceivably, there might be grounds for
overriding this obligation, just as there might be grounds
for public officials misleading their constituencies as
to military spending or aid to foreign dictatorship, etc.
But the moral burden must be assumed by those who would
defend CE, not those who would argue for its elimination.
In sum, the issues surrounding CE should not be thought
of as wholly or even primarily empirical - a matter of
contrasting the consequences for rational development of
CE and voluntarized alternatives.   CE, in its treatment
of children as subordinates whose private goal-rankings
have no intrinsic priority, mistreats them and hence
should be discarded unless powerful considerations can
be adduced in its favor.

These considerations would have to establish that there
are no alternatives to CE, that this practice furnished
the only - or at least the most effective - remedy for
overcoming the defects of childhood.   But as mentioned
earlier contentions such as these are speculative at
best.   There are no empirical studies comparing CE with
Illich's deschooled learning networks or Goodman's
'incidental education' in regards to facilitating given
educational objectives.   Does CE promote self-originated
learning and independence of mind more than a scheme in
which learners receive life-long subsidies to purchase
resources (tools, instruction, space, etc.) of the sorts
they desire, and in which support services such as
advisors, information clearing houses, evaluators, etc.,
are also provided?   At this point in the social science
of education, we simply do not know, though the Greene
and Lepper studies are strongly suggestive of a negative
response.

The conclusion to be drawn then is this: since CE's
accomplishments in reducing childhood deficiencies in
rationality are uncharted and problematic, the empirical
data necessary to defend it, to distinguish it from CR,
and to override its morally abusive treatment of children
are simply not available.   CE's failure to treat children
as ends is evident and inescapable; the claim that it
alone or best can develop rational decision-makers is at
most uncertain.   In brief, there would appear to be no
reason for preserving the practice, and a clear (and
hence decisive) one for eliminating it.

Let us return to CR and imagine a slight deviation
from Stewart's original text.   We shall suppose, that is,
that CR is applied not to all Auriana adults who reach

50, but only to those judged to be 'diminished in rationality.' Normal adults are left alone to find their own
favored forms of recreation, while the others, e.g. those
showing early signs of senility, are legally required for
ten years to join the games and enter the contests constructed for them. This modified system can be labeled
'CRD,' for Compulsory Recreation imposed on the rationally
Defective. Would CRD be a morally acceptable practice?

To answer in the affirmative would imply that the
liberty of those approaching senility can be set aside
as of no consequence. But if normal adults have a right
not to be burdened by CR, why should this right be denied
to those who have fallen below normality? If older adults
should not be subordinated to younger ones, why should
those with failing mental capacities be subordinated to
those whose ability to make choices is intact? The
Kantian imperative cited earlier would have all persons
(and not just 'normal' ones) treated as ends: it exhorts
us to honor the choices, the consent, the faltering (or
budding) powers of self-regulation of all individuals.
Kant's imperative, that is, gives no sanction or support
to a tyranny of normality.

Furthermore, the case for non-intervention gains
additional strength if there is uncertainty about CRD's
effects on senility or whether there are other equally
effective and less invasive policies for containing the
deterioration of rationality.

The relation of these remarks to CE is straightforward.
If the embryonic senility of those placed forcibly in CRD
does not decrease the moral illegitimacy of that practice,
then the rational deficiencies of children cannot offset
the case against CE. Once again, we are led to conclude
that the invasion and abridgment of children's liberty
represented by CE cannot be justified by their under-
development. For the connection between CE and the
development of rationality is at best speculative. More
important, as the case of CRD indicates, why should those
with substantial defects in rationality have lesser claims
to liberty than those of normal competence? A tyranny of
normality is as little justified for children as it is
for sub-normal adults.

2.3 'But you cannot deny that, because of their
deficiencies, we must sometimes protect children against
themselves, for their own good.' With this contention,
we reach the issue of 'paternalism': the deficiencies of
children, coupled with our obligation to guard them
against self-damage, require (supposedly) the imposition
of CE.

2.31 It is important to note, however, that in rejecting CE, no stand has been taken on the need or justification for paternalization of children by adults. In particular, I have not maintained either (a) that children should never be interfered with for their own good (never 'paternalized') or (b) that children should be paternalized no more than adults. Both of these seem to me false, though strong reasons could certainly be given for (b). In any case, neither is implied by what has been argued against CE.

Thus, to consider some specific cases, nothing has been said which denies or weakens our obligation to prevent children of 3 or 4 from playing in busy city streets or with chancy electrical appliances; allowing 10 year olds to sky dive or experiment with heroin injections is not an implication of rejecting CE's legitimacy. To generalize, paternalizing children can be acceptable when a child's health or life would otherwise be put in jeopardy. If CE were abolished, as we have been recommending, there would still be ample opportunity for adults to interfere with children bent on risking injury or death. The absence of that practice would in no way preclude such paternalization: children released from compulsory schooling could be supervised by adults authorized to protect them from self-damage but not to determine what, when, or how they should learn.

As for (b), nothing in the case against CE rests on viewing the capacities of children as equal to those of adults. At many points, the substantial defects of child rationality have been conceded, in order to argue that these defects fail to make CE defensible. On the other hand, the deficiencies of childhood might well make other types of paternalizing - those protecting health and life - both necessary for children and more frequent than with adults.

Our attack on CE does of course affirm that children can do without it. But this in no way implies that they can dispense with all forms of adult regulation and intervention. After all, adults can be justifiably paternalized even though they fall outside the scope of CE. Moreover, if children do not need CE, it does not follow that they require less protective interference than most ordinary adults. Elderly adults may need paternalization more than those of middle age, but this does not establish any obligation for the former to submit to CE.

Further, it would be a mistake to equate the view I am defending with the doctrine (c) that paternalism is morally unacceptable in educational contexts, i.e. that though children can be justifiably paternalized, this sort of interference can never be defended on exclusively educational grounds. Doctrine (c) seems to be a plausible enough doctrine, but it has not been defended or presupposed here. For CE is one, but not the only, form of educational paternalism. Consider a society which did not require the learning of any specific subject or skill, but which prohibited educational experiences thought to be (not dangerous or unhealthy but) time-wasting or intellectually discreditable. It might subsidize learners, telling them to use their subsidies as they desired, except for certain restrictions: e.g. not more than 5 per cent could be spent learning any given sport, interpretative and folk dancing were acceptable but contemporary dances such as the rhumba, twist, bump, etc., were not. Perhaps this sort of educational policy can be described as 'negative educational paternalism'; as opposed to CE, it makes no curriculum or learning environment obligatory, but it does constrict the boundaries within which educational choices are permitted (or will be supported). Now while what has been argued above is certainly incompatible with the positive sort of educational paternalism essential to CE, it raises no objection to the negative variety and hence contrasts sharply with (c).

2.4 What has been argued in responding to defenses of CE premised on the deficiencies of children can be reconstructed as follows. Three such defenses have been examined, each somewhat more complex than the preceding. The first claimed simply that children are defective or under-developed (Section 2.1). We conceded this claim, while pointing out that though the adults in 'Auriana' had deteriorated in several respects, this supplied no justification for CR: in short, inferior development, by itself, cannot warrant interference with personal liberty (2.11). The second defense appealed to the 'more fundamental' failings of children, those which adversely affect their capacity to make sound decisions (2.2). These defects, we maintained, also fail to provide a case for CE: other less restrictive policies could be introduced to remedy them and facilitate the growth of rational competency (2.21, 2.22); moreover, while CE's tendency to foster human learning is speculative and problem-ridden, its treatment of children as means rather than ends involves unmistakable moral abuse (2.23). Finally, we considered the view that the sub-rationality of children requires paternalistic intervention of various sorts by adults (2.3). Here it was argued that such paternalization, e.g. protecting children against self-destruction or serious self-injury, does not imply CE: one can endorse the former while finding the latter morally unacceptable (2.31).

In sum, neither the simplest nor the two progressively
more complex and sophisticated appeals to children's
deficiencies can provide a genuine moral contrast between
CE and CR; moreover, given 2.23's results, the two
practices are linked by a common thread of injustice.
To find such a contrast, if this is at all possible, it
appears that we must look beyond the supposed incom-
petencies of childhood.

3 THE SOCIAL INDISPENSABILITY OF EDUCATION

3.1 The second major contrast between CE and CR concerns
not who but rather what is compelled by each. Using this
contrast, it might be argued that, since the contributions of education to human welfare far exceed those of
recreation, there is a morally significant difference
between the two, and one that yields a justification for
CE. The appeal, then, is not to purported deficiencies
in those required to participate, nor even to their long-
term development or well-being. On the contrary, this
defense of CE is based on the (alleged) tendency of
education to promote certain of 'society's interests,'
i.e. certain morally important goals, a tendency not
shared, supposedly, by recreational activities.
    What are the social interests or moral goods which
education secures or helps to secure? A full list,
responsive to everyone's notion of education, would be
indefinitely long, but it would certainly have to include
the following:
  (A) The skills and attitudes necessary for an informed
and critical electorate and hence for a democratic polity.
  (B) Scientific, medical, and technological development
and the freedom from illness and impoverishment which
they enable.
  (C) The exposure to diverse beliefs and values - alternatives to those dominant within a child's family -
essential for a pluralistic and tolerant society.
  (D) The provision of educational resources, accredited
learning, and career training to vulnerable and disadvantaged groups (e.g. minorities, women, poor people),
and hence a minimal level of distributive justice.
    3.11 Though a detailed response to each of these
points is not possible here, there are certain considerations which have force against them all. For one thing,
do we know that education does in fact help secure these
admitted social goals? Suppose a non-interventionist
policy was initiated, whereby no educational venture or
association was to receive public support and none was

to be forbidden, except those in clear violation of
people's rights. Is it certain, or only speculative,
that goals A-D would be placed in jeopardy?

Prior to the seventeenth century, it was generally
thought that in the absence of publicly enforced and
supported religion, civilized values would swiftly succumb
to barbarian ones. Only a few decades ago, almost everyone held similar beliefs about the nuclear family. Today
these convictions strike us as little more than amusing
relics of historical gullibility. But is the contemporary
notion of education's social import any less amusing or
better grounded? It is highly doubtful, for example,
whether many entire public school careers have access
to as much diversity as the print, electronic, and film
media present within a single year.

3.12 Second, we should note that recreation, along
with art and medicine, also helps secure important social
goods. This, however, does not persuade us to define
publicly the games which all citizens must play, the forms
of art they should cultivate, or the kind of medical care
they must pursue. In general, no legal sanctions are
imposed on those who avoid altogether any or all of these
three worthy activities. Instead, people are often provided with publicly funded resources (parks, museums)
or services (clinics) as incentives to engage in them.
Why should education be different? Instead of compelling
participation in schools and curricula, why not distribute
resources and offer support services to make (or keep)
learning attractive and accessible?

In brief, the social benefits of recreation do not
justify CR, nor do those of art and health care justify
coercive, rather than voluntary, measures to promote
those activities. Hence, even if we concede that education does help realize important social interests, this
would not show that it should be made compulsory.

3.13 This conclusion can be strengthened by considering a design for facilitating, rather than compelling,
education. In this plan, public revenues would in general
be allocated directly to individual learners, rather than
to school distrcits, or to any other administrative unit
or 'authority.' Moreover, our subsidized learners would
have their choice as to what educational resources to
purchase, as well as from whom and at what periods of
their lives to make such purchases. Some might elect to
save up most of their educational subsidies until they
had reached 40 or 50, and were ready to begin a new
career or explore their full potential more deeply.
Nothing would prohibit the continuation of schools similar
to those we presently see all around us, but no one would

be subject to truant officers or legal penalties for keeping clear of them.

For the most part, the special occupation of 'Teacher' would disappear. Learning would in the main proceed through apprenticeships with those engaged in some craft or productive activity. We would not require learners to study under a separate group of 'professionals' who did nothing other than teach, and who by law pre-empted others with greater experience or capacity (but fewer teacher preparation credits) from receiving public educational funds. Thus, farmers could be hired to instruct city folk in how to produce subsistence on vacant lots or in city parks; poets, auto mechanics, lawyers, carpenters, musicians, etc., would all become available as educational resources. No requirements of age, prior schooling, degrees, etc., could prevent learners from contracting for the instructional services of anyone they wished to work or study with. In addition, as Illich points out, some learners would not want or need instruction, but access to equipment or materials (hand-tools, clay, telescopes) or to certain kinds of space or environments (an empty garage, open fields, a lake). The subsidies they receive could also be used to purchase or lease these, as well as the expertise and assistance of people with skills to impart.

To help make all this work, learners could be furnished with various types of support, for example:

(A) Information centers which publish and distribute material indicating what resources are available; when, where, from whom, and under what conditions they can be obtained, etc.

(B) Clearing houses which match would-be learners with needed human or material resources.

(C) The acquisition, maintenance, and distribution (by loan or lease) of educational equipment and materials. (This can be seen as an extension of the public library idea.)

(D) Advisors to work individually with learners, offering encouragement and criticism, pointing out unrecognized options, identifying and helping to overcome weaknesses and obstacles. (Advisors might set tests for their advisees, but the results would be privileged information.)

(E) Remedial programs for those having difficulty acquiring basic skills or with severe emotional or physical handicaps.

(F) Increased subsidies for those from low-income households.

Despite its brevity, this account of 'voluntarized

education' (VE) may suffice to indicate that there are
ways for education to promote socially beneficial goals
that do not depend on compulsion. (Much as medicine, art,
and recreation rely on voluntary sources of participation.) Earlier it was stated that claims concerning CE's
exclusive or preferred role in repairing childhood deficiencies can only be speculation; the same would now seem
to hold with respect to Section 3.1's social goods. In
both cases, the comparisons between CE and VE have not
been studied: the empirical issues remain entirely open.
    3.2 So much then for defenses of CE which rest on what
education is thought to contribute to the interests of
society. Against these defenses it has been contended,
first, that those contributions may involve more speculation than certainty; second, that even if they are conceded, this would not establish a need or justification
for educational compulsion; and last, that for all we
currently know, voluntarized forms of education could
promote society's interests as well as, or better than,
CE. In light of these contentions, however, the defenses
of CE considered in this section, like those in the
previous one, are either fallacious or heavily weighted
down by conjecture. Hence, since CE's moral abuse of
children is evident and not speculative, the case against
it, once again, would seem conclusive.

4 TWO PRACTICAL OBJECTIONS TO VE

Nonetheless, the grip of a long-standing custom, as Jake
Justin discovered, is not easily relaxed. Some residual
loyalty to CE, or antipathy towards its abolition, will
doubtless remain despite the preceding arguments. In an
effort to break through some of this resistance, I shall
discuss two practical objections to the notion that
education should be voluntarized. The first maintains
that eliminating CE, given present social conditions,
would have disastrous consequences, especially for groups
already suffering under inequitable treatment; the second
that CE is not abolishable anyhow, at least not from any
current or foreseeable industrialized society.
    4.1 The first of these practical objections is willing
to concede that, in theory, we should voluntarize education, i.e. that the ideal form of VE is to be preferred
over any form of CE But in practice - in any concrete
situation - the elimination of compulsory attendance laws
may not give rise to this ideal; instead, it may feed
the development of damaging and unjust institutions.
Thus, when the state of Mississippi discarded CE, the

prime victims were its poor and black children: they
are now even further removed from basic learning skills,
credentials, and access to decent jobs and life-
opportunities.

4.11   This objection is not lacking in force. But we
must be wary of inferring too much from it. What follows
here is not that CE is justifiable, but that, in certain
circumstances, we may have to tolerate it in order to
avoid even greater evils. Accordingly, as in other
'lesser of evils' cases, the present argument cannot
establish any obligation to support or to preserve CE.
On the contrary, our responsibility is to either eliminate the conditions forcing the dilemma upon us or extract
ourselves from those conditions: that is, to avoid both
lesser and greater evils altogether. Specifically, we
should work toward establishing in Mississippi some
variant of the VE design described in Section 3.13 above
or find ways to provide its blacks and poor people with
access to educational/life options external to that state.

The issues here are reminiscent of those arising from
the punishment of innocent persons. We may know, to
take the usual example, that a person charged with rape
did not actually commit the crime; if released from jail,
however, (s)he could not escape the town's desire for
revenge. Does this justify punishing the innocent as a
general practice? Clearly not: our obligation is to keep
the accused away from the lynch mob, not to deprive him/
her of liberty. If and as soon as possible, we should
contrive an escape both from jail and from the local
vigilantes.

In the same way, the intolerable consequences of alternatives cannot justify the imposition of compulsory
schooling. We remain obliged to protect children (those
innocent of crime) both from CE (punishment) and from
other injurious conditions. This duty of protection,
moreover, requires that we liberate children as soon as
and to the greatest extent possible. Our innocent victim
should be regulated and interfered with as little as
possible while in jail. Likewise, we should reshape CE
toward increasingly voluntary arrangements, e.g. by
ensuring public funds for experimental and community-
controlled schools, and by developing what might be called
a 'compulsory competence' system (CC). Here learners,
though entitled to conventional schooling, can gain
exemptions from it by demonstrating mastery of curriculum
objectives, say, by passing the same tests given to
regular students. When students earn exemptions, they
or their parents receive subsidies towards the cost of
educational resources of their own choosing. In short,

under CC only the 'what' and not the 'how' of education
would be compelled: in comparison with CE, infringements
on the liberty of children would be substantially
diminished.

Now this obligation to initiate something akin to CC
confirms once again what has just been argued about CE:
even where the wholesale abandonment of compulsory schooling would have consequences of hardship and inequity, our
obligation is not to retain CE but to eliminate as much
of it as we can without generating those consequences.

To sum up: this first practical objection fails to
distinguish CE from such clear moral abuses as punishing
the innocent (or CR). Quite the contrary, it leaves
intact our obligations (a) progressively to restrict the
scope of CE and of its interference with children and
(b) to create conditions in which any onerous consequences
of eliminating CE can be avoided and which enable us,
therefore, to develop VE as our primary form of education.

4.2   The second practical objection contends that
there is no escape from CE and hence that it is pointless
to discuss its moral acceptability or recommend its
abolition. Furthermore, since there would appear to be
no difficulty avoiding CR, we have here, supposedly, a
sharp contrast between the two practices.

Authors who disagree more than they agree reach consensus on this criticism of the aim of voluntarizing
education. Thus, Herbert Gintis, a radical economist,
appeals to an analysis of capitalism as sacrificing 'the
healthy development of community, work, environment,
education, and social equality to the accumulation of
capital' to argue that 'In the final analysis "deschooling" is irrelevant because we cannot "de-factory," "de-
office," or 'de-family," save perhaps at the still unen-
visioned end of a long process of social reconstruc-ion
tion.' (7) Alternatively, on behalf of the 'clods, the
piecemeal reformers, the people without a grand vision,
those who are simply trying to improve the quality of
the experience that real children have in schools,'
educator Neil Postman avows that 'American society is not
going to be deschooled! Not in the near future anyway -
and for the very reason Illich sees so clearly: the
schools function to perpetuate the established order.' (8)

4.21   A full reply to this objection would require
detailed treatment of such perennial philosophical issues
as the scope of prediction in human affairs, the role of
(autonomous) desires, beliefs, and decisions in shaping
social reality, the degree to which any one segment of
society (educational activities) is independent or the
product of another (productive forces and relations).

This is not the place to reiterate my discussions of
these issues, nor the arguments I have urged in support
of a libertarian conception of causality and explanation
in human life, one which rejects models of determinism
and prediction imported from natural science and which
is capable of recognizing and facilitating autonomous
activity. (9) Here, three more particularized remarks
will have to suffice.

In the first place, this objection appears to be a
product of conjecture: it lacks roots in any sustained
investigation of efforts to disestablish compulsory
schooling. In 1975, the task of abolishing CE may be
comparable to that of establishing representative democracy in 1750, or creating the right of labor to organize
in 1870, or 'de-asylumizing' mental health care in 1950.
That is, it is not as though people had been trying and
failing for decades: agitation against CE has just barely
begun. What evidence is there that CE is a fixed part
of the institutional environment, as opposed to having
reached a terminal phase of development - a phase which
in fifteen years will relinquish almost all involuntary
claims on those of high school age and permit exemptions
on an individualized basis to children under 12? (10)

I suggest (a) that whatever we see happening today is
no more compatible with the permanence of CE than it is
with the equally hypothetical view that voluntarized ways
of educating the young have begun to make their entrance
and will occupy primacy of place within industrialized
countries by the end of the 1980s, and (b) that the
dispute here involves, like so much else in social
science, a doctrine that is self-fulfilling: if people
ceased to believe in the intransigence of CE, they'd look
more readily and more successfully for ways to avoid and
replace it. But if (a) and (b) are true, the issue raised
by this practical objection is an open one; it can only be
resolved by examining what actually results from concerted
and tenacious efforts to introduce VE. Hence, the objection cannot show that such efforts will be futile, nor
can it reduce our obligation to work towards the voluntarization of education.

Second, to avoid the charge that CE's purported intransigence is a flight of untestable conjecture, this
objection is sometimes restated as the contention that
VE cannot be fully realized without the aid of fundamental
social changes of a non-educational sort, e.g. redistribu-
tions of power and resources, dispersion of child-rearing
responsibilities to persons outside the nuclear family.
Put in this way, the objection seems hardly disputable.
The trouble now is that, in this new form, it is

innocuous, entirely compatible with our position that CE can and should be discarded.

Consider: it is probably true that the aspirations of women and of racial minorities can be fully realized only where no individual or group (regardless of sex or race) can amass a disproportionate concentration of economic or political power, i.e. where there are social limits placed on the private ownership of land, capital and other resources. But this does not imply that, in the absence of such limits, racial and sexual equality are irrelevant or merely academic goals, nor that we can legitimately set them aside until those more general principles of distributive justice have already been achieved. The same holds for VE. Conceding that it can flourish only where child-rearing, ownership, and production have been substantially altered does not imply that, before those changes have been accomplished, we cannot or should not begin to substitute voluntarized for compulsory aspects of education. On the contrary, it suggests an hypothesis as to how those efforts can be most effective, i.e. by combining them with strategies designed to combat injustices other than those unique to education. Thus, on this hypothesis educational subsidies should be advocated not merely for minors but for adults as well. For this would not only curtail CE's present infringements on the liberty and development of children, but make further voluntarization more accessible by showing that it can work towards fulfilling demands made by working-class and low-income adults for a fairer share of resources and opportunities. But if this educational subsidy policy is supported by or compatible with the current formulation or our second practical objection, how can that formulation be used to contest either the feasibility or desirability of VE?

Last, there is a strange kind of callousness, one might even say 'age-ism,' in this objection's certainty concerning the perpetuation of CE and in the ease with which it sets aside the rights of children to be free of imposed confinement and of adult indoctrination. Sexism, racism, prisons, colonies, etc., like schools, all function to 'perpetuate the established order,' but we are not told to forgo support for anti-imperialist freedom fighters or for the 27th amendment on the ground that the system will remain what it is for the foreseeable future. Nor would most radical economists maintain that we must first 'de-factory' before struggling against the abuses of racism or to decrease the types of crime punishable by incarceration. Perhaps it has somewhere been discovered that only those features of contemporary industrialized

societies which affect children are beyond fundamental
change, or can only be altered after every other important
institutional change has been implemented? If not, children can be excused for thinking that once again they have
been put last, that their rights to self-determination
have been set aside on no defensible basis, and that this
objection manifests the very sort of arbitrary domination
exhibited by CE. ('Wait until you grow up, then we will
take the abuses you suffer seriously.') (11)

5   SUMMING UP THE CASE AGAINST CE

If the arguments advanced in the preceding sections are
sound, CE has nothing more to be said for it than CR;
any objection we may have to the latter applies with
equal force to the former. For both of the principal
contrasts alleged to distinguish these two practices -
the lesser competency of those compelled to participate
in CE and the greater contributions of education to major
social interests - have been found to be largely conjectural (2.11, 3.11). Moreover, even if we concede that
these contrasts do obtain, they fail to provide either
(a) any moral justification for compulsory rather than
voluntarized educational arrangements (2.21, 2.22, 3.12,
3.13), or (b) any evidence which denies or diminishes the
morally abusive treatment of children by CE or our consequent obligation to discard that practice (2.23, 3.12,
3.13).
     Nor were the two practical objections considered in
Section 4 any more successful in regards to (a) or (b).
As for the first, it was contended that injuries to
minorities and/or the poor (like those to an innocent
person) supposedly generated by voluntarizing education
(by imposing legal penalties upon him/her) may warrant
temporary tolerance of CE (punishment of the innocent)
but cannot reduce our general obligation to work toward
VE (to punish only the guilty) or to bring about conditions in which those injurious consequences are minimized
(4.11). The objection that CE is not eliminable from
industrialized societies was countered by the argument
that, taken literally, it seems to rest solely on unfounded (and age-discriminatory) speculation, while if
restated to affirm that implementing VE will require other
far-reaching changes in the distribution of power and
resources, the objection becomes true at the cost of
losing all of its bite: it no longer conflicts with the
advocacy of VE.
     Much more, of course, remains to be said on all of

these points. In particular, a complete account should
be furnished, first, of the many varieties of VE and,
second, of plausible strategies for diminishing the scope
of CE and for replacing it by voluntary activities
sensitive to the claims of distributive and compensatory
justice. (12) But enough, perhaps, has been presented
to indicate that the claims of CE on the lives and liberty
of children are very far from indisputable, and to shift
the burden of justification to those who would retain
CE at the cost of failing to promote voluntarized
alternatives.

NOTES

Many of the ideas and arguments in this paper have been
formulated or refined in the course of discussions with
my friends and colleagues, Phillip D. Jacklin, Jeffrey
Walter, and Phillip R. Wheeler. Others should have the
benefit of such painstaking and perceptive critics.

 1 C. Stewart, 'Auriana' (New Orleans, Louisiana: Gumbo
    Publications, 1965).
 2 J. Berke and Mary Barnes, 'Mary Barnes: Two Accounts
    of a Journey Through Madness' (New York: Ballantine
    Books, 1971).
 3 W. Godwin, Of the Communication of Knowledge,
    reprinted in L. Krimerman and L. Perry (eds), 'Patterns
    of Anarchy' (New York: Doubleday Anchor, 1966), p.421.
 4 D. Greene and M.R. Lepper, Intrinsic Motivation - How
    to Turn Play into Work, 'Psychology Today,' vol.8,
    no.4 (September 1974), p.50.
 5 Ibid., pp.51-2.
 6 See here ch.6 of Ivan Illich's 'Deschooling Society'
    (New York: Harper & Row, 1972).
 7 H. Gintis, Toward a Political Economy of Education:
    A Radical Critique of Ivan Illich's 'Deschooling
    Society,' reprinted in A. Gartner et al. (eds), 'After
    Deschooling, What?' (New York: Harper & Row, 1973),
    p.32.
 8 N. Postman, My Ivan Illich Problem, reprinted in
    Gartner et al., op.cit., p.145.
 9 These arguments appear in the introductions to section
    sections IV-VIII of my 'Nature and Scope of Social
    Science' (New York: Appleton-Century-Crofts, 1969),
    and in my article, Autonomy: A New Paradigm for
    Research, published as ch.XIII of the '71st Yearbook
    of the National Society for the Study of Education'
    (University of Chicago Press, 1972).
10 For a suggestive view on this point, see James

Coleman's article, The Children Have Outgrown the
Schools, reprinted in L. Bowman et al. (eds), 'Of
Education and Community' (Lincoln, Nebraska: Nebraska
Curriculum Development Center, 1972), pp.69-75.

11 Ch.5 of Allen Graubard's penetrating book, 'Free the
Children' (New York: Vintage, 1974), deals in much
greater detail with the issues raised by both of the
two practical objections examined in this section.

12 These two accounts are outlined in a position paper,
Should Education Be Compulsory?, by L. Krimerman and
J. Walter, available from the authors, c/o Childhood
and Government Project, Boalt School of Law, University of California, Berkeley, 94720.

Autonomy, freedom and schooling

part **III**

Autonomy as an aim of education

6

Brian Crittenden

INTRODUCTION

Individual autonomy is widely regarded as a fundamental
value in educational theory and practice. Supporters
of a systematic approach to knowledge in teaching and
learning often claim that one of the main outcomes, if
not the most important, of the educational process is
its contribution to the making of an autonomous person.
In the tradition of liberal education, the forms of human
thought and knowledge are to be studied for their own
sake, for the distinctive values they can bring to a
person's life, and not simply for the sake of an extrinsic
end they may happen to serve. It is not surprising that
the qualities of mind promoted through such disinterested
studies should be described in terms of personal freedom
and autonomy. Among the so-called radicals in education,
autonomy is not simply an achievement to be promoted,
but a condition to be respected even in children and thus
a basic criterion of the kind of educational procedures
that may legitimately be employed. Whatever other defense
may be offered for such practices as the open classroom,
participatory democracy in decisions of schooling, self-
directed and individualised learning, the stress on
creativity and learning by discovery, they are often
thought to be justified in the name of autonomy.

That such otherwise divergent theorists can so happily
appeal to autonomy suggests that the notion and its
relationship to education deserve to be examined more
closely. In the following discussion, I shall attempt
to pursue some aspects of this task. I shall be concerned, for the most part, with the practice of education
in so far as it involves a systematic introduction to the
main symbolic forms of culture. In this practice, the
enterprise of teaching and learning is not determined

primarily by the immediate interests of the child or the
society, but by the most significant human achievements
of knowing, interpreting, evaluating, expressing - what
we classify loosely as the sciences, the humanities, and
the arts. I take it that this view of teaching and learning clearly belongs within the tradition of liberal education. For the sake of brevity I shall therefore refer
to it by this title. There are of course other variations
on the theme of liberal education. In the interpretation
I have briefly sketched, the development of reasoned
thought and judgment is not restricted to exclusively
intellectual activities but extends to the moral and
aesthetic domains as well.

    Among my reasons for focusing on liberal education is
that its relationship to personal autonomy seems to be
a complex and ambivalent one. If we believe that children
are already autonomous (in a sense that demands moral
respect) and that their exercise of autonomy determines
what counts as education, it is obvious that the question
of the relationship between education and autonomy has
been drastically simplified. In this scheme, education
is to be defined as any activity that expresses a person's
autonomous choice and, presumably, increases his capacity
and opportunity for such choices. On the other hand, if
we believe quite strictly in the primacy of the social-
ising role of education, it seems that personal autonomy
can hardly be a serious candidate as an aim of education.
In the case of liberal education, the process is not
determined as a function of autonomy, but by the public
symbolic structures that make up a culture. At the same
time, proponents of liberal education would claim that
personal autonomy of any significance is achieved only
through initiation into these symbolic structures. While
this process of initiation, unlike socialisation, is not
crudely at odds with autonomy, there seems to be something
paradoxical about the claim that we achieve personal
autonomy through being encultured in such ways.

PERSONAL AUTONOMY AS AN 'IDEAL' TYPE

In order to give a positive sketch of autonomy as an
'ideal' type, I think it is useful, if not necessary,
to distinguish three overlapping basic aspects. These
may loosely be called the intellectual, the moral, and
the emotional. One may be autonomous in any of these
aspects without necessarily being autonomous in the
others. Under the intellectual I include the whole range
of one's beliefs, whether they are about the nature of

the world or the things that are thought to be worthwhile
or the standards of conduct. At an extreme limit, intellectual autonomy would require, in the first place,
that a person not accept any of his important beliefs
primarily on the authority of others, but on his own
experience, his own reflection on evidence and argument,
his own sense of what is true and right. For complete
intellectual autonomy it would also seem necessary that a
person should determine for himself the second-order
questions about what constitutes a true claim, adequate
evidence, a justifiable moral principle, and the like.
Even the crucial concepts in which he perceives and
understands should be of his own design or, at least,
accepted from others only because he is personally convinced that such concepts are satisfactory.

Moral autonomy, as I am using the expression, is
intended to embrace all forms of practical judgment and
action. Assuming that factual and normative beliefs are
relevant to the decisions we make on how we should act,
it is clear that moral autonomy depends in part on
intellectual autonomy. Of course, in the Existentialist
view, at least as Sartre has presented it, moral decisions
in the concrete situations of life are pure acts of the
will, choices in which belief and principle can play no
part. If moral autonomy is understood quite literally,
it will either include aspects of the extreme form of
intellectual autonomy or appeal to an interpretation of
moral choice in which such choice is the determining act
of an isolated personal will that is the core of the
self. As Iris Murdoch has shown, (1) this interpretation
finds support in contemporary Anglo-Saxon philosophy as
well as in Existentialism.

In addition to independence of thought in determining
and applying criteria of moral judgment, moral autonomy
also includes the executive capacities for carrying into
practice what one decides should be done. The possession
of these capacities is commonly described by such terms
as tenacity, resoluteness, strength of will, self-mastery.
Perhaps the last of these most appropriately designates
this facet of personal autonomy.

In relation to the exercise of political and other
authority, a morally autonomous person will not, in the
extreme view, obey or even acknowledge a command. 'For
the autonomous man,' says R.P. Wolff, 'there is no such
thing, strictly speaking, as a command.' (2) If such a
person acts as commanded it is only because he is personally convinced about the merit of the action independently
of the exercise of authority.

The third main aspect of autonomy, the emotional, is

also to be interpreted fairly broadly. It may be treated
as part of self-mastery in so far as the latter refers
to the control of one's emotions, desires, and feelings.
However, the point is not simply that a person would
exercise self-mastery in the face of strong emotional
involvement, but that he would remain emotionally detached
in his relationships to other persons and things. This
form of independence and self-sufficiency has a long
history as an ideal. It was illustrated in the life of
Socrates and cultivated as a central doctrine by the
Cynics and the Stoics.

Given the aspects of autonomy that I have been describing, it should be emphasised that even though a
person may reflectively accept the authority of others
in determining certain of his beliefs or actions, it is
nevertheless an abdication of his autonomy. This possibility illustrates the insufficiency of R.F. Dearden's
criterion of autonomy, namely, that the explanation of
what a person thinks and does in important matters
requires 'reference to his own activity of mind.' (3)
Obedience, even of a servile kind, is a human act and
thus cannot be explained without reference to the agent's
own activity of mind. Dearden's criterion may provide a
sufficient condition for ascribing responsibility. But
a person may be held responsible for what he does, without
necessarily having acted autonomously.

INTELLECTUAL AUTONOMY AND SUBJECTIVE EPISTEMOLOGY

Of the three aspects of personal autonomy that I have
just outlined, I shall give most attention to the
intellectual as a possible aim of education. This aspect
includes, of course, a significant part of what is often
claimed on behalf of moral autonomy.

At the present time there are probably very few serious
defenders of the complete subjectivism that intellectual
autonomy in the strict sense entails. However, in a
variety of recent relativist interpretations of knowledge,
the conditions of subjectivism on which a thoroughgoing
intellectual autonomy depends are substantially satisfied.
The trend is clearly illustrated in Feyerabend's 'anarchistic epistemology': he evens draws a connection between
his epistemological theory and the ideal of human freedom.
(4) A similar interpretation is defended by Kuhn in his
analysis of the changing models of epistemic procedure
to which scientists adhere. (5) Basically, the same kind
of relativism is also inherent in Wittgenstein's notions
of a form of life and a system. What is being claimed

in theories of this sort is that questions of objectivity, rationality and truth can only be raised in the context of a particular conceptual system. Different conceptual systems (whether, for example, the difference exists between cultures, or social classes, or interpretations of science, or science and religion) cannot be compared on criteria of objectivity, rationality and truth; they are strictly incommensurable. One's adherence to a particular conceptual system is treated as either an essentially arbitrary and non-rational decision to commit oneself or as the effect of a combination of psychological and social causal conditions. At least for those who make the issues of knowledge depend ultimately on a non-rational subjective commitment, a place for personal autonomy of a very significant kind in man's intellectual life is obviously secured.

A somewhat similar view of intellectual autonomy based on the relative nature of knowledge has recently been gaining favor in educational theory and practice. It is difficult to say whether, or to what extent, the philo-sophical views just mentioned have had any direct in-fluence. For the most part, the educationists have not developed the anarchistic epistemology that underlies their position. Kuhn's name is often quoted, but this may simply reflect a current fashion rather than a studied acceptance of his theory. In any case, the relativism of the educationists may have been fueled more by some recent popular social theorists than by the philosophers. Certainly, the vision of small local groups determining their own curriculum of learning and making their own knowledge can be nourished from the writings of a Theodore Roszak of a Peter Berger (although the latter eschews any epistemological stand). (6)

The trend in educational thought and practice to which I am referring incorporates much of what has now become the established doctrine of progressive education - in particular, the belief that each child's education should be determined primarily by his or her felt needs and interests. What has been added (or reiterated more force-fully, if we recall the Instrumentalist branch of earlier progressive education) are some elements of a theory of knowledge in which the claim to objectivity for any form of thought and inquiry is radically challenged. The favored alternative is either a version of subjectivism or, for those who find its individualist aspect repugnant, a relativism of small local groups made up of freely and fully participating members.

The flavor of this theory as it is proposed by educa-tionists can be gained from the efforts of Charles H.

Rathbone and Roland S. Barth to set out the interpretation
of knowledge that they themselves support and that they
believe is commonly assumed in the practices of open
education. (7) Among their tenets are the following:

Knowledge is idiosyncratically formed, individually
conceived, fundamentally individualistic. Theoretic-
ally, no two people's knowledge can be the same, unless
their experience is identical.

Because knowledge is basically idiosyncratic, it is
most difficult to judge whether one person's knowledge
is 'better' than another's.

Knowledge does not exist outside of individual
knowers: it is not a thing apart. The data that goes
into books and into the Library of Congress is not
the same as the knowledge people know.

Knowledge is not inherently ordered or structured
nor does it automatically subdivide into academic
'disciplines'. These categories are man-made, not
natural. (8)

In relation to these views on the nature of knowledge,
it is useful to notice what Rathbone takes to be the
underlying assumption or 'the basic idea' among supporters
of the open classroom on how children learn:

Open education views the child ... as a self-activated
maker of meaning.... Learning is seen as the result
of his own self-initiated interaction with the world:
the child's understanding grows during a constant
interplay between something outside himself - the
general environment, a pendulum, a person - and something inside himself - his concept-forming mechanism,
his mind...

... in a very fundamental way each child is his own
agent - a self-reliant, independent, self-actualizing
individual who is capable, on his own, of forming concepts and of learning. (9)

Of course, Rathbone also reaffirms the Rousseauist
faith of progressive education generally in the natural
goodness of the child. This attribute of the child
together with his autonomy as a learner form the basis of
his general autonomy as a moral agent. Each child 'has
the right to elect what he will do and what he shall be';
'to pursue whatever question interests him'; 'what he
does and who he becomes are his to decide.' In the
theory of open education, as Rathbone interprets it,
each child is thus already an autonomous agent, and this
is a fundamental condition that any effort claiming the
name of education should respect.

Given these beliefs about the nature of knowledge and
the autonomy of the child as learner and moral agent, it

is not surprising that the ideal teacher-student relationship bears no resemblance to that of master and apprentice.
The key words in Rathbone's description of the teacher's
role are 'assistant' and 'facilitator.' (10)

It is beyond the scope of this essay to provide an
adequate critique of the varieties of relativist epistemology that underlie the assertion of an unqualified
intellectual autonomy for the learner in the process of
education. In relation to both the philosophical and the
educational positions that have been mentioned I shall
merely point to what I take to be their most serious
shortcomings. No doubt, many of their supporters are
reacting to the excesses of the mechanistic, positivist
account of knowledge - in particular, to its notion of
objectivity; (11) and many are probably motivated by a
proper moral revulsion at the inhumane uses to which knowledge, especially science, is frequently put. However,
in attacking these philosophical and moral defects, it
is not necessary to promote the role of the individual
human agent in knowing to such an extent that any notion
whatever of objectivity is undermined. In fact, once
this has been done, the philosophical and moral criticism
simply collapses into an expression of one ultimately
non-rational commitment against another. The critical
notes I here wish to make on recent forms of relativism
have for the most part been developed by Roger Trigg in
'Reason and Commitment.' (12)

1 When the standards of truth and reasonable belief
that apply to any individual are those, and only those,
that the individual decides to accept for himself, then
it is not possible for him (provided he observes the
standards to which he subscribes) to hold a false belief
or to believe or act irrationally. In these circumstances,
no distinction between knowledge and belief can be drawn,
and there is no ground for claiming that anyone is
fanatical or prejudiced. As Trigg observes,'"truth"
becomes a consequence of belief and commitment and not a
reason for it.' (13) In such a scheme, it is not simply
that we can only speak of what is true or rational for
this or that person, but we cannot intelligibly employ
the concepts of true and rational at all. For where it
is not possible to distinguish error or irrationality,
neither is it possible to distinguish truth or rationality.

2 Human beings who hold radically different beliefs
do communicate with one another through language, and
translations are effectively made from one language or
conceptual system into another. An essential condition
for such communication and translation of beliefs, as
well as for genuine argument, is that claims may be true

or false, may constitute good or bad reasons, as such -
and not simply from the point of view of the speaker.
This, in turn, presupposes that there are not as many
worlds as there are ways of talking, but various conceptual perspectives from which the same world may be described and interpreted in ways that may be true or false.
Anyone who followed a relativism of conceptual systems
or forms of life quite literally would be forced to
restrict his assertions about what is the case to those
who share his form of life.   Even his account of relativism could claim to be true (and intelligible?) only from
the viewpoint of that group.

3 If the commitment to conceptual systems on which
issues of truth and rationality depend is finally non-
rational, it must be assumed that we cannot question
whether the beliefs that characterise such a system may
themselves be mistaken, or whether it may be more reasonable to accept one system rather than another.   To support
this assumption it would have to be further supposed that
these conceptual systems (forms of life, etc.) exist
as completely self-contained units and that there are no
general or commonsense criteria for true or reasonable
belief.

It also seems to be assumed that we may choose whether
to be committed to the conditions of rationality or not.
But these conditions apply to us regardless of our commitment.   We may of course choose to reject them, but still
we cannot escape acting irrationally.

The talk of ultimate non-rational commitments seems to
reflect the image of man referred to earlier in which each
individual is, at centre, an isolated will that is not
constrained by reasons, but in a pure act of freedom
determines what it shall find acceptable as reasons, not
only in morality but in science as well.   In this context
I can only refer the reader again to Iris Murdoch's
critical discussion of this view of man.   In summary, the
alternative she defends is expressed as follows:

> Man is not a combination of an impersonal rational
> thinker and a personal will.   He is a unified being
> who sees, and who desires in accordance with what he
> sees, and who has some continual slight control over
> the direction and focus of his vision. (14)

4 Serious exponents of relativism are not able to
maintain a strict and consistent relativist position.
The general problem they face is that anyone who adopts
a thoroughgoing relativism, who rejects the possibility
of objective criteria of truth and rationality, cannot
even consistently assume that he is correct.   Even if he
begins to argue seriously, he must assume inconsistently

that the claims one makes may be true or false.

The problem is illustrated in Kuhn's interpretation of scientific knowledge. Although he asserts that different paradigms of scientific inquiry are incommensurable, he confidently undertakes a comparative and historical study that yields conclusions about what is presumed to be, in some sense, a common enterprise. He even suggests that scientists can go wrong in following a given paradigm, and detects a pattern of progress, not simply change, within science. Kuhn also accepts the truth of the psychological and sociological explanations as to why scientists at a given time support a particular paradigm. If he were consistent, he would have to treat such explanations as relative to the conceptual schemes within which their proponents work. In terms of his relativist assumptions, Kuhn's own conclusions cannot even make a claim to be true - except on those who find themselves committed to the paradigm of inquiry that he himself employs.

The relativists among the philosophically inclined sociologists of knowledge, such as Karl Mannheim, have also inconsistently supposed that they were giving a true account of the group-relative nature of belief (both as a matter of fact and as an epistemological theory). In theories of this kind there is often an elite (e.g. Mannheim's 'socially unattached intelligentsia') that excapes the conceptual boundaries of this or that social group, and to which their authors belong. Despite the inconsistency with relativism, it is argued that the conceptual perspective of the elite is preferable to that of any other group.

Anything like an adequate critical comment on the beliefs about knowledge and learning that, in Rathbone's view, are presupposed in the practice of open education would take us far beyond the limits of this paper. Yet, as we saw earlier, these beliefs offer a rationale for treating what approaches the limit of unqualified intellectual autonomy as a basic normative factor in the conduct of education. I should therefore at least refer briefly to some respects in which I believe the theory is mistaken.

1 Perhaps the most serious weakness is the theory's simplistic image of learning: each human organism independently interacting with its environment and deriving its own concepts out of this experience through the workings of its 'concept-forming mechanism' or mind. There is a substantial range of concepts for which this abstractionist view simply cannot account. (15) But, in any case, as human beings we are not isolated individuals

constructing our private realm of concepts out of the data
of our raw experience. We acquire concepts, and learn to
apply them in interpreting and understanding our experience, through the social process of learning language
as an integral part of various human practices. The
theory's individualistic view of man ignores the fact that
each human being develops as such in the context of a pre-
existing world of shared meanings, that mind is not simply
a given, there to be flexed like a muscle, but an
achievement that depends largely on our gaining access
to the inheritance of shared meanings. (16)

2   There is an obvious sense in which all the ways of
classifying knowledge are man-made. However, it does not
follow from this, as Rathbone seems to suppose, that they
must be entirely matters of convention, or if conventional, that they are necessarily arbitrary. One need not
even argue, as Hirst has done, (17) that there are several
logically distinct basic forms of knowledge. It is sufficient to point out that a particular method of inquiry,
a group of closely related key concepts, a significant
common human purpose may severally or together provide a
non-arbitrary basis for the organisation of knowledge.

Apart from incurring the general criticisms against
subjectivism, the emphasis that Rathbone places on the
idiosyncratic character of knowledge seems to reflect a
confusion between the sequence of psychological activities
in which a person learns and the logical criteria that
apply to the outcomes of his learning (that is, whether
what he has learnt is knowledge or false belief, whether
he has acquired a moral concept of honesty or a scientific
concept of energy, and so on). In relation to the practice of education, the consequence of this confusion is
that an account of how children learn is also thought
to determine what they should learn.

A curious feature of the theory of open education as
Rathbone presents it is that, despite the uncompromising
rejection of objective forms of knowledge, it seems only
to entail that 'in certain rather basic situations, traditional academic objectives are not considered to be the
first order of priority.' (18) On the basis of the
general claims about the nature of knowledge, one would
expect that such objectives could have no place in the
order of priorities at all.

3   Rathbone's discussion of the theoretical assumptions
of the open classroom also illustrates the general problem
of inconsistency that relativists face. If the supporters
of the open classroom consistently accept the anarchistic
epistemology that Rathbone describes, they cannot argue
that the assumptions of traditional schooling are mistaken

or that their own style of education embodies correct principles and priorities. They can merely state that the position they take is true for them because they believe it to be so, and acknowledge that the same must be said for the supporters of any other view of education.

As we have seen, various forms of anarchistic epistemology (including the relativism of conceptual systems to which people ultimately adhere by virtue of a non-rational commitment) allow for, and in fact require, the exercise of 'pure' intellectual autonomy. I have suggested briefly why the price they exact for this autonomy is intolerably high. It can be bought only at the cost of eliminating in effect the distinction between knowledge and belief, between rational and irrational thought and action. Certainly, the kind of personal autonomy that makes these demands cannot be an aim of liberal education. For liberal education is primarily an induction into the standards of truth and rationality and other domains of value as they have been articulated in the ongoing public traditions of human understanding.

It is difficult to know what kind of education could be justified, given the assumptions of unqualified personal autonomy. If human beings are thought to be autonomous from birth, or, at least, if it is supposed that the potentiality unfolds spontaneously, there is clearly no need for an education that promotes autonomy. In so far as such autonomous beings can be said to be educated, the only appropriate method would seem to be that of personal discovery. But if this method were taken quite literally, its effectiveness for most individuals would be very limited, and it would make impossible the cumulative achievement of knowledge and skill from one generation to another. Nor would it be possible to apply any public criteria to the quality of what an individual discovered for himself. It could not be said, for example, that a conclusion he had reached was false, or insignificant, or biased. It is difficult to see how we can speak seriously at all of the education of human beings if they are interpreted as asocial and ahistorical atoms. Even the environment that A.S. Neill established at Summerhill was not entirely consistent with his beliefs about the complete autonomy of each child's wants, and the dire consequences of any kind of uninvited adult influence. He did not seem to notice, for example, that children at Summerhill were not necessarily free to do what they wanted when left alone; both the wants they had and the ways they satisfied them depended upon the options available at Summerhill.

The general objections that have been raised do not

necessarily apply to emotional autonomy. It is an argu-
able moral ideal and can probably be promoted by some form
of liberal education. At least, there does not seem to
be any incongruity between the general characteristics of
liberal education and this ideal. Given the role of the
emotions in human action and the consequences of involvement and commitment, the question is whether there is more
loss than gain in attempting to achieve emotional autonomy.
Without arguing the case here, I believe that the loss
does outweigh the gain. The detachment by which a person
refrains from egoistically consuming what he loves seems
to me a more admirable ideal to develop than the egoistic
detachment by which one carefully avoids loving, or loving
too much.

KANT'S DEFENSE OF RATIONAL AUTONOMY

To come back to the question of intellectual and moral
autonomy; although an anarchistic epistemology provides
the basis for a substantial form of personal autonomy,
I have argued that it cannot be justified and that autonomy of this kind cannot be an aim of liberal education.
The question now is whether there can be a significant
version of personal autonomy that is nevertheless hedged
in by the conditions of rationality and morality in human
thought and action. Whether such a concession seriously
dilutes the claim about autonomy clearly depends, in part,
on how the conditions for rational and moral behavior are
interpreted. Historically, the main effort to defend
autonomy in a strong sense, while still acknowledging the
constraints of rational criteria, has been made in the
moral sphere. Kant's defense of moral autonomy of this
kind is, of course, the most distinguished and influential.
It clearly reverberates in the contemporary theories of
moral development proposed by Piaget and Kohlberg.
    According to Kant, who in turn was influenced by
Rousseau, each individual is autonomous in that he decides
upon and legislates to himself those principles of action
which he sees are fitting to his nature as a member of a
community of free and equal rational beings. In the moral
sphere each one of us is usbject only to his own will as
a rational being. But, of course, the principles that we
prescribe for ourselves in this way must also be willed
as universal laws applying equally to all free and
rational beings. For Kant, the basis of autonomy is 'the
idea of the will of every rational being as a will which
makes universal law.' (19)
    The first difficulty with this doctrine is that an
individual cannot seriously will a universal law without

being prepared to challenge the autonomy of everyone else.
(20) No conflict arises as long as every individual does
in fact will the same law for himself and everyone else.
But it is not the case that human beings always agree
about universal laws of morality. And we cannot suppose
that they must necessarily agree, without questioning the
autonomy of their decision. Of course, Kant tried to
ensure a consensus of sovereign wills by appealing to an
obscure metaphysical entity, the rational self.

A second and more basic problem is that of making sense
of individuals legislating universal laws to themselves.
In Kant's theory the plausibility of the metaphor of self-
legislation depends again on the metaphysical distinction
he draws between the noumenal or rational self and the
phenomenal self. But apart from the difficulty with this
distinction, there is, as Kurt Baier has recently argued,
a logical impossibility in claiming that each individual
is subject only to laws of his own making: 'If no member
of a society were subject to the will of any other, then
there would simply be no law and so no legislation including self-legislation.' (21)

As Baier also points out, the metaphor of legislation
is inappropriate to the activities of accepting, applying,
criticising, or even reforming moral principles. To the
extent that Kant's criterion of universalisation is useful,
it is not a legislative mechanism, but a guide for judging
the moral adequacy of a rule. While various aspects of
Kant's moral theory may consistently be adopted in the
practice of education, there is one decisive reason why
his ideal of the autonomous rational self-legislator
cannot be an aim of education: it is simply that there
cannot be such a person.

MORAL AUTONOMY AND OBJECTIVITY

In the contemporary view of moral autonomy, there seem to
be elements of both the Kantian self-legislator and the
older belief in the supremacy of individual conscience,
shorn now of its religious affiliations. The latter holds
that an individual must be completely free to follow his
own moral beliefs and that his own conscience (or what
he judges he should do) is the final arbiter of morality
in his case. Where this element dominates, autonomy slips
from the hold of rationality that Kant attempted to place
upon it. It is simply another way of talking about pure
autonomy in the moral sphere, and is subject to the
criticisms that have already been made. I wish to consider here more closely whether the not uncommon mixture

of the self-legislator and personal conscience theories
of autonomy can perhaps escape the charge of subjectivism.

H.D. Aiken illustrates the attempt to interpret moral
autonomy in this fashion and yet to argue for a form of
moral objectivity that is compatible with it. According
to Aiken, objectivity in making a moral judgment amounts
to an impartial consideration of all the moral values to
which one is committed that are related to the decision.
As he says, when there is question of the objectivity of
a moral judgment we have made, 'our task is always and
cnly to look beyond it to the other relevant commitments
which we ourselves acknowledge.' (22)   Aiken also seems
to claim that a moral judgment is verified if it satisfies the conditions for objectivity. (23)   While his
interpretation places stress on internal consistency and
authenticity, it is really only a demanding form of
subjectivism rather than a version of objectivity.
Perhaps it permits us to say that an individual is inconsistent with his own moral beliefs in reaching a certain
decision or holding a particular principle. However, if
a person sincerely claims that he is not being inconsistent, I am not sure that on Aiken's theory anyone else
can justifiably challenge the claim. Certainly, the
theory does not allow for the possibility that anyone
could sincerely and consistently hold moral principles
and make moral judgments that were nevertheless false or
inadequate.

Aiken's own reference to moral communities within which
argument is possible provides the context for a more
satisfactory account of moral objectivity. But if we are
talking about a genuine moral community of beliefs and
practices, and not simply the fortuitous agreement of
isolated individual wills, it then becomes necessary to
modify the notion of moral autonomy from which Aiken
starts. I would wish to go further still in drawing the
boundaries of moral objectivity. No doubt serious moral
argument is empirically very difficult among those who
belong to different moral communities, and some agreement
on moral beliefs and practices would seem to be a necessary condition for such argument. However, Aiken seems
to suppose a series of discrete moral communities rather
than a pattern of significant common and overlapping
elements among all moral communities. Moreover, as he
allows that the autonomous person is a rational self-
legislator, he can hardly reject the possibility of comparatively assessing the adequacy of different moral
practices and systems against criteria of rationality.
It is outside the range of this paper to develop this
point any further. A clear illustration of the kind of

dimensions that may be applied is given in Morris
Ginsberg's 'On the Diversity of Morals.' (24) As Ginsberg
notes, the relativists, whether individual or social, are
in an awkward position in that their views are more likely
to encourage the imposition of moral beliefs and practices
rather than respect for those who differ, unless they
inconsistently assert the universal validity of a principle of tolerance.
     Whatever may distinguish personal autonomy in the moral
domain once due regard is given to the criteria of rationality and the communal character of moral practices, I
think it is clear that objectivity, to the fullest extent
that it can be achieved, is an essential characteristic
of moral maturity. We should not confuse, as Aiken seems
to, the questions of objectivity and truth. Although the
two are closely related, objectivity is predicated of
attitudes and procedures, while truth is predicated of
statements. The development of objectivity in a moral
agent - e.g. critically reflecting on one's own assumptions, being aware of the conditions that shape one's
values, understanding other points of view, submitting
one's principles and judgments to the criticism of others
- is an outcome to which liberal education is immediately
and evidently directed. Whether autonomy is also an aim
depends on the extent to which it can be reconciled with
the practices required for objectivity.

AUTONOMY AS AN AIM OF LIBERAL EDUCATION

If there is question of trying to achieve personal autonomy in anything like the strict sense, then it is clearly
paradoxical to suggest that this can be done through
induction into the main public traditions of rational
thought and expression. Of course, from the point of view
of classical rationalism, these traditions and the nature
of personal autonomy are interpreted in such a way that
the paradox is avoided. The condition that autonomy
should be rational is not regarded as a restriction on
personal self-determination. In the classical rationalist
interpretation (of which Kant's self-legislator is one
version) personal autonomy consists in willing what one
knows to be rationally necessary. Thus initiation into
the forms of understanding is not only compatible with
personal autonomy but a necessary condition for its
attainment. (25) I shall not comment on the adequacy of
this concept of autonomy or the distinctive beliefs of
classical rationalism that underlie it. Assuming that the
defense of objectivity and rationality against the claims

of anarchistic epistemology does not depend on these
beliefs, what I wish to ask is whether there is a sense
in which 'autonomy' can appropriately describe a fundamental aim of liberal education.

In relation to this question, I am assuming two general
conditions that the practice of liberal education should
satisfy. The first concerns the way in which the traditions of rational inquiry are interpreted. The crucial
difference is whether they are seen as immutable and
unquestionable moulds of human thought and action or as
ceaseless efforts at understanding and achievement carried
forward from one generation to another - in Eliot's
phrase, 'the common pursuit of true judgment.' I am
referring to the kind of liberal education that reflects
the latter of these interpretations. The continual,
critical reform of the traditions of rational inquiry is
itself a tradition. However, it does not exist independently, but is a way of engaging in any of the particular
traditions.

The second condition is that the dominant emphases in
the procedures of liberal education should be upon the
understanding of what is learned; the acceptance of
methods and theories on the basis of the evidence that
justifies them, not simply on the authority of the
teacher or the experts; the development of the skills of
inquiry in a way that depends on reflection and imagination, a combination of what is fashionably called conver-
gent and divergent thinking; the critical appreciation of
the scope and limitations of each of the main forms of
thought and expression and the relation in which they
stand to one another.

Granted that liberal education in practice attempts to
satisfy these two conditions as fully as possible, it is
clear that it must be aiming at the development of some
degree of intellectual autonomy. However, I am still
not satisfied that we should describe the outcome in these
terms. When the qualifications have been duly acknow-
ledged, we can speak of autonomy only in an attenuated
sense. Even those who have achieved the mastery of
experts in any field might initiate a significant revision
or breakthrough - particularly affecting its basic methods
- is relatively restricted. And, of course, even in these
cases, the judgment of significance has to be upheld by
the community of experts. (26)

If these are the sorts of limitations on the autonomy
of those who have achieved mastery, how much more so for
those who have achieved the level of understanding and
competence that may reasonably be expected through liberal
education? For while liberal education may provide the

basis for mastery in some aspect of science, or the human- ities, or the arts, its direct purpose is to achieve an integrated induction into the broad range of these public symbolic structures. Even if liberal education were restricted to an intellectual elite, it would not aim at developing the level of mastery at which one might exer- cise some degree of significant autonomy. The language of autonomy seems even more unrealistic and misleading, if we are prepared to entertain the radical possibility of providing liberal education for the majority of people in our society; and, apart from any other reasons, as long as we are serious about having everyone participate intelligently in political democracy, I do not see that we have any alternative but to try.

Being reasonable does not depend on being autonomous, even when autonomy is interpreted as discovering for oneself the rules that apply rather than deciding on one's own rules. In fact, there would be little scope for reasonable thought and action if we did not, for much of the time, employ theories and rules that have been worked out and tested by others. Whether we consider, for example, learning and using language in everyday life, or examining the validity of an argument or the claims of a scientific experiment, or even making direct observations, we must inevitably rely to some extent on the authority of others.

As I have already suggested, a fundamental aim of liberal education is the development of the skills, attitudes and values that are bound up with objectivity. This aim cannot be adequately realised unless we also learn to reflect critically on the traditions of rational inquiry themselves. It might be said that here the objective of liberal education is to encourage personal autonomy. However, I would point out that the habit of critically assessing the 'conventional wisdom' is not promoted for the sake of personal autonomy as such, but as the best way of ensuirng that our beliefs and values will be as thoroughly justified as is possible. Indepen- dence of judgment, whether on moral or other issues, is a desirable characteristic only to the extent that a person is qualified to judge. An educator may not justifiably encourage critical inquiry except in the context of trying to develop skills and knowledge relevant to making judgments in a given area.

In relation to the other outcomes of liberal education that are loosely, if not misleadingly, described as personal autonomy, I think it preferable to speak of them in such terms as the following: to gain an understanding of the main methods of thought, conceptual schemes and

bodies of knowledge, together with a critical appreciation
of their strengths and limitations both in themselves and
in relation to one another. The level of understanding
should be sufficient for intelligently interpreting one's
own experience, for expressing oneself with clarity and
precision, for making informed and responsible choices,
for following intelligently the debate of experts -
especially when their claims affect the general conduct
of life, for critically assessing the programs of political leaders, for seeing through and resisting persuasive
strategies of empty rhetoric and propaganda, for responding with discrimination to fashionable trends whether in
art, life-styles, political theories, popular entertain-
ment, or whatever. This list is not intended to be
exhaustive. It mainly stresses aspects of a constructive or critical response, rather than a contribution,
to the forms of culture. This emphasis reflects, I
believe, the character and scope of liberal education.
For while it is a desirable, if not necessary, basis for
a constructive - perhaps even creative - contribution,
it is not sufficient.

     In regard to the process of liberal education, teachers
who are committed to the kinds of outcomes I have listed
must, if consistent, be prepared to observe the conditions
of objectivity in their own teaching, and always to provide the most adequate reasons that are within the
capacity of their students. While there are moral grounds
for acting in this way, it is not necessary to appeal to
the students' actual or potential autonomy. It is sufficient for the teacher to recognise them as persons in
the process of developing their capacity to choose on the
basis of reasons, and that reasons may be good or bad.
It is precisely in reference to the criteria of objectivity and reasonable belief, which are such primary concerns of liberal education, that such questions as what
conditions distinguish educating from indoctrinating,
what kind of persuasion is rationally and morally defensible in teaching, when a teacher should and should not be
neutral on an issue, are to be resolved.

     I do not wish to imply of course that liberal education
is not closely related to the achievement of human freedom.
In gaining familiarity with the main symbolic forms of
culture one also greatly enlarges the range of significant
choices that one can make. The outcome also involves a
change in the quality of choice, not simply in its scope.
The fundamental objective of learning with understanding
cannot be realised unless the learner comes to grasp
principles for himself, and thus to achieve intellectual
independence from the mere authority of teachers, text-

books, experts and cult heroes. So if the engagement
in liberal education is conducted properly, a person
should reach the point at which the important choices he
makes are his own in the sense that he applies for himself the relevant criteria of criticism and evaluation,
and sees for himself why these criteria are the relevant
ones to employ. Provided we recognise the public criteria
of knowledge and the public standards of excellence within
which an individual exercises such intellectual independence, we may metaphorically refer to him as autonomous
in contrast to the person whose choices are in effect
usually made for him by others.

However, to speak in terms of autonomy versus hetero-
nomy is, I believe, to draw the line of distinction too
sharply. The question is not whether we accept the public
forms of reasoned inquiry, moral practice, artistic
expression, or the authority and judgment of others, or
deeply felt commitments, but how we accept them. The
fundamental distinction is between a blind, unreflective,
mechanical acceptance and one that is informed, critical,
discriminatory, adaptive. If the latter (which includes
the reasoned acceptance of the authority of others) is to
be described as intellectual autonomy, there is no difficulty in counting autonomy as an aim of liberal education.
However, it must be recognised that this is a substantially different concept of autonomy from the one that
is related to an anarchistic epistemology and widely
invoked in contemporary educational theory. It is precisely because of this difference (and because educationists often leave the underlying epistemological issues
unexamined) that the invocation of personal autonomy,
whether as a criterion for the process or the outcome of
education, tends to function as a slogan. In fact, it
seems that personal autonomy has become one of those
idols in whose name the effort to make liberal education
available to as many people as possible is being betrayed.

NOTES

1 I. Murdoch, 'The Sovereignty of Good' (London:
   Routledge & Kegan Paul, 1970).
2 R.P. Wolff, 'In Defense of Anarchism' (New York:
   Harper & Row, 1970), p.15.
3 R.F. Dearden, Autonomy and Education, in 'Education
   and the Development of Reason,' ed. R.F. Dearden,
   P.H. Hirst and R.S. Peters (London: Routledge & Kegan
   Paul, 1972), p.453.
4 'Such an anarchistic epistemology - for this is what

our theories of error now turn out to be - is not only
a better means for improving knowledge, or of understanding history.   It is also more appropriate for a
free man to use than are its rigorous and "scientific"
alternatives'   (Against Method: Outline of an Anarchistic Theory of Knowledge, in 'Minnesota Studies in
Philosophy of Science,' vol.IV, ed. M. Rodner and
S. Winokur (Minneapolis: University of Minnesota
Press, 1970), p.21).

5   T. Kuhn, 'The Structure of Scientific Revolutions,'
2nd ed. (University of Chicago Press, 1970).

6   T. Roszak, 'The Making of a Counter Culture' (London:
Faber & Faber, 1970), especially ch.VII; Science:
A Technocratic Trap, 'Atlantic Monthly' (June 1972),
pp.56-61; P.L. Berger and T. Luckman, 'The Social
Construction of Reality' (New York: Doubleday, 1966).

7   C.H. Rathbone (ed.), 'Open Education: The Informal
Classroom' (New York: Citation Press, 1971); R.S.
Barth, 'Open Education' (New York: Agathon Press,
1972).

8   C.H. Rathbone, The Implicit Rationale of the Open
Education Classroom, in Rathbone (ed.), op.cit.,
p.102.

9   Ibid., pp.100,104.

10   Ibid., pp.106-8.

11   Some of the contemporary critics (E.G. Roszak) seem
to have confused the general question of objectivity
with the particular interpretation of it in the
positivist tradition (the doctrine of objectivism).
It is not uncommon for writers to refer to Michael
Polanyi's 'Personal Knowledge' as a decisive refuta-
tion of scientific objectivity. What he attacks to
good effect, however, is the doctrine of objectivism.
What he tries to construct - whether successfully or
not is another matter - is a theory of knowledge at
once personal and objective. In supporting objectivity in knowledge, I am not assuming the rationalist
view that, in our attempts to understand the physical
world or the normative standards of human action, we
must suppose a perfectly consistent system. But if
the world (or human conduct) is such that it cannot
be accounted for in strictly consistent theories,
then this is itself a fact about the world and our
efforts to know it.

12   R. Trigg, 'Reason and Commitment' (Cambridge University
Press, 1973).

13   Trigg, op.cit., p.23.

14   Murdoch, op.cit., p.40.

15   Cf. P. Geach's criticism of abstractionism in 'Mental

Acts' (London: Routledge & Kegan Paul, 1957). For
a general critique of the theory of knowledge
supported by Rathbone, see L.F. Claydon, Content and
Process in Curriculum Construction, 'Educational
Philosophy and Theory,' vol.6, no.2 (October 1974),
pp.43-53.
16 This view is developed by a number of recent philosophers of education. See, for example, R.S. Peters,
Education as Initiation, in 'Philosophical Analysis
and Education,' ed. R.D. Archambault (London:
Routledge & Kegan Paul, 1965); I. Scheffler, Philosophical Models of Teaching, in 'The Concept of
Education,' ed. R.S. Peters (London: Routledge &
Kegan Paul, 1967); P.H. Hirst, Liberal Education and
the Nature of Knowledge, in Archambault (ed.) op.cit.
17 Ibid.
18 Rathbone, op.cit., p.105.
19 I. Kant, 'Groundwork of the Metaphysic of Morals,'
translated and analysed by H.J. Paton (New York:
Harper & Row, 1964), p.98.
20 As Berlin has pointed out, Kant's individualistic
doctrine lends itself ironically to a totalitarian
interpretation:
     If I am a legislator or a ruler, I must assume that
     if the law I impose is rational (and I can only
     consult my own reason) it will automatically be
     approved by all the members of my society so far
     as they are rational beings. For if they dis-
     approve, they must, pro tanto, be irrational;
     then they will need to be repressed by reason:
     whether their own or mine cannot matter, for the
     pronouncements of reason must be the same in all
     minds.
See 'Four Essays on Liberty' (Oxford University
Press, 1969), pp.152-3.
21 K. Baier, 'Moral Autonomy as an Aim of Moral Education,
in 'New Essays in the Philosophy of Education,' ed.
G. Langford and D.J. O'Connor (London: Routledge &
Kegan Paul, 1973), p.102. On Kant's idea of legis-
lating for oneself, G.E.M. Anscombe comments that it
     is as absurd as if in these days when majority
     votes command great respect, one were to call
     each reflective decision a man made a vote
     resulting in a majority which as a matter of pro-
     portion is overwhelming, for it is always 1-0.
     The concept of legislation requires superior power
     in the legislator.
See Modern Moral Philosophy, in 'Ethics,' ed. J.J.
Thomson and G. Dworken (New York: Harper & Row, 1968),
pp.187-8.

22   H.D. Aiken, 'Reason and Conduct' (New York: Alfred A.
      Knopf, 1962), p.162.

23   Ibid., p.168.

24   M. Ginsberg, 'On the Diversity of Morals' (London:
      Mercury Books, 1956), title essay, especially pp.121-6.

25   As Berlin notes in describing the rationalist view,
      'Knowledge liberates not by offering us more open
      possibilities amongst which we can make our choice,
      but by preserving us from the frustration of attempt-
      ing the impossible' (op.cit., p.144).

26   The relationship between intersubjective agreement and
      the attainment of objectivity and truth is a complex
      one. Such agreement functions both as a criterion
      and a condition of objectivity. However, in neither
      case is objectivity just a matter of agreement. In
      relation to the former, a claim is not held object-
      ively - much less is it true - simply because a large
      number of people agree about it. As Michael Scriven
      has pointed out, it is an error of positivist method-
      ology to confuse the qualitative and quantitative
      senses in which 'objective' and 'subjective' may be
      contrasted (Objectivity and Subjectivity in Educa-
      tional Research, in 'Philosophical Redirection of
      Educational Research: The Seventy-First Yearbook
      of the National Society for the Study of Education,'
      ed. L.G. Thomas (University of Chicago Press, 1972),
      pp.95-7). However, even when qualitative criteria
      are observed, agreement does not constitute object-
      ivity or truth, although it provides a crucial test.
      Some measure of agreement at the methodological
      level on the qualitative criteria of objectivity, as
      well as on the use of concepts, is a necessary con-
      dition for making and settling claims to objectivity
      in particular cases. However, this does not mean that
      the question of objectivity must in the end be just
      a matter of convention. For what may justifiably be
      agreed upon is constrained by characteristics of the
      world and of human beings that do not depend on con-
      vention. For a discussion of objectivity see D.W.
      Hamlyn, Objectivity, in 'Education and the Develop-
      ment of Reason,' ed. R.F. Dearden, P.H. Hirst and
      R.S. Peters (London: Routledge & Kegan Paul, 1972).
      I am not convinced that Hamlyn gives a satisfactory
      account of the ultimately non-conventional nature
      of 'forms of life.'

Ambiguity and constraint in the 'freedom' of free schools

7

David Nyberg

'Lyberte or freedome is a moche swete thynge.' Freedom
is an idea, like justice or education, that is used to
defend and to embellish social policies and institutions
of almost all persuasions. Freedom is one of the most
important words in our language, not so much because it
helps resolve disputes or solve intricate dilemmas, but
because to consider it and its diversity of meanings is
inevitably to learn something more about civilized human
life and values. The word is important because it represents an idea that we cannot do without, and because it
has survived the persistence of philosophers and poets
and politicians to reduce it to a single operational
definition. Some would argue that this characteristic
ambiguity of the word is evidence that its worth in terms
of human knowledge has been overestimated, and that it
may even be an impediment to 'philosophically sound'
cultural advancement, that is to say, meaningless. To
conclude of freedom, on the grounds that its 'real meaning' eludes analysis, that the word must be meaningless,
leads one to the same conclusion about the Tao, the
Pentateuch, most of Plato, Shakespeare, Marx, and Freud,
most music (excluding, perhaps, military marches and the
mnemonic alphabet songs of childhood), and the Constitution of the USA, for example.

The silliness of such conclusions is less ambiguous,
I think, than is the meaning of freedom. But this introduction to the difficulties of the idea of freedom should
not be read as praise for ambiguity itself. Ambiguity is
no more a 'good' than is precision; these are aspects of
language, not virtues, notwithstanding Russell's remark
that the demand for certainty is natural to man, 'but is
nevertheless an intellectual vice'. Across the breech
from the analytics' antipathy toward ambiguity, gloat
the family of romantics whose devotion to the ambiguous

in language, if not in ideas, is no more defensible for
its fervor, than is the analytics' denial for its chill.
It is not defensible for two reasons. First, some types
of ambiguity serve the intention to deceive, either in
disguising the fact that a speaker or author does not
know what he would have the listener or reader believe
he knows, or by creating an emotional response in connection with a slogan that is meant to carry conviction
along with ignorance. (In fairness it must be said that
sometimes the sloganeer is as ignorant as he must count
on his audience being, and therefore we should not impute
to him culpability for deception which is more inevitable
than deliberate.) The second reason comes as a response
to the romantic claims that since important words, like
freedom, have several meanings, then it doesn't really
matter which we choose, and it is pointless to debate
justifications for our choices. This position rests on
the common and mistaken belief that, lacking certainty,
there are no standards by which choices and meanings can
be assessed for their relative and potential worth, and
that because there are alternatives on a given issue,
the alternatives are coequal. This simply is not the
case. Aside from the obvious reminder that 'equal' is
one of our most important words, too, and it has its own
ambiguities which must be observed before it can be
invoked to defend the subjective construct view of 'freedom' and of meaning in general, there is a more generic
objection. The objection has two parts: 1, the value of
a meaning of freedom cannot be justified without appeal
to other values, and the meaning of these other values
may or may not be consistent with a given meaning of
freedom; 2, it is not possible to endorse all meanings
of freedom, all freedoms, without contradiction.

The argument for the first part of the objection is
roughly this: If A claims that freedom means 'whatever
one can do and wants to do, one may do', and that this
meaning of freedom is coequal with any other, then A must
answer for B's challenge that for him (B) freedom means
'whatever one can do and wants to do, one may do, except
if it causes pain to anyone else', and that what A pro-
poses to do (e.g. burn B's manuscript to keep warm) will
cause B pain, therefore, A is not free to do as he can
and wishes to do. If these meanings of freedom are
coequal and conflicting, we have a dilemma: both A and
B are restricted by the other's view of freedom. A is
prohibited by B from burning B's manuscript on the ground
it would interfere with both A's and B's conception of
freedom (B can and wants to protect his manuscript, so
he may protect it; B also claims that if A exercises his

freedom it would cause B pain). B is restricted in a
slightly different way; he is forced to be vigilant of
his manuscript so that A won't get a chance to burn it,
and this robs his attention from other matters. The
dilemma remains unresolved until an appeal is made to
another value, which could be any one of several (respect
for private property, compromise, friendship, the communal
authority of civil law, etc.). In this example, B's
meaning of freedom is more consistent with an appeal to
another value, because of its conditional clause, and
therefore might be considered a 'better' meaning so long
as the resolution of conflicts over freedom is also held
to be a value. It should be noted in conclusion that some
other value must be held for freedom itself to be of any
value. Calling the ideal of freedom 'good', or 'humane',
or 'democratic' is only to put off the question 'For
what?' And when that question is answered, the basis for
assigning value to a meaning of freedom will have been
laid, or mislaid, depending on whether the meanings are
shown to be compatible. (If the answer to the question
'For what?' is 'Nothing', then what would be lost without
freedom? If the answer to that question is also
'Nothing', freedom is neither gain nor loss; it has no
apparent value.)

The argument for the second part of the objection to
the romantics' view, namely, that one cannot endorse all
meanings of freedom, all freedoms, without contradiction,
can be elucidated in a single example. If all freedoms
are allowed, A is free to arrogate B's freedoms, even to
take B's life. If to give A all freedoms is to make a
slave of B, and if slavery is taken to mean unfreedom,
then to endorse all freedoms is to endorse unfreedom as
well; both justified under the same principle. It takes
considerable guile and dexterity even to a defense of
such a position.

Freedom is a swete thynge, but it is a complex thing,
too. Many persons have died for it, killed for it, some
long for it while others fear it, some have got great
government grants to figure out how to keep it for allies
and take it away from enemies, who are often defined in
terms of what meanings of freedom they hold and what
they are willing to do to get it and keep it. It is
important to continue trying to understand the idea of
freedom, because the idea is crucial in human life. No
less important is the idea of education, and no less
ambiguous, as one is bound to judge who is concerned with
understanding the enchanting controversy over the re-
appearance of 'free schools'.

'A foolish consistency is the hobgoblin of little

minds, adored by little statesmen and philosophers and
divines. With consistency a great soul has simply nothing
to do....' Emerson goes on in this most celebrated of his
essays, Self-Reliance, to pick at the intellectual glue
of the arguments just presented, namely that thinking of
freedom in relation to other values is worthy and best
done with respect both for the systematic and productive
ambiguity of our most important ideas and words, and for
consistency in reasoning. In his tribute to individualism
and nonconformity, he foreshadows the spirit of the free
schools that would follow him by more than a century:

> Society everywhere is in conspiracy against the manhood
> of every one of its members...
>
> Whoso would be a man, must be a nonconformist....
> Nothing is at last sacred but the integrity of your
> own mind.... No law can be sacred to me but that of
> my nature. Good and bad are but names very readily
> transferable to that or this; the only right is what
> is after my constitution, the only wrong what is
> against it....
>
> Life only avails, not the having lived. Power
> ceases in the instant of repose; it resides in the
> moment of transition from a past to a new state, in
> the shooting of the gulf, in the darting of an aim....

These snippets of Emerson are used as a beginning for
a discussion of freedom and schooling, free schools in
particular, because of their sententious economy not
because of their chronological significance. In fact,
Emerson's essay fits in between Fichte's considerations
of freedom based on a sort of instinct of self-respect,
and Tolstoy's concept of non-interference, all three of
whom wrote later than Montaigne, Rousseau, and Pestalozzi.
None of these others, though, seems to remain as contemporary with modern educational-freedom thinkers such as
Kozol, Goodman, and Rogers, whose works are cited below
as evidence that while the issues and convictions have
not changed much, our progress toward their elucidation
has been slow.

'Sir, We know our will is free, and there's an end
on't.' In the 200 years since Johnson made this rather
imperious remark to Boswell, we have not been able to
produce the evidence for the great man's conviction.
Professor Skinner has recently produced a volume, 'Beyond
Freedom and Dignity', which manages only to claim that he
knows our will is not free, and there's the real end on't,
while at the same time managing to detract from the
character of the debate. But to speak of Johnson and
Skinner in the same context is to compare Sabatiers with
screwdrivers.

Like the bullish and opposite beliefs contrasted above,
we have, in deciding how to stand as educators these days,
a rather mean pair of alternatives offered by the proponents of free schools.

One can either come out for 'love and freedom', and
learn to believe that no learning can take place unless
the pupil's environment is loving and free; or one feels
pressure, failing this alternative, to say that something
else is better for learning than 'love and freedom', and
that learning most likely occurs when the pupil is not
free, but rather is well disciplined and diligent, loved
or not. The charge against this view is that 'fear and
authoritarianism' are the other sides of 'love and
freedom', and that no right thinking, warm blooded adult
educator could still make policy on 'fear and authoritarianism' grounds, when the disastrous results of such
policy are so embarrassingly apparent in our massive
cowering crowds of obedient consumers, our bourgeois
bureaucracies, our bellicose nationalism, our chauvinistic
social constructs, and our sundry asylums. It is not
difficult to see that this bifarious scene would be much
improved by an appreciation of at least some of the complex reasoning that sustains it, however much wanting
it is for utility in generating premium policy.

A complex combination of appealing principles and of
some stupefying practices has a confounding effect on
the policy questions of free schools, and open education
in general. One is as naturally drawn to most principles
of freedom as one is drawn to uncontaminated air. One
is 'for' them, but they are hardly thought of until they
are taken away, or slip, during the night, out of our
control. (But who ever worried about controlling fresh
air until recently?) On the other hand, when certain
principles of freedom are used in defining and endorsing
educational policy in schools, especially free schools,
awesome things occur. For example, in one free school
I know of, en dome in Illinois, the cooperative board of
directors voted to allow the pupils freedom in using any
means they wished for settling disputes that arose during
the course of a free school-day. The vote was not unani-
mous, but the policy was adopted. In a few weeks' time,
the directors were troubled and rent as a policy-making
body over the issue of violence among the pupils. Some
of the disputes were being settled in brutish fashion,
and in fact some disputes were being generated by the
more pugnacious of the pupils so they could 'pick a
resolution' with their meeker peers.

There were arguments for the cathartic benefits of
expressed aggressions, which, it was assumed, would

disappear as they were freely discharged. And there were
arguments from the vanquished that such individual therapy
came at too high a price, that it was not in the community's better interests, that the long term effects of
such unruly and careless behavior would be destructive to
the school's reputation and to the learned values of
cooperation and compassion that had been assumed to underlie the whole notion of free schools. For bullies they
had public schools.

This is a long hand way of illustrating Camus's remark
on freedom, 'Your freedom ends where my nose begins.'
But he was speaking of adults. When speaking of children,
it is crucial to remember that important as the nose is,
behind it lies a brain, and a bloodied brain is not so
easy to spot and mend as a bloodied nose. What counts
as behavioral freedom for one may indirectly, through
fear and persuasion, wreck the psychological freedom of
another.

In the next few pages, the words of three well known
advocates of free schools will be used to expose three
major theoretical claims about freedom, claims that are
appealed to, mistakenly I think, in debates over free
school policy. The first is Jonathan Kozol's view about
the function of free schools in the realization of the end
of liberation, of freedom.

Kozol, like many others, tries to define 'free school'
contra traditional school, or public school, assuming
that the latter already have an adequate definition,
especially as the definition would concern freedom. This
is an unsupportable assumption, surely, due to the difficulties we have seen in overcoming the ambiguities of
freedom, and another of our most important words, education. What a traditional school 'is' depends so much on
what the speaker means by 'education' and by 'freedom'
that one would think a definition of the former would rely
so heavily on the latter that, given the ambiguity of the
latter, agreement on what a traditional school is would
come hard, and seldom, if at all. However, the assumption
apparently prevails that 'traditional' or 'public' school
is a standard referent.

In 'Free Schools', Kozol reasons that 'Free School, as
the opposite of public school, implies not one thing but
ten million different possibilities.' However, this
admission does not serve to caution its author from
asserting with considerable certainty his own 'true'
definition of 'free school': 'The true, moral, political
and semantic derivation of "Free School" lies in "Freedom
School". It is to the liberation, to the vision and to
the potency of the oppressed that any Free School worth

its derivation and its photographs of Neill, Tolstoy or
Eldridge Cleaver must, in the long run, be accountable.'
A free school, then, is an organization dedicated to the
condition of liberation, i.e. freedom, of the oppressed,
and further characterized by Kozol as being outside the
public education system, inside cities, outside white
man's 'counterculture', in direct contact with needs of
the poor and dispossessed, as small as can be managed,
and unpublicized.

Kozol's vision of the eventual condition of liberation
as the organizing principle of free schools, contrasts
with another common emphasis on what is 'free' about free
schools, an emphasis that is, like Kozol's, primarily
sociological. Paul Goodman believed that we can educate
the young (1968, pp.73-5):

> entirely in terms of their free choice, with no pro-
> cessing whatsoever.... It seems stupid to decide a
> priori what the young ought to know and then to try
> to motivate them instead of letting the initiative
> come from them and putting information and relevant
> equipment at their service. It is false to assert
> that this kind of freedom will not serve society's
> needs - at least those needs that should humanly be
> served; freedom is the only way toward authentic
> citizenship and real, rather than verbal, philosophy.
> Free choice is not random but responsive to real situ-
> ations; both youth and adults live in a nature of
> things, a polity, an ongoing society, and it is these,
> in fact, that attract interest and channel need.

Continuing his policy of nonencroachment, he claims,
a few pages later, that 'Voluntary adolescent choices
are often random and foolish and usually transitory; but
they are the likeliest ways of growing up reasonably.
What is most essential is for the youth to see that he is
taken seriously as a person rather than fitted into an
institutional system.' Goodman clearly believes that
being 'taken seriously as a person' means being given
virtually unlimited free choice, at least in one's
education. Goodman has switched the emphasis from the
end of freedom, to the means of freedom employed for the
ends of 'authentic citizenship and real, rather than
verbal, philosophy', as well as due service to society's
needs. Living with such faith must have been invigor-
ating.

A third usage of 'freedom' in education, one that has
some, yet little, in common with the other two, has been
tirelessly written about by Carl Rogers. I quote from a
section called The Meaning of Freedom of a chapter called
Freedom and Commitment in his book called 'Freedom to
Learn' (1969, pp.268-9):

the freedom that I am talking about is essentially an
inner thing, something which exists in the living
person quite aside from any of the outward choices of
alternatives which we so often think of as constituting
freedom.... It is the realization that 'I can live
myself, here and now, by my own choice.' It is the
quality of courage which enables a person to step into
the uncertainty of the unknown as he chooses himself.
It is the discovery of meaning from within oneself,
meaning which comes from listening sensitively and
openly to the complexities of what one is experiencing.
It is the burden of being responsible for the self one
chooses to be. It is the recognition of a person that
he is an emerging process, not a static end product.
The individual who is thus deeply and courageously
thinking his own thoughts, becoming his own uniqueness,
responsibly choosing himself, may be fortunate in
having hundreds of objective outer alternatives from
which to choose, or he may be unfortunate in having
none. But his freedom exists regardless.
And there's another end on't.

In the remainder of this paper I will deal with three
issues raised by these excerpts: 1, freedom as a goal of
schooling; 2, the implication that taking one seriously
as a person means giving one unlimited choice in one's
education; and 3, the reification of freedom.

'Oh, Lord, I want to be free, want to be free; Rainbow
round my shoulder, wings on my feet.' The words of this
old song capture in simple grace the sense of freedom as
a goal. But freedom as a goal, like a rainbow, is an
image that inspires pots of gold. The inspiration is of
more substance than the pots.

Kozol has spoken for the ambition of producing a
condition of liberation as a result of free school
experience. The ambition is common among free school
theorists, but not all limit the conditions of liberation
quite as Kozol does. Nonetheless, Kozol's position can
serve as an example of the faulty reasoning behind the
ambition itself. Kozol argues that a free school is an
organization dedicated to the condition of liberation,
freedom, of the oppressed. But not all qualify as 'the
oppressed'. In fact, Kozol accuses other free school
people, e.g. those who retreat from urban terror and
degradation to the country and the copse, the sylvan
communities devoted to spontaneous behavior and simple
values, of 'running away' to a 'moral vacuum', and thus
contributing to the oppression of those left behind in
the cities; never mind what reasons or conditions were
responsible for these people's need to escape the clamps

of urban life. Kozol uses an ugly simile to emphasize
his view: 'In my belief, an isolated upper-class rural
Free School for the children of the white and rich within
a land like the United States and in a time of torment
such as 1972, is a great deal too much like a sandbox
for the children of the SS Guards at Auschwitz.'

We have here in Kozol's own position the grounds for
questioning the reasoning behind freedom as a goal. If
the condition of liberation, of freedom, is to be sought a
as a good, as a goal, one would assume that as a good,
freedom would be a legitimate goal for everyone. But
this is not the case for Kozol, who claims that the
freedom some seek is immoral (like the SS), or at least
amoral (a vacuum). The problem comes of a difficulty in
defining 'the oppressed' who need 'freedom'. Kozol
rightly and passionately points out that economic and
racial oppression should not be tolerated and that is
what his notion of a free school is designed to fight.
But what about the emotional retardate of any economic
or racial group, the academic 'success' who is also help-
lessly hypochondriacal, the children of sadistic parents,
the wives of wife-beaters? Are they, too, rightly considered in any sense oppressed, and in need of 'liberation' from their oppressive circumstances? It is not
immediately clear why it is less moral, or even immoral,
to attempt to free someone from neurotic constraints
(e.g. authoritarian compulsions, xenophobia, excessive
greed), than to attempt to liberate someone from economic
or racial constraints. Regardless of whether it is clear
or not, it does seem to be the case that for most of us,
some groups deserve freedom more than others, some
sandboxes become evil for us depending on who plays in
them.

When we speak of freedom as a goal, we do not generally
mean freedom as a universal goal. To be free to do as one
likes is to be free to oppress, to murder, to degrade, to
take freedom from others. This clearly is not what Kozol
or any other free school theorist is after, yet they go on
speaking in a way that leaves them open to this sort of
criticism. What seems to be the real intent is to
remediate certain freedoms that a depressingly large
number of politicians, landlords, money lenders and others
of the lesser species exercise at the expense of those
who are defenseless against them because they have not
the power; power to fight other powers with in order to
gain the opportunity to do something else. 'Liberating'
might mean 'empowering', but this is not the same as
'being free'. One needs the power to choose of course, or
one has no power at all. But what one does with this

power, what one chooses, what turns out to be the something else that one does, is the nub of moral education,
not merely the condition of being able to exercise the
power of choice. As Arnold put it in 'Culture and Anarchy
Anarchy' (1935, p.74):

> What is freedom but machinery?... In our common notions
> and talk about freedom, we eminently show our idolatry
> of machinery. Our prevalent notion is.... that it is
> a most happy and important thing for a man merely to
> be able to do as he likes. On what he is to do when
> he is thus free to do as he likes, we do not lay so
> much stress.

But we have trouble thinking of freedom as machinery.
There is a general presumption for defending the right of
people to do what they want. We demand reasons for
limiting this right, as if it were the sole means for
happiness itself, and social well-being. But as Peters
has pointed out recently, and as the literature of
alienation in the 1950s has documented copiously, happiness does not necessarily follow freedom, for gains in
freedom often cost the security of the familiar, and the
contentment of reliable companionship. It is simply not
realistic, given our experience with social groups, to
expect that the inherent good will and decency, let alone
the intelligence and imagination, of a given group will
ensure the freedom to do as each one wants. The diversity
of wants, and their equality under the goal of freedom,
the condition of liberation, will not allow it. The condition where freedom is desired needs rules, consistent
order, to protect against the inconsistency of men. In
fact, the choice as we have it is not 'for' or 'against'
freedom, but for and against certain restraints and not
others. There is no concrete and general problem, or
condition, of freedom. But there are concrete problems
of what some people want to do and what it is that hinders
or prevents them. The general aim or goal of 'freedom',
then, does not make sense.

The development of civilization is possible not when
individual freedom is supreme, but when the individual's
power to satisfy instinctual needs, part of which are
aggressive, is replaced with the community's power to
ensure security from one's aggressive needs to satisfy at
the expense of another. Although an argument can be
raised that this plea of necessity as justification for
limiting the freedom of some, is the plea of tyrants,
this is not to argue that the necessity for order is
wrong when compared to freedom. It is only to argue that
tyrants misuse their freedom when not restrained from
doing so by the power of the community.

The goal of freedom is a false goal for educators. The
goal of acquiring due power for the disenfranchised to
choose well and effectively for themselves is a legitimate goal, as is the goal of influencing any student's
ability to discriminate for worth and fairness between
possible wants. This position leads to the next issue
raised by the free school literature, namely, that
respect for another person means giving unlimited free
choice in educational matters.

'... we should deal with children as God deals with
us, for He makes us happiest when He lets us grope our
way in a pleasant illusion.' Just about the time I let
Goethe's words convince me, a little poem by J.P. Donleavy
jangles in the back of my mind:

At the rate
The world
Is going
It will
Be
Poor old
Everybody

Does respect for students mean that we should let them
grope away in their pleasant illusions; will this groping
lead us to poor old everybody? This is a question of
normative freedom, perhaps the central question of free
school policy.

Goodman's belief that we can educate the young 'entirely in terms of their free choice, with no processing
whatsoever' is a belief that either 1, students' reasoning
is intrinsically as valid, useful, and moral as anyone
else's, or that 2, students' reasoning is beside the point
of educating. If one believes the former, then the next
step is to believe that everyone's reasoning is just as
valid, useful, and moral as anyone's reasoning. This
amounts to a denial that there is any criterion at all
that we can agree on for objective justification, even
consistency. That being the case, then, if the next
utterance by the believer of such a doctrine is a negation
of the doctrine, it must be taken as equally valid as the
original statement. We are asked to believe that A is
both A and not-A, and not to fret over it, or fret over
it; whatever we like. It is both easy and difficult to
argue against this claim. It is easy because there is an
abundance of examples that show the claim false (e.g. the
proper, correct, change for 5 dollars on a 1 dollar purchase is 4 dollars; New York is larger than Rhode Island;
as of the summer of 1974 Richard Nixon is the only
president in USA history to resign his office; ½ means
the same as 'one half', etc., in spite of anyone's opinion

to the contrary). There are criteria for objective veri-
fication and justification that we can and do agree on,
and consistency underlies them all. But it is also difficult to argue against the subjective view of knowledge,
and the idiosyncratic view of reasoning because those who
hold such views don't care about consistency in argument
so much as they care about their rights to learn what and
how they please, to grope their way in their own pleasant
illusions, just as we others grope our way in the illusion
of consistency and the possibilities of objective justification. John Gardner put it well in 'Grendel': 'All
order, I've come to understand, is theoretical, unreal -
a harmless, sensible, smiling mask men slide between the
two great, dark realities, the self and the world - two
snake pits.' But if Gardner succeeds in making us understand his meaning through our common use of language, he
in some measure succeeds also in making an argument
against himself, for surely there is order in the language
itself, insofar as we use it with mutual understanding?

It is equally indefensible to claim that reasoning is
beside the point of educating, especially in the common
free school principle of educating the 'whole child', for
reasoning is a part, a significant part, of a person's
integrity as a 'whole' person. To ignore reasoning is to
do mental mayhem, a character amputation. And Goodman
himself aims for 'authentic citizenship' and 'real philosophy' through education, neither of which is conceivable
without highly developed reasoning. In fact, connecting
the accomplishment of any aim at all with any preferred
or necessary means is an act of reasoning in and of
itself, so any policy for educating on purpose would rely
on reasoning from the start.

The spirit of this normative freedom survives such
analysis, however, even if its sense fades a bit. And
this is because we do want students to make choices for
themselves, and to be responsible for their educations
to a large, and in the end, controlling degree. The
problem is that we are reluctant to assume the authority
in teaching them how to make choices when their own education is the subject, and a 'free school' is the object
model. We have trouble holding in mind at the same time
both the principle that freedom in choosing is a desirable
end, and the principle that good choices do not happen
spontaneously or by gift alone, but one must learn how to
make good choices by learning how to reason and to perceive oneself accurately in many various circumstances.
We make the mistake of believing that the best way to
achieve an increase in some sort of freedom, e.g. in
choosing well among alternatives, is by way of freedom

itself, by way of noninterference on the adult's part.
That freedom leads to freedom is a dubious formula,
however.

And here is the question of the role of adults in free
school education, a question still the subject of enormous
debate. The alternatives that seem to exhaust the
imaginations of the debaters are Abdication and Non-
interference, Love and Be Loved, or mere Environmental
Design. The first is weak because it is hypocritical,
unreal; it denies participation in the natural and necessary relations between people who share the same space
and so much time. The second is unclear because if 'love'
is meant as caring and being cared for, we are left with
no way of evaluating the many different ways one can
'care for' another; it does not take an unusual imagination to conceive of the circumstance in which caring, or
loving, means taking away certain freedom. The third,
Environmental Design, 'providing a rich environment',
is insufficient because all hinges on what the designers
consider 'rich', and it is distressingly similar to the
behaviorist response to questions of education, namely,
contingency management, which can be an insidious in-
fringement on freedom through its indirect coercion and
structured limitation of access.

I think this unsatisfactory situation can be improved
significantly with regard to the role of adults in the
development of a student's freedom, by using a conceptual
scheme presented by Joel Feinberg (1973).

Since Mill's classic statement that the absence of
coercion is the sufficient and necessary condition for
freedom, the individualist/liberal view has been enlarged
to include two amendments: 1, other than human coercion,
there must be an absence of natural conditions that prevent the chosen activity, and 2, one must have the executive power to do that which one wishes. This view split
of its own ripeness into two halves, a double concept:
freedom from..., and freedom to.... At this point Feinberg
offers a single concept analysis to replace, and simplify,
the double concept analysis. He does this by defining
'constraint' as anything that prevents one from doing
something, and then proposing that all constraints can
be considered along two dimensions: the positive/negative
dimension, and the internal/external dimension. Combining
these dimensions yields four categories of constraint:
1 Internal Positive, such as headaches, obsessive thoughts,
compulsive desires, etc.; 2 Internal Negative, such as
ignorance, weakness, deficiencies in talent or skill;
3 External Positive, such as barred windows, locked doors,
and pointed bayonets; 4 External Negative, such as poverty,

lack of transportation, and the like. It might help to
remember the categories if they are presented like this:

CONSTRAINTS

	Positive	Negative
Internal	(obsession)	(ignorance)
External	(guns, locks)	(poverty)

(By 'positive' he means 'the presence of', and by 'negative' he means 'the absence of' a thing or condition.)

Now if an adult wishes to expand a student's range of
possible alternatives, to ensure against useless deliber-
ations that are a nuisance or impossible or insignificant
alternatives, then the adult can diagnose, with Feinberg's
four categories, what the nature of the relevant constraint is for the accomplishment of the chosen objective.
Teachers, naturally, will have more direct dealings with
internal constraints, both positive and negative. In
fact, a strong case can be made in the name of freedom
for the direct, intentional interference on the teacher's
part when the student finds himself in a condition of the
internal negative constraint of ignorance. The internal
positive constraints would be more to the taste of those
who follow Rogers's therapeutic facilitation of learning,
rather than, say, a Bereiter's unabashed skills teaching
regimen.

A note on the notion of autonomy will conclude this
section. Feinberg contrasts the condition of autonomy
with that of anomie, a contrast that will be useful in
resolving policy debates over the most effective and
desirable, and consistent, means for generating free
school curricula, and perhaps for training free school
teachers.

Anomie, according to Durkheim, is a defective condition
of persons who have no success at ordering within themselves their ideals, desires, intentions, and commitments
into some sort of hierarchy. The lack of such ordering
leaves the person subject to internal action jams and
motivation jumbles. Free to do anything, one has difficulty deciding what to do; when there is no hierarchy of
reasons or values for doing this rather than, or before,
that, there is virtually no point in doing this or that.
This condition is a sort of inhibiting disorientation,
an internal constraint, that stands in the way of accomplishing objectives. Such absence of order, or rules, or
structure is what people often call freedom; the existentialist might call it dreadful freedom. From outside,

though, it looks very much as if the person thus free is not free to act in ways that he might wish, or even, finally, to wish at all. Instead of conduct regulated and assisted by a system of stop and go, yield and 'caution when wet', one is bashed and bandied about in the fashion of the amusement park ride called 'Bumpers Cars' (a large rink-like arena in which one drives an electric car, flat out and careening, trying to butt and bump others for the fun ... Poor old/Everybody).

Autonomy, though, can mean quite another thing from 'being free to do anything'. It can mean self-governing. 'Autonomic' has the sense of self-regulation while still part of a large whole. The autonomic nervous system, for example, is concerned mainly with regulating the smooth muscles and glands, but it is not subject to strict voluntary control; nevertheless it is dependent on the brain and spinal cord. It is a system, with organization and uniformity, it is self-regulating but not free of the larger whole which sustains it. In the same way, one can speak of a person's behavior being probabalistically determined by the (social and physical) system which sustains him, but not wholly determined if at any time a mental state can influence the function and effect of that system, say, by acting morally without reward. Such a mental state which serves to regulate behavior in the absence of external conditioners, may be called autonomy.

'Philosophy is a battle against the bewitchment of our intelligence by means of language.' Reification means 'To convert mentally into a thing; to materialize' and it is about the same as 'to hypostatize' which means 'To make into or treat as a substance' ('Oxford English Dictionary'). Freedom has been reified into a 'thing' worth fighting for, as a condition which exists and deserves homage, as the 'substance' of various forms of government, as the idol of humanism. This is a similar birthing phenomenon as that undergone by Western religions. Feuerbach sums up his analysis of the mystery of religion in 'The Essence of Christianity' this way: 'Man - this is the mystery of religion - projects his nature into objectivity, and then makes himself an object of concern for this new "subject," for this projection of his nature.' In this sense, then, religion, is man's alienation from himself. One might replace 'religion' with 'freedom' in this though thought to get at the problem of the creed of freedom in much of the free school argument that we have considered here. Ollman (1971) suggests further that 'by attributing an independent life to the various forms of value, people succeed in transferring to them certain powers for regulating their own existence.' As these forms take on

'existence' they influence the way we see and how we judge
what we see. An example of this might be the Constitution
of the USA which manipulates the people (as in 'We the
people...') who wrote it, and which in some cases inspires
a sort of patriotism, a service to an abstraction, at some
considerable expense to service to real living persons.
The 'freedom' of such a patriot is illusory, as is the
'state' which he fervently serves.

This sort of reification of values is an attempt to
rescue the chosen value from the influence of context,
from the ambiguity of these values in the generation and
refinement of civilization. But such influence cannot
be avoided any more than being in a context can be avoided.
Being in a context means being influenced. One cannot
escape influence just as one cannot excape context.

If we are born into a community, we are not born free,
Rousseau's exhortations to the contrary notwithstanding.
Perhaps the most comprehensive and brief introduction to
this condition of human life is Freud's 'Civilization and
Its Discontents'. The principle thesis of this book is
that civilization progresses as the individuals in a
culture learn to trade their instinctual 'happiness' for
the security they need to live among others, both within
and without their given community. One aspect of the
security thus gained is freedom from the potential oppression of others' instinctual needs. Freud's analysis of
the 'happiness for security' bargain in civilization is
useful in developing a perspective on the plural nature of
freedoms, on the lost values of freedom-as-instinct-
happiness v. freedom-as-security-from-alien-oppression.
Following these points in social psychology made by both
Feuerbach and Freud, one can dereify freedom and argue
that education has a central role in developing freedoms.
Education for freedoms is certainly conceivable as education for better trading, for self-governance, for the
powers of discrimination among desired and desirable
wants.

As we have seen throughout this paper, the generic
terms of freedom are 'you' and 'me' and 'us'. Your freedom, my freedom, and our freedom may not be compatible:
we cannot affirm them all without some appeal to another
value that governs not freedom, but particular freedoms.
Because freedoms entail more than one person and at least
one context of their behavior, the issues raised in dis-
cussing freedoms are inevitably ethical ones, involving
the rights of each to be granted, taken, or denied.
Adler sums up this point well in 'The Idea of Freedom'
(1961, p.617):

If some tension between self and other is involved in

any conception of freedom, then law plays one role when
it represents a power alien to the self, and another
when the self is able to make the law somehow its own
or an expression of its power. In the first role,
law is an obstacle to freedom; in the second, it is a
source of freedom, or even part of its substance.
Again, there is no general issue of freedom, but issues of
particular freedoms. Freedom can be defined in terms of
independence, power, autonomy, choice, 'doing what one
wants', and so on. None is sufficient for defining the
magnificent singular Freedom, but each can be useful in
defining the more diminutive freedoms. In education,
these diminutive freedoms do not lead to an abdication
of instructional responsibilities on the grounds that
presenting alternatives is enough for a teacher to do.
To know of alternatives is not the same as having a
choice, any more than to know of theoretical justifications for freedom(s) is the same as being free. What one
does with one's knowledge, subjective or objective as it
may be, is the more important indication of one's degree
of freedom(s), of one's education, and most important, of
one's values for conduct. Freedom is machinery that makes
various modes of conduct more or less possible, it is not
an idol to which one appeals in a solemn invocation for
happiness.
    Care for the freedoms of others, in my view, is more
clearly demonstrated when the people of an institution,
such as a free school, or a public school, care for the
cultivation of discrimination in judgment and in those
other values that ultimately govern manifestations of
freedom, than by their studied reluctance to instruct in
methods of judging, observing, and valuing. I think,
further, that instruction in Feinberg's four categories
of constraint, and pursuant diagnosis of students'
conditions of constraint, especially the internal negative
constraints of ignorance, or lack of skills, would be an
admirable and practicable initial move toward a policy
of educational liberation, freeing schools from an unnecessarily constraining sense of freedom.

SELECTED BIBLIOGRAPHY

ADLER, MORTIMER J. (ed.), 'The Idea of Freedom', New
York: Doubleday, 1958, 1961 (2 vols).
ANSHEN, RUTH NANDA (ed.), 'Freedom: Its Meaning', New
York: Harcourt, Brace, 1940.
ARNOLD, MATTHEW, 'Culture and Anarchy', Cambridge Uni-
versity Press, 1935 (1869).

EMERSON, RALPH WALDO, Self Reliance, in 'The Complete Works of Ralph Waldo Emerson', ed. E.W. Emerson, Boston: Houghton Mifflin, 1909.

FEINBERG, JOEL, The Idea of a Free Man, in 'Educational Judgments', ed. James F. Doyle, London: Routledge & Kegan Paul, 1973.

FEUERBACH, LUDWIG, 'The Essence of Christianity', Edited and abridged by E.G. Waring and F.W. Strothman, New York: W.W. Norton, 1962.

FREUD, SIGMUND, 'Civilization and Its Discontents', New York: W.W. Norton, 1962.

GOODMAN, PAUL, Freedom and Learning: The Need for Choice, 'Saturday Review', 18 May 1968.

HOOK, SIDNEY, 'The Paradoxes of Freedom', Berkeley: University of California Press, 1962.

KOZOL, JONATHAN, 'Free Schools', Boston: Houghton Mifflin, 1972.

LEWIS, C.S., 'The Abolition of Man', New York: Macmillan, 1947.

LEWIS, C.S., 'Studies in Words', Cambridge University Press, 1960.

MULLER, HERBERT, J., 'Issues of Freedom', New York: Harper, 1960.

OLLMAN, BERTELL, 'Alienation: Marx's Conception of Man in Capitalist Society', Cambridge University Press, 1971.

PARTRIDGE, P.H., Freedom, in 'The Encyclopedia of Philosophy', ed. Paul Edwards, New York: Macmillan, 1967.

PETERS, R.S., 'Ethics and Education', New York: Scott, Foresman & Co., 1967.

ROGERS, CARL R., 'Freedom to Learn', Columbus, Ohio: Charles E. Merrill, 1969.

SKINNER, B.F., 'Beyond Freedom and Dignity', New York: Knopf, 1971.

Equality and pluralism

part IV

Cultural diversity and education

8

Richard Pratte

INTRODUCTION

The general purpose of this paper is to examine the
phenomenon of cultural diversity with a view to drawing
out the relevance and significance for educational policy
and public education.

Today, as perhaps never before, there is an expanded
interest in cultural diversity and ethnicity. This is
true not only of the USA but of many developed and un-
developed countries of the world. Both have asserted
themselves forcefully and demands related to them are
among the most persistent and troublesome for educational
policy-makers. Many ethnics are particularly sensitive
to what they regard as their changing status resulting
from recent social revolutions and the result has been a
demand for greater expectations and outcomes to be had
primarily through schooling. Educational authorities have
been pressured on many fronts either to take greater
account of cultural diversity or to suppress it altogether. In most cases, administrators, school board
members, teachers, etc., have been ill-prepared to deal
with such attacks and reluctant to institute changes
because the content of their training has left them un-
prepared for an intelligent appraisal of the situation.
The basic issues remain unarticulated, the forum of understanding not made ready. This paper, then is an attempt
to contribute to the articulation and the making. And
although its main focus is the USA, the issues and problems are applicable to other countries as well.

It is important, moreover, to note that this paper is
neither an attempt to justify ethnicity nor an attempt
to make capital of the problems of culturally diverse
societies. Rather, it is an attempt to explore the
fundamental question: What is called for regarding the

making of educational policy and the functioning of public
education in a culturally diverse society?

'CULTURAL DIVERSITY'

The initial question I wish to pose is: Just what is
cultural diversity? 'Cultural diversity' is a much
bandied-about term that bears examination, for it is
central to many present-day discussions concerning the
role and future of public education. What is less
obvious, although closely related, is the term 'diversity'
itself. In what situations, under what conditions, is
the term 'diverse' or its cognate 'diversity' used?
Oftentimes there is great variability rather than sameness
exhibited in employing these terms.

    To explain how different human groups were originally
distinguished is beyond the scope of this work; such an
undertaking would require an extensive historical/socio-
logical/anthropological study. Suffice it to say that
two facts do stand out. First, it is clear that 'human
groups do not exist in nature, or rather, the part of
difference that exists because of nature is unimportant.'
(1) Whenever distinctions are made and groupings result,
it is we who make them. Second, the distinctions that
men make to create groups or factions may be drawn along
regional, economic, ideological, political, occupational,
etc., lines, and among the most persuasive distinctions
that divide mankind are those which we designate as
'ethnic,' that is, those distinctions based on race,
religion, or national origin. (2)

    There seems to be no end to human ingenuity in thinking
of characteristics that can set groups apart. Hence, we
are all familiar with the realization that diversity may
and does take different forms. But what is claimed here?
what does it mean to say that some group is diverse? At
rock-bottom we would say that the decision to regard any
group as diverse signifies a decision on somebody's part
to single out different factors in the group - such as
skin color, beliefs, ancestral heritage, language - and
establish these as criteria for the basis of the so-called
diversity.

    The point is, of course, that diversity of some sort
exists everywhere and is visible everywhere. Every
society is diverse in some respects, but this observation
can only be made from a certain point of view. It could
be made only by somebody who looks at a number of people
and because of some reason or other finds it important to
observe that some members are different. While seeing

that every society is diverse in some respect, it should not go unrecognized that we make certain criteria count in establishing differences. To turn the coin over, when we say that a particular group is homogeneous, we mean simply that the ways in which the members differ are unimportant or irrelevant to any practical concerns. However, we do not suggest that there are no differences. When we say that a society is diverse, we are saying that from a particular vantage point we find something relevant, interesting, and for some reason important to mark off a group or groups as different. Thus, we may identify differences of exclusiveness along the lines of cultural difference, and group identity may be ordered along the lines of ritual, dietary habits, beliefs, folk tales, and language pattern. One or a combination of these aspects generally is regarded as necessary for identifying a group as culturally diverse.

But is this sufficient for establishing cultural diversity? No analysis of cultural diversity is complete without a recognition that the selection differences between groups must be viewed as fundamental enough to be capable of producing values and dispositions that contribute to significantly different outlooks on the world. The variety or variegation of unlikeness among groups must be capable of making a difference. The difference must have reality in the minds of men, not just in the eye of the beholder. The point to be observed is that cultural diversity within society must have a concrete social reality; it must be made incarnate within the behaviors of the people. It must be expressed in a concrete situation which bears on political, economic, and social policy. Hence, the second condition that must be met for a society to be culturally diverse is that diversity go beyond being merely visible; diversity must be exhibited in the social behavior of groups who wish to embody their views in choosing among the various social arrangements which determine the division of advantages for underwriting an agreement on the proper distribution of goods and services.

But even this is not sufficient: Diversity is not a matter of genetics; it is a matter of cultural transmission across generations. Hence, a third condition of cultural diversity would require that a sense of historical and participational identity and the peculiar traits which mark the identity must be transmitted from generation to generation if the group is to continue to maintain its identity. It is doubtful that any group could long maintain its peculiar features if it did not jealously guard them and limit the member's sphere of relations, particularly in the decisive period of formation, namely childhood. (3)

With these three conditions in mind, we may further
identify what 'cultural diversity' expresses. We can
start with its descriptive use. As a descriptive term,
at the very least 'cultural diversity' refers to the co-
existence of unlike or variegated groups in a common
social system. It makes no judgments about this situation, for it is employed simply to record the fact that
different groups are able to live together in such a way
that allows the society to accomplish the basic functions
of producing and distributing goods, defining social
arrangements and institutions which determine collective
goals, and providing security.

But 'cultural diversity' may be also used normatively
to express a social ideal. As a social value, the phrase
goes beyond the descriptive sense to emphasize the value
of freedom of association, the so-called 'democratic
ideal.' That is, a culturally diverse society is commonly
portrayed as a cooperative venture for mutual advantage -
everyone profits from a plurality of groups expressing
different values and interests. Thomas F. Green expressed
this point most eloquently:

> The view is that any society is richer if it will allow
> a thousand flowers to blossom. The assumption is that
> no man's culture or way of life is so rich that it may
> not be further enriched by contact with other points of
> view. The conviction is that diversity is enriching
> because no man has a monopoly on the truth about the
> good life. There are many ways. Diversity is further
> valued because it provides any society with a richer
> pool of leadership from which to draw in times of
> crisis. (4)

Green develops this position by observing that the value
of diversity entails two further assumptions.

> In the first place it means that there must be contact
> between the divergent groups in society. A household
> may be richer for including persons of different
> aspirations, values, dispositions, and points of view.
> But these differences will not be enriching to any
> particular individual unless he talks with, eats with,
> or in some way has an exchange of views with those
> who are different. The value of diversity implies con-
> tact between persons, and not simply incidental, tem-
> porary, and casual contacts. Secondly this fundamental
> value implies that the diversity which is enriching
> is not itself endangered by the contact which is
> valued. The diversity must be sustained through
> contact. (5)

If Green is right, and there is good reason for thinking
he is, then it seems that cultural diversity as a social

ideal wraps up certain fundamental values or beliefs. It demands that different groups coexist with one another, having more than mere fleeting or casual contact, and it presumes that such contact will not limit or endanger but will enrich the diversity.

Cultural diversity as a social ideal is immensely significant for public education. Our understanding of the ideal could influence the positions we take on the issue of informal or casual education versus formal education or schooling as well as determining the flex- ibility we allow to public education in accommodating religious and language differences. But if the ideal of cultural diversity is to have any influence in determining practical educational issues, it will do so to the extent that the ideal is embodied in and expressed through the decision-making of men in voting their various agendas of politics. In other words, the ideal of cultural diver- sity will or will not be expressed in no other terms than in the reality of American social structure.

From the view of social structure, American society has had difficulty in accepting cultural diversity. There is strong evidence that cultural diversity has been viewed as potentially divisive. The point is that the USA has been seen as a congerie of culturally diverse (and poten- tially divisive) groups, most with distinctive social, economic, and political concerns, who prefer living with other members of their group and take pride in efforts to sustain and build up group self-confidence and self- assertiveness. The divisive tendencies of cultural diversity have been seen as promoting a view of politics which makes of local and state government a federation of groups, with protected and excluded turfs.

Reasons for the lack of congruence between cultural diversity as social ideal and as realized in social in- stitutions are found in the hard core of the American experience. Since most Americans have no ethnic roots in past millenia, as do so many other peoples of the world, the Americanization process has taken on a central role in the formation of a national identity and self- concept. What is unique in the American experience is not the fact that the naturalization of immigrants has taken place, but rather that we have the example of a new nation starting from scratch, as it were. In fact, to question the wisdom of the necessity for engaging in the Americanization of immigrants has struck many as question- ing the very possibility of America's continued national and cultural well-being. Both the explanation and the fact of Americanization have affected the nature and function of cultural diversity, and both have done so in a cumulative and accelerating fashion.

Nevertheless, a double anomaly is hidden in this phenomenon. The first anomaly is that so many could be de-ethnicized so easily. The second is that having apparently been de-ethnicized, they have not become more indistinguishable than they are.

TWO ANOMALIES

The first anomaly has received much attention. The Americanization of immigrants has been explained by scholars and laymen alike in terms of one or another combination of the following: the destruction of immigrant family patterns under the impact of rapid industrial- ization and urbanization; the American emphasis given to childhood and youth, and the outdating of adult values and patterns; the attractiveness of American culture coupled to an 'old world' weariness which immigrants wished to be rid of; the openness and ampleness of the American reward system gained primarily through public education- and, finally, American nationalism was non- ethnic from the very first, and to become the 'ideal' American, immigrants were encouraged to repudiate their older life-styles, customs, and language. (6)

The fact of the matter is that any immigrants who thought moving to the USA made them masters of their own fate - or of their economic well-being - were in for a rude shock. In the USA, as in Europe, power flowed from above. And power - the capacity to get other people to do what you want them to do - was found at the level of management and ownership of the industrial-corporate order orbbeing a politician on practically any level. Moreover, patterns of ethnic stereotypes dictated a clear pecking order for immigrants from eastern, central, and southern Europe. Many Americans thought that such immigrants were plodding but industrious, and that, because they had brought little cash from the old country, they had to work or starve; particularly they would work in menial occupa- tions which were spurned by non-immigrants. In short, the immigrants were considered mentally and socially inferior. They were seen as a group to be basically uneducated, ignorant, and easily misled by labor agitators and by politicians. Above all, immigrants were considered unfit for the industrial discipline needed in the factory or workshop. (7)

The net result was the de-ethnicization of the immi- grant. Its story is largely a tale of transforming the immigrant and his children into a stable, quiescent labor

force. The process, where effective, conceded very little
to racial or national diversity. Many immigrants, almost
as soon as they had established residence in America,
took for their own the slogan, 'Americanize the immigrant.'
The years from 1880 to 1923 witnessed a great deal of
unanimity in the shaping of the American ideal of nation-
hood. First- and second-generation immigrants collabor-
ated with the descendants of earlier, more respectable
and more prosperous immigrants to define '100 per cent
Americanism.'

Lest the reader be misled, it must be remembered that
the immigrants had come to America to gain freedom and
opportunity, and most were willing to sacrifice, to shift,
to change, both personally and culturally, in order to
acquire the benefits of being in America. America was
regarded as a land of great opportunity, and the immigrant
visualized his children becoming American. Hence, while
the first generation themselves might be called Hungarians,
for example, and their sons and daughters would be called
Hungarian-Americans, they dreamed of the day when their
children's children would be called American. Most
immigrants appeared to be willing to cast their lot with
a new land, a new culture, and a new image.

But it is significant that over fifty years after mass
immigration from Europe to this country ended, the culturally diverse pattern is still so strong. Thus, we come to
the second anomaly.

The second anomaly is indeed a curious one. Ethnic
groups and ethnicity, language loyalty and language maintenance, abound on the present American scene. Many
Americans of today, the progeny of the immigrant folk of
decades ago, wear lapel buttons that say 'Irish Power,'
'Kiss me, I'm Italian,' 'Viva la Raza.' In addition, some
Navajos these days drive cars with bumper stickers pro-
claiming 'Dine Bizell' ('Navajo Power'), and there are
Sioux headbands and Afro hairdos. Comedians rejoice in
the fact that ethnic jokes and dialects of yesteryear are
no longer regarded as vices to be indulged in behind
closed curtains in discretely defined neighborhoods. Even
some Americans of northern and western European origin -
German, French, Norwegian, Swede, etc. - recognize their
ancestry and partially define themselves in accord with
it. For reasons that seem to be little understood, many
American groups have not lost themselves entirely within
their American surroundings even after three, four, and
more generations, although there have been coercion and
opportunity enough to do so. Hence, cultural diversity
is a constituent part of American life and politics.

Is it the case that industrialization and the much-

touted economic and social mobility of America contains
limits which non-Anglo-Saxon ethnics cannot transcend?
Have recurring anti-foreigner sentiments elicited protective withdrawal and insularity in their threatened
targets? Is the threat of de-ethnicization in America so
conducive to anomie and alienation that the retention of
cultural diversity of some kind is called for to perform a
an orienting and stabilizing function?

These questions, according to Michael Novak (8) -
a primordialist who celebrates ethnicity as a basic
attribute of men which, when suppressed, will always rise
again - have yet to be answered. His contention is that
the resurgence of ethnicity today is a fact all too well
ignored by most. American society, although paying lip-
service to the ideal of the melting pot, maintains or
permits ethnicity beyond the point of cultural assimilation. The surprise, according to Novak, is not that
cultural diversity is still alive and kicking, but rather
that all of a sudden a great many people are rediscovering
this.

There is, however, a curious fact to observe about the
phrase 'resurgent ethnicity.' Ethnicity, as a concept,
suggests a movement of affection and identity, enriched
perhaps by the subtle, provocative ways in which one
differs from others, and reinforced by a strong attachment
to family and relatives. 'Resurgent ethnicity' lends
itself to an interpretation of ethnicity which suggests
that the immigrants' experiences in America were those of
continuous pressure to conform to an alien culture, but,
paradoxically, the immigrant and his children's ways were
never accepted. Despite enormous pressure to 'Americanize,' the Americanization process, although outwardly
successful for a period of time, could not ultimately
succeed due to some sort of ethnic 'unmeltableness.' This
rather awkward term catches precisely Novak's claim that
human nature demands ethnic identity and many Americans
today are simply exhibiting the remarkable recuperative
power of men, who in the face of serious social and
psychological adversity, seek a return to their most basic
and rewarding source of identity. According to Novak,
'The new ethnicity is a form of historical consciousness.
Who are you? What history do you come from? And where
next? These are its questions.' (9)

At the core of the slogan 'resurgent ethnicity' lies
an extremely seductive line of thinking, particularly
when the phrase is given Novak's metaphysical formulation.
It is seductive insofar as its unquestioned acceptance
points us to the conclusion that the immigrants' experiences in America were those of facing discrimination and

privation, and ultimately the immigrants' children and their children could not repudiate their ancestral past, at least not without doing a disservice to their basic humanness.

Novak paints in broad outline the dimensions of resurgent ethnicity. He contends that ethnics have proved themselves to be a dynamic force in American politics and culture, and he claims that the 1970s is the 'decade of the ethnics.' But on the periphery of Novak's works lies a relatively unexamined assumption that a 'crisis of identity' exists in America today and this crisis is the cause of resurgent ethnicity. Novak claims that 'the new ethnicity - [is] a movement primarily of personal and social identity -....' (10)

How does this explanation compare with others? It seems that Novak's position is parallel to the view advanced by the historian Marcus Lee Hansen in his study 'The Problem of the Third Generation Immigrant.' In this work, Hansen suggested that 'What the son wishes to forget, the grandson wishes to remember.' (11) Hansen's Law stipulates that assimilation characterizes the second generation, but when the second generation throws off its immigrant skin, the third generation suffers an identity crisis. That is, Hansen's Law contends that changes in the attitudes of social groups correspond to generational changes. Put in other terms, in a truly diverse society it is not enough to be just an American. The question becomes 'What kind of American are you?' According to Hansen, the third generation falls back upon the social identity of its grandfathers.

Glazer and Moynihan, in a pioneering study of ethnicity and politics in New York City (1963), said, 'We have precious few studies of ethnic identity, despite the increasing prominence of its role in the mass media in recent years....' (12) They do, however, suggest the following reasons for the revival of ethnicity.

1. Ethnic identities have taken over some of the task of self-definition that occupational identities, particularly working-class occupational identities, have formerly given. The status of the worker is downgraded; as a result, apparently, the status of being an ethnic, a member of an ethnic group, has been upgraded.

2. International events have declined as a source of feeling of ethnic identity, except for Jews. Identification with homelands (involvement in and concern for) declines, and more and more the sources of ethnic identification are to be found in American experiences, on American soil.

3. Along with occupation and homeland, religion has

declined as a focus of ethnic identification, particularly in the Catholic Church. For the first time, the
Catholic Church does not complement the conservative
tendencies of Catholic ethnic groups. (13)

Glazer and Moynihan offer some basic insights into the
nature of the problem of cultural diversity. Their hypothesis is best stated in their own words:

The assimilating power of American society and culture
operated on immigrant groups in different ways, to
make them, it is true, something they had not been,
but still something distinct and identifiable.... The
ethnic group in American society became not a survival
from the age of mass immigration but a new social
form. (14)

According to the authors, ethnic differences remain
with us but they also assume new social meanings and
functions. Such membership is a form of social identity,
a way of knowing who you are, within the larger society.
Moreover, each of the so-called hyphenated-American
minorities (Irish-American, Italian-American, etc.)
represents a political interest group. Each group, in New
York City, has become politically organized in order to
reap its share of the goals and services of society.

In short, it has been argued, both explicitly and
implicitly, that a 'crisis of identity' is sufficient to
account for resurgent ethnicity. Novak, Hansen, Glazer
and Moynihan, and others are in agreement that resurgent
ethnicity today is merely a response to an identity crisis.
But to establish why this is, is perhaps to accept a too
facile explanation. While it is not denied that identity
is connected in some way to the phenomenon of resurgent
ethnicity, it may be unwarranted to claim that a 'crisis
of identity' is a sufficient condition (or even a necessary one?) for the phenomenon. It may be the case that
a too ready acceptance of the identity factor as the only
or even the most plausible explanation of resurgent
ethnicity is unfounded.

For example, it may be granted that the identity factor
is connected in some way to the phenomenon of resurgent
ethnicity, but to what extent this needs to be connected
to a historical identity (ethnicity) is a moot question.
If we limit the sources of identity to those rooted in
race, religion, or national state, have we in effect
excluded a great many categories of identity commonly
known to operate in today's society? For example, the
identification of someone with a 'reform' political candidate, some political action group, an Archibald Cox,
a Henry Kissinger, Martin Luther King, Ralph Nader,
The Beatles, or what have you? In short, it seems to be

the case that the single path of personal identification
with the traditional ethnic sources commits us to too
narrow an explanation of resurgent ethnicity.

There is another possible explanation to be considered.
Our first step is to ask a prior question, namely, 'Just
what is resurgent ethnicity?' 'Resurgent ethnicity' may
be explained in part by noting that the term 'ethnic'
has been broadened to include 'life-style.' Mary Anne
Raywid has pointed out that the phrase 'ethnic group'
was 'previously restricted to national groups, often in
religious combination (as, for example, in Irish Catholic)'
but 'the term has recently come prominently to apply to
blacks as well.' (15) She contends that:

> We've not given much attention to the considerable
> switch this represents in identifying cultural differ-
> ence or ethnicity: from acquired or learned difference
> like nationality, to biological differences such as
> race. According to current usage, blacks are an
> ethnic group, and at least some women have acquired
> that particular consciousness of kind entitling them
> to ethnic group status too. And this, of course,
> represents an even further extension of ethnicity,
> from a racial to a sexual basis. (16)

I agree with Raywid that a broadening of ethnicity has
occurred. Indeed it is a 'considerable switch ... in
identifying cultural difference or ethnicity ... from
acquired or learned difference like nationality, to biological differences such as race.' However, what is
important in this shift is the fact that certain sub-
cultural groups have 'asserted' their fundamental claim
to ethnicity. What is indicated here is that blacks and
women have asserted that they have a distinct sub-culture
or life-style that is sufficiently different to warrant
their having ethnic group status.

What can we say about such a shift? (17) If we recall
the three criteria for cultural diversity established
earlier - 1, we make certain criteria count in establishing differences; 2, the selected differences between
groups must be viewed as fundamental enough to produce
values and dispositions of a significant sort; and 3,
there must exist a sense of historical and participational
identity capable of being transmitted across generations -
then we see that the inclusion of blacks and other minority groups as well as women as 'new ethnics' is permitted.

But what needs clarifying here is that the locus of
the first criterion has shifted. Previously in the
Americanization movement culturally diverse groups were
'labeled' as such by the 'older' established Americans
who claimed a cultural superiority. Immigrants were told

explicitly and implicitly to become aware of how much
they differed from the host or dominant culture. Such
a labeling rarely accommodated ethnic identification and
dignity marching hand in hand. Oh, dignity could be had
from bearing insult and assault without rancor, but it
was rarely granted the ethnic through a show of acceptance
and kindness. The labeling process easily descended into
a squalid form of cultural debasement and gross prejudice.

   In this shift from a group being labeled ethnic to a
group asserting its fundamental ethnicity is the fact
that the new ethnics themselves elect to make certain
criteria count in establishing differences; but today
the criteria are not necessarily nationality, culture,
language, and religion. Rather they are of the ascriptive
sort, and should be recognized as such. Ethnicity appeals
to and is fast taking hold among many Americans who know
that they cannot shake or be rid of certain identifying
characteristics such as skin color or sex. Thus, the
phenomenon of broadened ethnicity is indicative of more
than resurgent ethnicity; something larger is taking place.
It is caught, in part, by what Ralf Dahrendorf has
referred to as the 'refeudalization' of society - the
return to ascriptive rather than achieved characteristics
as determinants of social stratification. (18) Moreover,
as Daniel Bell put it, 'Ethnicity has become more salient
(than class) because it can combine an interest with an
affective tie....' (19) Apparently, the strategic
efficacy of ethnicity is seen as a major focus for the
mobilization of group interests. It is a strategy for
asserting claims against the institutions of society, for
any oppressed group has the best chance of changing the
system if it raises the communal consciousness of its
individual members.

   It is important, therefore, to recognize that broadened
ethnicity suggests the past experiences of oppressed
minorities as merely the starting point of a strategy
calculated to cash in on today's rapidly changing political situation. The common elements fashioning broadened
ethnicity are the crucial considerations of deprivation,
powerlessness, alienation, frustration, and the like.
In the not too distant past, such conditions were viewed
largely in terms of individual-personal discontent, and
help was sought from relatives and friends. But today
individual-personal discontent has been replaced with
collective-political discontent and the new organizations
of broadened ethnicity seek significant power to harness
the sources of discontent and to establish a political
and a moral base under the emotive slogan of cultural
pluralism. (Curiously, the political interest-defined

group is now behaving as an ethnic group, whereas in the past the ethnic group behaved as a political interest-defined group.)

The second factor challenging the thesis that 'resurgent ethnicity is caused by a crisis of identity' has to do with the fact that many of America's ethnic whites belong to America's working class. In the mid-1960s, the working class discovered that the old rules of the game through which they would supposedly share in the bounty of America were suddenly changed. Welfare, for some, had become an acceptable way of life; police officers were called 'pigs' and those who flaunted the law were not punished; and flag burning and draft evasion were condoned by some. By the late 1960s rampant inflation caused an economic squeeze and many family breadwinners were hard put to meet the family budget. Inflation made it next to impossible for the average family to save and it appeared that only the children of the very rich or the very poor (scholarship grants and aid) were able to meet the problem of spiraling costs of a college education. Labeled or characterized as racist pigs, honkies, bigots, the Silent Majority, and hardhats, many white ethnics felt that there was little hope that any foreseeable change in American life would likely benefit them. To them, the social revolution of the 1960s had changed the 'rules of the game' and the change was largely made at their expense.

Hence, today's white working-class ethnic wants it known that his ancestors' early experiences were not easy ones; that they had to work tremendously hard to 'make it' in America, that they were oppressed and exploited; and in addition, they, too, were the targets of pseudo-scientific racial theories. It is apparent that the message of the third- and fourth-generation offspring is this: Whatever progress or success they have achieved, it was due to hard work, struggle, and self-sacrifice, and no one gave their forebears and themselves anything 'on a silver platter.'

Finally, the 'crisis of identity' cause of resurgent ethnicity can be challenged in terms of yet another phenomenon, namely, the collapse of accommodative or 'machine' politics. The rather sudden collapse of accommodative politics - that curious blend of ethnic groups and local and state-elected officials - has changed significantly the political and social mobility of white ethnic groups, such as the Irish, Jewish, and Italian. The long-term contribution of accommodative politics was its providing of political stability facilitating the mobility of white ethnic groups within a permissive political environment. For example, accommodative

politics is reflected in the Irish-Catholic transition
from a despised and feared outgroup to one for whom the
traditional American holders of institutional power had
to make room or 'accommodate.' Indeed in Boston they
became a despised and feared ingroup - The Irish Mafia!
The primary political benefactors of accommodative
politics shaped public policy in the Democratic party
coalition and, to a lesser extent, through the labor
unions and fraternal associations of America.

Accommodative politics was largely ethnic, with
political candidates showing up at, say, a local picnic,
attempting to enjoy an athletic feat or perhaps a polka,
and attempting to say a few words in another tongue.
But this was changed in the 1960s. The 'new politics,'
made up of groups representing the 'new' minorities
(ethnics?) - women, blacks, Chicanos, native Americans,
Puerto Ricans, etc. - displaced the white ethnic coali-
tions and claimed for themselves the political rewards
of exercising power.

My major point is that Novak and others, who stress
the importance and significance of a resurgent ethnicity,
also justify it in terms of its being caused by a 'mass
society' type of social order inimical to identity
stability. Now it is true that ethnicity and its
accounterments are 'in the air' at present, but it is not
necessarily true that the phenomenon is caused by a
'crisis of identity'; other factors also appear as
possible causes. A minor point, but an important,one, is
'What counts as resurgent ethnicity.' This is not just
a nit-picking question, but one which is crucial if we
are to make judgments about cultural diversity, particularly in the schools. The question is not whether
cultural diversity in the form of multi-ethnicity is
undesirable. It is rather that since many, perhaps most,
Americans desire some sort of sub-cultural identity or
life-style, we should not necessarily connect this
phenomenon to the historic past of racial, religious,
and national groups. My concern here is that we ought
not be too quick to join those who insist that no
separation of the older and traditional view of ethnicity
and today's so-called 'resurgent ethnicity' is necessary.

EDUCATIONAL POLICY AND CULTURAL DIVERSITY

To see public policy as a product that authorizes the
distribution of benefits and prerogatives in society,
and educational policy as performing the function of
ensuring the acceptance and maintenance of such policy

is to appreciate the instrumental function of public education in providing stability to a society. Thus, to consider public education apart from policy-making is to run the risk of confusing the cart with the horse. This is the reality: Public education is, and always has been, inseparable from broader social, political, and economic goals.

We must now consider some points which, if recognized, might have the positive effect of creating public education within the parameters of a democratically conceived culturally diverse society.

First, the bulk of the evidence is in and it indicates that most Americans desire some sort of group affiliation tie or ties. If my analysis is correct, we are in the presence of more than simply a renascent ethnicity. The pattern of cultural diversity emergent in our society is both broader and deeper. It encompasses sex, occupation, race, age, etc. People are rejecting the goal of a monolithic American culture and are discovering themselves to be members of groups distinguished by interest-defined concerns. Since the goal of a monolithic American culture is no longer acceptable to the many self-identified sub-groups or to the dominant core culture itself, public education should attempt to secure some workable expression of cultural diversity, although not necessarily as a response to Novak's (et al.) claim that it is a 'resurgent ethnicity.'

My objection is not to the notion that an ethnic factor remains with us, although colored by assimilation, for Glazer and Moynihan's observation that ethnic groups assimilate but remain distinct is a most important one for us to remember. But in discussions concerning the role of public education in a culturally diverse society we should note the brute fact that for some Americans today acceptance of the notion of a 'resurgent ethnicity' requires no more than the politicalization of passions along black-white lines to fan the flames of a latent racism. In a word, the need is for stability, particularly in the area of race relations, because for some ethnics, white and black, the resurgence of ethnicity is simply a cover for racism.

My point is a simple one: the need for stability in a society dominated by a broadened ethnicity may turn into a mockery of a great society. We may note a pragmatic folly in easy accommodation to the 'new ethnic consciousness' celebrated by Michael Novak. For the poor and the victimized it could be nothing more than a cruel hoax, since it could be made to exploit the reactionary potential of the not so recent American past. Stability, at

any cost, however, might lend support to the glorification
of racial and religious peculiarities offering as a viable
alternative a federation of races - each with its own
territory or elected representative. Such a proposal
would assure freedom for the group, but not for the
individual. The individual's fate would be predetermined
on the basis of his cultural identity.

A system of public education sympathetic to a legitimate cultural diversity demands standards drawn from more
than one culture. In this context, the curriculum
requires that due recognition be given to all who contributed to our national heritage. The tokenism of 'Black
America Week,' 'Columbus Day,' or male heroes only, simply
will not suffice. Public education must deny the position
that has consistently refused to recognize that a legitimate cultural diversity exists, or even that it should
exist. Implied here is the notion that schooling that
dicounts cultural diversity by ascribing to cultural
differences all kind of demeaning terms - culturally
deficient, culturally disadvantaged, culturally deprived
(culturally depraved?) - is no longer acceptable - it
simply cannot be tolerated any longer. But neither can it
substitute a new kind of advocacy which emphasizes the
racist and ethnocentric aspects of American life.

The revival of ethnicity is growing and will continue
for some time to come. The new-found pride and economic
power of native Americans, blacks, Chicanos, Puerto Ricans,
women, and others will result in a growing assertiveness
aimed at reshaping occupational, housing, and educational
patterns. In particular, the positive aspects of ethnicity will call into question the failure of the neighbor-
hood school to prepare adequately children for successful
roles in adult life. Hopefully, the realization of the
inadequacy of the old accommodation model of politics to
deal meaningfully with this problem should be seen as the
starting point of most discussions on educational policy.
But the search for something more adequate in shaping
public education based on the recognition of cultural
diversity should not encourage exclusivist tendencies.
Divisive groups who wish to achieve separation should be
recognized but not encouraged.

My contention is that the ethnic factor remains with
us, although colored by cultural assimilation and the
'broadening effect.' And if ethnicity is honest and is
viewed as a source of cultural strength rather than of
personal deprivation, then public education may help
develop a cultural stability rooted in youths who are
open to change, who are flexible, adaptive, and receptive.
This means introducing the student to many life-styles,

not superficially, but in depth. Students should study
the variety and richness of America's multicultural
history. Hopefully, such an education would defuse a
latent racism and provide a solid, stronger type of social
stability.

The problem of resurgent ethnicity, minority group
assertiveness, and the need for stability is directly
related to two further consequences for public education.
We can see this as follows: For one thing, the problem
may produce a willingness to compromise on vital matters.
This practice was defended in the 'accommodation model'
as not only a necessity of politics and white ethnicity,
but also as the supreme virtue. As previously mentioned,
the long-term contribution of the model was that it provided stability facilitating the mobility of white ethnic
groups within a somewhat adaptive political environment.
But it is entirely conceivable that the very broadening
of passions and cultural issues in current 'ethnic
politics' makes such facile pragmatic accommodation, even
if one is willing, all but impossible to achieve. That
is to say, the policy at present is too broad, too
involved in scope to make possible easy accommodation of
all interests involved. As John Dewey foresaw in the late
1920s, the sentiments and symbols of shared cultural
attachments are themselves too varied, disparate and
incomplete. He said 'The social situation has been so
changed ... that traditional general principles have
little practical meaning.' (20) Further on he commented,
'Symbols control thought, and the new age has no symbols
consonant with its activities.' (21) And 'Our Babel is
not one of tongues but one of signs and symbols without
which shared experience is impossible.' (22)

The essential point here is that the newer collective
strategies and methods - such as the use of skyjacking
commercial aircraft, political assassination and kidnap-
ping, economic sanctions against supermarkets, etc. - have
outrun mere mediation and negotiation efforts aimed at a
compromise. This points toward major reconsiderations
which involve educational policy conceived primarily as a
function of informative criticism, inquiry, and publicity.
The need, in other words, is the improvement of the
methods and conditions of discussion and debate. There
being no universal arbiter who decides which ethnic
demands are just and which are not, relevant data must
penetrate the whole system of decision-making and policies
must be developed that reflect the bearing of knowledge
supplied by the various groups.

Second, the implementation of cultural diversity
studies as part of the curriculum of public education

would involve, minimally, a school setting in which programs are designed to help students learn about and possibly appreciate the many diverse American life-styles
as well as learning to interact productively with people
from different backgrounds. The teacher would teach
students not to stereotype others and how to prevent
alienation in social intercourse.

Hopefully, teachers would engage students in a number
of learning activities designed to accomplish inter-group
understanding. The curriculum would in part be derived
from the many cultures and problems of a culturally
diverse society and would be related to academic subjects
of study such as language arts, social studies, and the
physical sciences. Projects involving in- and out-of-
school activities would be utilized to help students
better understand the roots of prejudice, the consequences
of ethnocentrism, the strengths and weaknesses of local
ethnic groups, the search for individual identity within
a multi-culture, and how to become facile in the dominant
culture as well as in the sub-culture.

There is, however, a need for a cautionary note. I am
not advocating a multi-cultural education per se. Rather,
I wish to suggest that schools can be utilized as vehicles
for fostering tolerance and understanding among culturally
diverse groups. But if this is to be accomplished,
teachers must conduct a careful assessment of the impact
of their work and their knowledge of the political as well
as the self-serving purpose of schooling. The rhetoric,
promises, trappings and symbols of, say, a 'problems of
democracy' course for students simply will not suffice.
Tolerance and understanding will not be fostered in the
area of forced consensus nor by adherence to an ideology
of social reconstructionism. What seems to be indicated
instead are discussions and situations focusing on primary
associations wherein students interact more fully as
people who learn about and share a number of common interests and concerns. Schooling would thus provide an
opportunity for the gathering of heterogeneous or homogeneous groups to examine and discuss issues of mutual
concern. The major thrust of schooling would be reflection and deliberation, clarity before commitment, and
above all, commitment.

There is no good reason why schools cannot foster the
kind of learning suggested above by pursuing a great
number of dialects, values, languages, historical accounts,
interpretations of events, etc. In a society such as ours,
in which many culture groups exist, massive areas of disagreement about public education will abound, but we
should not overlook the agreement, the shared or common

concerns. Both disagreement and common concerns are
possible because of the acceptance of the fundamental
principle of equal citizenship which grants a prima facie
right to all individuals, even the right to disagree.
Our ability to construct a viable system of public education that recognizes bases of agreement may well provide
the acid test of the old 'melting pot' ideal.

NOTES

1   Nathan Glazer and Daniel P. Moynihan, 'Beyond the
    Melting Pot,' 2nd ed. (Cambridge, Mass.: MIT Press,
    1970), p.xiv.
2   Perhaps the most common use of the term 'ethnic'
    connotes a group or person. Historically, this use
    was restricted to nationalities (French, Greek, Poles,
    Germans, Irish, etc.) and then it was broadened to
    include religious affiliation as well - as, for
    example, German-Lutheran, Irish-Catholic, etc.
    Recently, however, the term has been applied much
    more broadly and includes Latin Americans, blacks,
    and so on as ethnic groups. This is an important,
    but often unnoticed observation that I owe to Mary
    Anne Raywid, Pluralism as a Basis for Educational
    Policy: Some Second Thoughts, presented to the Lyndon
    B. Johnson Memorial Symposium on Education Policy,
    Glassboro, N.J., May 25, 1973.
3   It would be wrong to assume that explicit sanctions
    would be needed to enforce expression of cultural
    diversity. Nothing more than a carefully nurtured
    sense of historical identity and well-defined and
    available satisfying participational roles within
    the group and the large society are needed.
4   Thomas F. Green, Education and Pluralism: Ideal and
    Reality (Twenty-Sixth Annual J. Richard Street Lec-
    ture, Syracuse University School of Education, 1966),
    p.10.
5   Ibid., p.11.
6   For early documents on the immigrant problem and a
    workable bibliography of this aspect of the American-
    ization movement, see Edith Abbott (ed.) 'Historical
    Aspects of the Immigrant Problem: Select Documents'
    (University of Chicago Press, 1926). See also Andrew
    M. Greeley, 'Why Can't They Be Like Us?' (New York:
    Dutton, 1971); Marcus Lee Hansen, 'The Atlantic Migra-
    tion, 1607-1860' (Cambridge, Mass.: Harvard University
    Press,1940); Edward Hartmann, 'The Movement to
    Americanize the Immigrant' (New York: University of

Columbia Press, 1948); John Higham, 'Strangers in the Land: Patterns of American Nativism, 1860-1925' (New York: Random House, 1970); Dwight Macdonald, 'Against the American Grain' (New York: Random House, 1962); Roger Portal, 'The Slavs' (New York: Harper & Row, 1969); Richard Scammon and Ben J. Wattenberg, 'The Real Majority' (New York: Coward-McCann, 1970); George M. Stephenson, 'A History of American Immigration, 1920-1924' (New York: Russell & Russell, 1964); Rudolph S. Veceli, European Americans: From Immigrants to Ethnics, in 'Reinterpretation of American History and Culture,' ed. William H. Cartwright and Richard L. Watson (Washington DC: National Council for the Social Studies, 1973).

7   Gerd Korman, 'Industrialization, Immigrants, and Americanizers' (Madison, Wisconsin: The State Historical Society of Wisconsin, 1967).

8   See Michael Novak, One Species, Many Cultures, 'The American Scholar,' Winter, 1973-4; The New Ethnicity, 'The Humanist,' May/June 1973; 'The Rise of the Unmeltable Ethnics' (New York: Macmillan, 1971). For a variation on this theme, see Peter Schrag, 'The Decline of the WASP' (New York: Simon & Schuster, 1970).

9   Novak, 'The Rise of the Unmeltable Ethnics,' pp.xviii.

10 Ibid. p.xxiv.

11 Marcus L. Hansen, 'The Problem of the Third Generation Immigrant' (Rock Island, Illinois: The Augustana Historical Society, 1937), p.15.

12 Glazer and Moynihan, op.cit., p.xxxiv.

13 Ibid., pp.xxiv, xxv, xxvi.

14 Ibid., pp.13-14, 16.

15 Raywid, op.cit., p.6.

16 Ibid.

17 Although the precise import of the shift is notoriously difficult to characterize, it is caught in part in the following:
    Nowadays, it appears a cultural demand can no longer be weighed on the scales of seriousness and depth. Eventually all demands are to be taken seriously. Indeed, the point about ethnicity and ethnic consciousness is that no group submits to the judgment of others. By their very nature ethnic claims do not allow of a universal scale against which they can be measured.
    See Norman Glazer, Ethnicity and the Schools, 'Commentary,' vol.58 (September, 1974), p.58.

18 See Nathan Glazer and Daniel P. Moynihan, Why Ethnicity, 'Commentary,' vol.58 (October, 1974), p.36.

19 Ibid., p.37
20 John Dewey, 'The Public and Its Problems' (Chicago:
    The Swallow Press, 1927), p.133.
21 Ibid., p.142.
22 Ibid.

9   Equality of educational opportunity

Robert H. Ennis

In which of the following cases do we find the educational
opportunity of one member of the pair equal to that of
the other?

(A) Edward Tudor and Tom Canty, born on the same day,
were raised respectively in the Palace of Westminster and
Offal Court. Edward had a series of private tutors who
gave him a strong academic education. Tom Canty learned
by experience in the streets of London. The Earl of
Hertford deemed the education of each to be fitting
(characters from Mark Twain's 'The Prince and the Pauper').

(B) Jill and Jack, born on the same day in a small
rural Illinois town to lower class and upper/middle-class
parents respectively, went to the same tax-supported
Illinois schools through age seventeen. Their inherited
mental ability was about the same. In their early teens
both entertained the idea of becoming electrical engineers.
Jill was discouraged by her gasoline-delivery-truck-
driving father, who scoffed at her 'uppity' thoughts, and
who himself did not go beyond the eighth grade. Very few
magazines and books were to be found in her home, which
contained two bedrooms and housed six people. Jack had
a private bedroom; and his physician father encouraged his
engineer aspirations and subscribed to 'Scientific
American.' Right after high school, Jack went on to
engineering school, and Jill married locally, becoming a
housewife with children.

(C) Fraternal twins, Bonnie and Clyde, came out differently in what John Rawls (1971) called the 'natural
lottery.' At age six Bonnie's and Clyde's scores on the
Wechsler Intelligence Scale for Children are about 130
and 70 respectively, and the disparity in scores is consistent with their parents' and teachers' appraisals of
their conceptual development and ability to learn. Clyde
can look forward to special classes for the 'educable

mentally handicapped' in tax-supported schools through age eighteen. Bonnie can expect to progress through the tax-supported schools and, with some financial help from their middle-class parents, the state university.

(D) White identical twins, Alpha and Beta, who are children of school teachers, came out the same in the natural lottery of mental ability, but throughout school, Beta was not interested in acquiring an academic education. Rather he wanted to hunt, fish and tend horses. Alpha sought an academic education. In elementary school Beta was pressured to learn to read and work with numbers sufficiently to cause him to keep up with Alpha in elementary school, but by the time they completed secondary school, Beta's academic achievement level was well below that of Alpha. The school system offered no courses in hunting, fishing and horsemanship, and their parents tried to discourage Beta's interests therein.

(E) Another of Alpha's classmates is Running Deer, a full-blooded American Indian coming from a tribe that values prowess in hunting, fishing, and horsemanship, but does not value academic accomplishments. Running Deer and Alpha are born with similar capacities, but are brought up differently. At the end of their compulsory education Alpha scores higher on academic tests than does Running Deer.

People with whom I have discussed these cases generally agree that Edward and Tom, the prince and the pauper, did not have euqal educational opportunity, and I agree, though I shall contend that the case is not conceptually inconsistent with this ideal. But people vigorously disagree about the other four cases. These disagreements are indicative of some deep-seated policy issues that trouble us these days.

Why is it that even though there is so much agreement on equality of educational opportunity as an ideal, there is so much disagreement about its application? A first approximation sometimes offered as an answer is that different people have different definitions of equality of educational opportunity. For those who view definitions as simply arbitrary rules for the use of terms, this first approximation results in the disagreement's being simply an arbitrary matter to be settled by the flipping of a coin, or some such maneuver. Clearly the disputes are not such as can reasonably be settled that way.

For those who view such definitions as things that need more justification than is provided by flipping a coin, the first approximation provides some insight, albeit oversimplified. The problem with this oversimplified answer is that it leaves confusion about how to proceed

in trying to settle the disagreements. This is because
there are different sorts of definition, requiring different sorts of justification. When I have encountered this
first approximation, it has generally not been accompanied
by an understanding of these different sorts of non-
arbitrary definition.

Embodied in this paper is an attempt to make more clear
the nature of equality-of-educational-opportunity disputes,
especially those that develop even when people appear to
be looking at the same set of facts. Greater understanding of disputes about cases like the five I offered is the
modest first goal.

The disputes involved, I shall claim, are often about
the value judgments required for the application of the
concept equality of educational opportunity. If I am
right, there is some advance over the first approximation.
Although settling value issues is often a very difficult
matter, there is an advance in knowing that this has to
be done, as opposed to mucking about in the typical confused argument over, or 'search for,' a definition. (1)

In order to achieve this first goal of understanding,
I shall offer an analysis of the concept of equality of
educational opportunity, an analysis that ultimately
focuses on our ideas of education and of having an
opportunity as the sources of controversy. I believe that
this analysis does justice to the concept that is employed
by intelligent, sensitive educational policy makers. Its
elaboration and defense is a second goal of the paper.
The defense depends on the ability of the analysis to
explain the way we think and argue about cases like the
five given earlier.

EQUALITY, A DYADIC RELATIONSHIP

Equality is a relationship between two things, a dyadic
relationship. To say that something is equal, without
specifying something else (or in the often trivial case,
itself) to which it is claimed to be equal, does not make
any sense. To say that Jack has equality of educational
opportunity all by himself does not make sense. There
must be someone who is claimed to be equal to Jack in
amount of educational opportunity for the claim to get
off the ground.

In discussions of equality of educational opportunity
we are often interested in relationships between groups,
so one might wonder how such a dyadic relationship fits
groups, since it is individuals, not groups, that have
educational opportunity. One way to express this interest
is to look at average or representative individuals for

each group, and see whether their educational opportunities are equal. I am not meaning here to suggest a mathematically precise way of reducing the problem about groups to one about individuals; I am only indicating a general approach. As a first approximation, one might say that two groups have equal educational opportunity just in case a pair of average members, one from each group, have equal educational opportunity. Alternatively one might pair comparable children of various sorts and see whether the educational opportunities of the pairs are equal.

Statisticians, methodologists, and philosophers have work to do here prior to the execution of studies. I am only suggesting that they build their methods on the concept of the comparison of a pair. Discussions of equality of educational opportunity have not and need not wait for the methodological refinements, however. Once we make decisions about pairs (the hardest part of the conceptual problem, I believe), we can make rough, intuitive estimates for groups that can be useful in policy discussions. First things first.

THE ANALYSIS

Because equality of educational opportunity is a dyadic relationship, I shall take as the object of my analysis an expression that clearly indicates this dyadic relationship and that facilitates thinking about what must be equal to what. This form is called 'contextual definition' by Hempel (1952, p.4) and others. I think a more informative name is 'equivalent-expression definition' (Ennis, 1969, pp.217-21). The expression on which I shall focus then is the following:

    1 x and y have equality of educational opportunity
This expression, which is in the form of a sentence, exhibits the fact that equality is a dyadic relationship. As an analysis I suggest that expression 1 is equivalent in meaning to the following:

    2 x and y have the same amount of opportunity for an education
This proposed analysis is not immediately startling, but there are advantages.

CONCEPTS AND CONCEPTIONS

In terms of the concept-conception distinction used by John Rawls (1971), the offered analysis outlines the concept of equality of educational opportunity; to specify in addition what constitutes education and having an

opportunity would be to offer a conception of equality
of educational opportunity. Rawls in talking about
justice explains the concept-conception distinction as
follows (1971, pp.5-6):

> It seems natural to think of the concept of justice as
> distinct from the various conceptions of justice and
> as being specified by the role which ... different
> conceptions have in common. Those who hold different
> conceptions of justice can, then, still agree that
> institutions are just when no arbitrary distinctions
> are made between persons in the assigning of basic
> rights and duties and when the rules determine a proper
> balance between competing claims to the advantages of
> social life. Men can agree to this description of just
> institutions since the notions of an arbitrary distinc-
> tion and of a proper balance, which are included in
> the concept of justice, are left open for each to
> interpret according to the principles of justice that
> he accepts. These principles single out which similar-
> ities and differences among persons are relevant in
> determining rights and duties and they specify which
> division of advantages is appropriate.

Using this language, I have offered a concept of
equality of educational opportunity, feeling that people
can agree to it, but have not set forth any conceptions
of equality of educational opportunity, nor any principles
embodied by any conceptions. The notion having an
opportunity and the notion education are 'left open for
each to interpret according to the principles' that she
or he accepts.

Furthermore, the analysis enables one to make the
important point that application of the concept equality
of educational opportunity requires value judgments in
addition to that required for the endorsement of the
concept as a guide to life. This point has been made
before in the philosophy of education literature, by Myron
Lieberman (1961), B. Paul Komisar and Jerrold Coombs
(1964), R.S. Peters (1966) and Thomas Green (1971). The
point should be made, but prior work does not adequately
explain why the point is a correct one. Nor does the
prior work indicate focal points for deciding whether
there is equality of educational opportunity. I shall
attempt both.

The point that additional value judgments are required
enables us to explain why there is so much agreement that
equality of educational opportunity is a good thing and so
much disagreement about what to do in specific cases. We
are generally agreed that the concept should be
implemented, but we are often not agreed upon any

particular conception of equality of educational opportunity. More specifically we are often in disagreement about
what is to count as education and what is to count as
having an opportunity. To decide these matters requires
one or more value judgments. To show that value judgment
is generally required for the specification of what is to
count as required for education is relatively easy. To
show that value judgment is required for application of
the concept having an opportunity is more difficult, but
I shall attempt to formulate a defense. Defense of both
points will be aided by an examination of the previously
described cases.

EDUCATION

In Case A, most people would agree that Edward Tudor and
Tom Canty did not have equality of educational opportunity.
On most views of education and of having an opportunity,
Edward and Tom had different amounts of opportunity for
an education. Education, most would think, was brought
to Edward on a silver platter but was systematically
denied to Tom. Tom had less opportunity, I suppose most
people would say. (2)
     However, one who thinks that Tom's education in the
streets is every bit as good an education as Edward's
(not merely good for Tom, given his destiny), and thinks
that Tom had just as much opportunity as Edward (which
he presumably did) for his good education, then that
person should judge them to have equality of educational
opportunity. Furthermore, if one judges Tom's prospective
education in the streets to be appropriate education for
everyone, in contrast to what some might call an 'empty,
bookish, academic' education, then, since Edward had less
opportunity for the street kind of education, the conclusion should be that Edward had less educational
opportunity than Tom.
     This all goes to show that one's judgment about whether
there is equality of educational opportunity depends at
least in part upon one's judgments about what constitutes
an education. In most equal-opportunity contexts this
determination requires value judgment.
     One's judgments about education also play a significant
role in Case D, in which identical twins, Alpha and Beta,
have different interests. If one judges an academic
education to be proper, as contrasted to an education in
hunting, fishing, and horsemanship (or alternatively, if
one makes the value judgment that mastery of hunting,
fishing, and horsemanship does not constitute an educa-

tion, whereas academic mastery does constitute an education), then presumably one would judge Alpha and Beta to have equality of educational opportunity. One would presumably also say that Beta just did not take advantage of his opportunity.

Suppose that one instead judges an education to be proper to the extent that it is in accord with a student's interests, but that their school provides only an academic education. Then presumably one would judge their educational opportunities to be unequal, since Alpha's academic interests were better provided for by the system than Beta's outdoor interests.

A parallel problem arises in making judgments about equality of educational opportunity for people whose background is other than the dominant culture in a school. Let us assume that to be academic, white, and middle class, for the sake of discussion, in comparing Alpha with his classmate, Running Deer (Case E). Running Deer's culture encourages hunting, fishing and horsemanship, but Running Deer's days in the compulsory school are spent in attempts to develop him academically.

Granting these typical conditions we can see that the issue of whether or not they have equal educational opportunity depends in part on one's value judgments about what constitutes an education. If one judges that a genuine education is primarily concerned with introduction to and absorption of one's culture, then Running Deer and Alpha do not have equality of educational opportunity. Running Deer's culture is not promoted by the compulsory school.

If, however, one judges academics to be the core of an education, then the decision problem (comparing Running Deer and Alpha) becomes somewhat like that of Case B, in which Jill and Jack, coming from different backgrounds, go to the same school with a common goal assumed. These two cases bring out a type of controversial issue often embedded in comparing amounts of opportunity, when agreement on the goals (or nature) of education is assumed. Settling this sort of issue, I shall urge, requires one or more other value judgments.

In previously discussed cases I bypassed this type of problem, assuming that all of us would line up on one side of the question about opportunity, enabling me to focus on the controversial goals (or nature) of education. For example, in Case A concerning Tom Canty and Edward Tudor, assuming that an academic education of the sort given to Edward Tudor was the right kind of education for both, I suggested that all would agree that Tom had less educational opportunity than Edward; and assuming that a

street-type education was the right type for both, that
Tom had more opportunity than Edward.

HAVING AN OPPORTUNITY

In Cases B and E, however, assuming academic educational
goals and the same inherent ability, the environmental
differences are such that people with different value
orientations can understandably still come up with
different equality-of-opportunity judgments when looking
at the same situation. I shall at first focus on these
cases involving environmental differences. Later on I
shall examine Case C as a representative of situations
involving people with natural differences.

In Case B some would say that Jill had less educational
opportunity than Jack, because Jill's background was not
academically stimulating, because her father scoffed at
her academic ideas, because of the lack of quiet privacy
for study, because of 'hidden tuition' costs, etc., items
for which the schools did not deliberately attempt to
compensate through such things as Head-Start programs.
Let us call this the 'Liberal Position.'

Others would say that the educational opportunity was
the same, since the schools were there to serve both Jill
and Jack, giving them equal attention, and the factors
mentioned were merely conditions of the situation. What
really matters, so the position goes, is the fact that
there was nothing restraining Jill from going on to
engineering school and absorbing what it had to offer.
It was up to her to take advantage of what was there.
If she failed to do so, the responsibility is hers. She
just was not sufficiently motivated. Let us call this
the 'Conservative Position.'

One interesting feature of the Liberal-Conservative
dispute is that opposing parties have difficulty seeing
the rationality of the other position. The Liberal tends
to think that the Conservative has simply failed to take
account of some obvious basic facts, while the Conservative tends to think that the Liberal has introduced
irrelevancies. Each has trouble seeing how the other
could think the way she or he does, and suspects that
ulterior motives must be operating. My proposed explanation of the situation is that the controversy is often not
about a matter of fact, as many think, nor about a concept,
as some think, but rather about the buried value judg-
ment(s) that one makes in applying the concept, 'to have
an opportunity.' This explanation is fairly complicated
with some gaps in detail. But on the whole it appears to

be a likely candidate because it explains how we handle
difficult issues, and it makes understandable the feelings
that some have that their opponents are irrational.

POSITIVE AND NEGATIVE ASPECTS OF HAVING AN OPPORTUNITY

Roughly speaking, x's having an opportunity to do z consists of the presence of positive factors combined with
the absence or insufficiency of negative factors. The
positive factors are environmental facilitators; that
is, environmental features that could enable (or help) x
to do z. Examples are the presence of an engineering
school and Jack's father's help, which facilitated Jack's
learning engineering.

Negative factors, the insufficiency of which is the
other constituent of x's having an opportunity to do z,
are environmental factors that could deter (or are deterring) x from doing z. An example of an environmental
deterrent (at least from the point of view of Tom Canty)
is the fence that kept him out of Westminster.

THE PERSONAL-ENVIRONMENTAL DISTINCTION

Only environmental, as contrasted with personal, factors
are constitutive of having an opportunity. (3) Personal
factors include motivation, traits, abilities, decisions,
ideas, beliefs, and goals of the person involved. That
Jill did not in the end decide (a decision is a personal
factor) to learn engineering does not by itself count
against her having had the opportunity to learn engineering. That people do not choose to take advantage of their
opportunities does not automatically show that they do not
have the opportunities.

Some might point to her lack of motivation as evidence
of environmental factors that would count directly against
the presence of opportunity. For example, the Liberal
might claim her lack of motivation to be evidence of the
existence of deterrents, such as lack of privacy, lack
of encouragement, scoffing, etc., perhaps grouped together
as family background. One sort of evidence of the
efficacy of something is the identification of the chain
of events through which it operated. Lack of motivation
could be one element in the chain. But being evidence for
a state, s, does not make something constitutive of s.

Although traits and abilities are not constitutive of
having or having an opportunity, the absence of some
ability might make it pointless to talk about a person's

opportunities. For example, it would be pointless,
perhaps a cruel joke, to say of Clyde (IQ 70) that he has
an opportunity to learn engineering.

The distinction between environmental and personal
factors is very important in discussions of equality of
educational opportunity. In Jill's case the deterrent
alleged by the Conservative (lack of motivation) is a
personal factor; personal factors are not constitutive of
having (or not having) an opportunity. Those alleged by
the Liberal are environmental factors; environmental
factors are constitutive of having (or not having) an
opportunity. More generally when there is an issue, the
issue is usually one of determining the environmental
facilitators of and deterrents to x's doing z. Roughly
speaking the presence of an environmental facilitator
augments and the presence of an environmental deterrent
diminishes, the amount of opportunity that x has to do z.
How then do we determine what are (or were) the facilitators and deterrents to someone's doing z?

For the sake of brevity I shall look in some detail at
the determination of deterrents only. In our current
milieu, there is considerable expressed interest in
deterrents, so I pick them. However, the upcoming
discussion could be extended in parallel ways to facilitators.

PRESENCE AND ABSENCE

Conceptually, deterrents can be either the presence of
something or the absence of something. The fence was a
presence-type deterrent. Lack of money and lack of
private study space, if they were deterrents, consisted of
the absence of something. Although Liberals and Conservatives will disagree about whether those two absence
factors were deterrents to Jill's learning engineering,
presumably everyone would agree that there can be absences
that are deterrents. For example, the absence of food
can be a deterrent to someone's learning engineering.
A mother's lack of sympathy can be a deterrent to a
child's emotional development. And many would hold that
the absence of a public school system in Prince Edward
County, Virginia, in the early 1960s, was a deterrent to
the education of many children. The absence of a
facilitator that should exist is a deterrent.

Descriptions of presences and absences can be at least
roughly converted into opposite-type descriptions though
the conversion is often awkward. 'Lack of food' can be
roughly converted into 'presence of food deprivation,'

'lack of sympathy' into 'presence of non-sympathy,' and
'presence of a fence' into 'lack of unblocked space.'
For our purposes it does not especially matter whether
presence or absence formulations for deterrents are used.
It is largely a matter of convenience and linguistic
habits. The main point is that a factor should not be
ruled out as a deterrent simply because its formulation
is of one sort or another.

DETERRENTS, CAUSES, MAKING A DIFFERENCE, RESPONSIBILITY

Since a deterrent is one kind of cause - the kind that
holds back or prevents something - I shall apply with
appropriate modifications an analysis of specific causal
statements for which I have elsewhere argued (Ennis,
1973). Following this analysis (4) there are two
decisions to make in determining that a factor is a deterrent: 1, Determining that the elimination of the factor,
other things remaining the same, would have made x's doing
z more likely. (It could not be a deterrent unless it
made a difference. (5)) There are many factors that can
satisfy this criterion. When we look at any occurrence
or state of affairs, we can see that a very large number
of things could have made a difference. For example, if
Jill had been offered 50,000 dollars per year plus free
tuition, room and board to learn engineering, she probably
would have done so. Hence the absence of such an offer
satisfies the first criterion. (The elimination of the
absence would have made her learning engineering more
likely.) It gives a necessary, but not sufficient,
condition for something being a deterrent. A second
decision, involving a responsibility judgment, is needed:
2, Selecting from those factors that satisfy Criterion 1
the one (or ones) to deem responsible (or in part responsible) for the lessened likelihood of x's doing z.

Most of us would not want to deem the absence of the
annual-payment-plus-tuition-room-and-board responsible
for Jill's not learning engineering. That explains why
we would not judge the absence to be a deterrent to her
going to engineering school. But other candidates are
more controversial.

Suppose the Liberal and Conservative to be in agreement
on the empirical point that if Jill had decided to try to
learn engineering, it would have been likely that she
would have done so. For them, then, Criterion 1 would
have been satisfied for establishing absence-of-a-
decision-to-try as a deterrent. Suppose them also to be
in agreement that having given Jack's family background

to Jill (instead of hers) would also have made it likely
that whe would have gone on to engineering school and
learned engineering. So for them Criterion 1 would have
been satisfied for another factor, Jill's family background.

But they part company on Criterion 2. The Conservative
might deem the lack of motivation responsible, and thus
conclude that it was the deterrent to her learning
engineering. Since this alleged deterrent would be a
personal factor, its existence would not count as
diminishing the amount of opportunity that Jill had.

The Liberal, on the other hand, does not deem the lack
of motivation responsible, and thus for the Liberal this
lack was not the (or a) deterrent. The Liberal deems
her family background responsible, which for the Liberal
then satisfies Criterion 2, and was the deterrent. Since
family background is an environmental factor, its being
a deterrent would count as a reduction of Jill's opportunity. Now we are beginning to see how the Liberal and
Conservative can disagree, even when given the same
empirical facts. In principle at least, disputes about
the satisfaction of Criterion 1 can be settled by
scientific investigation. But how are disputes about
Criterion 2, the responsibility criterion, to be
settled? There are empirical and value elements.

The empirical element is the determination of the other
consequences of a change in any factor that satisfies
Criterion 1. For example, what would be the other consequences of intervention focused on Jill's family background? We need to know these consequences in order to
evaluate the intervention. We need this evaluation
(which introduces the value element) in order to determine
responsibility. That is, we deem responsible the thing
(or event, or state of affairs) that we think should have
been the focus of change, if the result in question were
to have been avoided. And we decide what should have been
the focus of change on the basis of costs and benefits,
using empirical and value beliefs and assumptions to
decide what are costs and benefits, and to what extent
they are so. Thus values play a significant role in
deciding what was a deterrent.

The Liberal picks family background as the (or a)
deterrent to Jill's learning engineering, because the
Liberal feels that the best way to have avoided Jill's
non-learning (or a good way to have helped avoid it) was
by altering the functioning of her family background.
The costs of so doing (greater taxes, interference with
the family, etc.) are acceptable to the Liberal, who thus
has picked an environmental factor, one that would count
against Jill's having had full opportunity.

The Conservative picks Jill's lack of motivation as the deterrent, feeling that a change in her motivation was the best way to have avoided her non-learning of engineering. And that was up to her, this Conservative thinks, though we might have given her some help by pointing out the (alleged) advantages of going on to college. The frequently presented chart depicting expected life-time earnings for people of different levels of education is what the Conservative might offer, plus a good commencement address and other exhortation. But to reach into her background would involve costs unacceptable to the Conservative (greater taxes, interference with the family, etc.); her background would thus not be an appropriate focus of change, would not be responsible, would not be a deterrent, and thus for the Conservative would not be relevant to opportunity judgments.

I do not propose here to suggest how to settle the empirical and value questions raised in deciding whether someone has an opportunity. Presumably we each already have ways of settling such empirical and value questions (though many, including me, are not completely happy with our methods). The contribution I am trying here to make is to show how to locate and separate these issues.

THE GENERAL APPROACH

The location and separation of the issues in the Jill and Jack case is fairly typical. Assuming some set of goals of education for a pair of people, we decide that the two have equal educational opportunity just in case the environmental facilitators minus deterrents for one balance the environmental facilitators minus deterrents for the other.

The balancing of factors is not a matter for which we have precise techniques, though we do generally manage with our imprecise methods. Perhaps it would be desirable to develop precise techniques, perhaps not. Current cost-benefit analysis strategies leave me pessimistic.

The approach is the same in the Alpha and Running Deer case. In contrasting minority groups and the majority group, in addition to the controversy over aims of educa-tion that can result in disagreements about the presence of equality of educational opportunity, there is the con-troversy about the value judgments used in judging the best way to have avoided (if we had wanted to) what would otherwise occur (or has occurred), a controversy that must be faced in making judgments about opportunity. Assuming an academic goal, settling this case requires (in addition

to the empirical judgments) value judgments which are
no doubt embedded in broad value positions dealing with
the desirability of paying more tax money for the education of lower-class children and of minority children
than for white middle-class children, etc. I have illustrated this general picture with an example of an American
Indian, but the picture fits representatives of any
minority group.

DIFFERENCES IN GENETICALLY DETERMINED NATURAL ABILITY

The approach for Case C, in which fraternal twins, Bonnie
and Clyde, differ in their mental endowment, also follows
the guidelines suggested. We consider what would constitute an appropriate education for each. If an academic
education is deemed appropriate for Bonnie, while training
in basic unskilled job-holding skills together with
aesthetic and social development is deemed appropriate for
Clyde, then their not ending up with comparable academic
competence would be irrelevant to a judgment about equality of educational opportunity. What would be relevant
would be the balance of the environmental facilitators
and deterrents to their achieving the appropriate goals.
They are balanced just in case Bonnie's environmental
facilitators minus deterrents equal Clyde's environmental
facilitators minus deterrents. If there is an unbalance,
then the opportunity judger should deem the opportunities
to be unequal.
     To be more specific, with me serving as the opportunity
judger for the real case I know (there are significant
differences from one real case to the next), I judge them
to have equality of educational opportunity for the
following reasons:
     1 I believe academic education to be appropriate for
Bonnie and rudimentary vocational training plus aesthetic
and social cultivation for Clyde. Hence inequality of
academic results is irrelevant.
     2 Special classes are provided for Clyde. The inter-
vention I recommend is thus occurring in a chain of events
that would otherwise have led to his failure to achieve
his goals. The facilitator is there, and I believe the
only significant deterrent to be junk television programs.
But these are not a strong-enough deterrent for me to
judge that Clyde does not have an opportunity to achieve
the specified goals.
     3 Similarly, an academic curriculum for Bonnie is
provided and it is adequate. Thus a facilitator is there
and the same deterrent, junk television, is also present.

I judge that Bonnie does have an opportunity to achieve academic goals.

4   Now why are their educational opportunities equal? It is impossible for me (or anyone) to describe the rich complexity of the situation in sufficient detail to provide full justification. But it does seem that overall the environmental factors that facilitate and deter do balance out.

So far in the Bonnie and Clyde case I have assumed different educational goals for each. Suppose on the other hand that we judge that an (appropriate) education for each would be an academic education. On that assumption (one that I would not make), if the only thing I judge to be deterring Clyde (in addition to the things deterring Bonnie) is his low mental ability, then (since that is personal) I judge them to have equal opportunity. What I would be doing in making such a judgment is saying that his mental prowess is the appropriate focus of interference, if we could and if we wanted to so interfere.

If, in addition, I judged lack of additional compensatory facilities for Clyde to be a deterrent, then I would judge Bonnie to have greater educational opportunity. This judgment incorporates the judgment that an appropriate focus of change in the chain of events is in the lack of compensatory facilities and that the costs of such change are acceptable. Actually I do not make such a judgment, because I think additional compensatory facilities would make no difference, an empirical judgment.

My consideration of this and previous cases is oversimplified, because we do in fact take more factors into account than I have indicated. Even with the oversimplification the account may at first appear complicated, but the proposed depiction of our conceptual structure does account for what we do, it accounts for our occasionally believing other people to be irrational for not agreeing with us, and it accounts for the disagreements that so trouble us beneath the veneer of agreement.

PROSPECTIVE RETROSPECTION

So far my emphasis has been on judgments about whether there is equality of educational opportunity between two people at some particular point in time. This is the basic conceptual case from which results can be extended to questions of greater political interest. Earlier I mentioned extension to groups. Another useful extension is to a total period of development from birth to maturity or beyond. Our interest in justice warrants concern about whether there was equal educational opportunity over the growth periods of the parties concerned. We are not merely interested in whether, given the parties' motivation, knowledge, and ability at some advanced point in their development, they have equal opportunity for an education.

This long-range interest for mature parties is retrospective: Did they have equal educational opportunity? For unborn and immature parties it is prospectively retrospective: Will they, when mature (or beyond), have had equal educational opportunity? Answers to this question follow the general outline developed earlier: a decision about what constitutes a good education is required; and the environmental facilitators and deterrents over the years must be balanced. Part of the determination of the facilitators and the deterrents over the years is empirical; the other part is evaluative, involving value judgments. Given that the empirical question (about what will and would have made a difference over the years and at what consequence) has been answered, the ascription of responsibility to certain of these factors (and thus their selection as facilitators and deterrents) requires value judgments. The value judgments are involved in deciding what costs and benefits are acceptable, the costs and benefits being those involved in changing the functioning of factors that over the years will and would have made a difference. Environmental deterrents and external facilitators thus selected are then balanced off to make equality-of-opportunity judgments.

GOING ALL THE WAY

Some writers (e.g. Myron Lieberman, 1961, p.142; R.S. Peters, 1966, p.140; James Coleman, 1968, pp.21-2; and Thomas Green, 1971, p.137) have avoided endorsement of full equality of educational opportunity, because they apparently believed that this ideal implies control of too many things, including 'early upbringing, size of families, and breeding,' as Peters put it. They need not have felt so restrained. One can consistently endorse full equality of educational opportunity without being committed to control of such things, for there are other possibilities.

1 One is to pick motivation as the responsible factor when people with backgrounds that make a difference do not generally achieve up to the level of people with other backgrounds. This is a Conservative response. All they (the lesser achievers) had to do was make up their minds

and be steadfast. The Conservative much prefers this
cost to the individual over the cost in terms of freedom,
family, taxes, and bureaucratic frustration, which results
from interference with early upbringing, size of families,
and breeding. This response in terms of value judgments
does assume that people have some freedom of choice,
even given their early upbringing, the size of their
families, the breeding they do have, etc. This response
is not open to someone who denies the existence of free
choice, but I have found very few people who consistently
do that.

2 A second alternative is to locate other environmental factors that also would make a difference. For
example some kind of compensatory education including
very small classes, special attention, and scholarships
might well also make a difference - just as much difference as early upbringing and family size (breeding makes
a special problem here that I shall look at soon), and
that is an empirical question which certianly has not yet
been conclusively resolved. The value question is whether
we should tax heavily enough to make such things available
to the poor - perhaps leaving as is the treatment of folks
who are better off. One could well decide that the costs
of this kind of intervention (taxes, challenges of unfair-
ness to the better-off, etc.) are far more bearable than
the costs of interference with early upbringing and family
size. If one so decided, then one might conclude that
full equality of opportunity would be achieved by introducing those changes, because they would bring about a
balance of environmental facilitators and deterrents for
the parties of concern. The intervention would provide
greater opportunity to the recipients, bringing them up to
equality without 'going all the way,' given the above
empirical and value assumptions, assumptions that many
reasonable people are willing to make.

With respect to the 'breeding' suggestion presumably
this means that various selective genetic practices
would be needed in order to achieve full equality of
educational opportunity. An initial problem with this
suggestion is that people who otherwise would not have
had equal opportunity are simply avoided. They do not
come into existence. Who then benefits from this equal-
izing? But leaving that aside, selective genetic practices, because of their costs in human intimacy, dignity
and freedom, might be judged to be completely unacceptable; thus the absence of genetic practices, since there
is an alternative candidate for responsibility, could
reasonably be deemed not responsible and they would thus
not be judged a deterrent. The selected deterrent might

instead be mental incapacity, which being personal, does not count against the existence of opportunity. This could be selected even though we know of no way to get rid of it (other than breeding). In selecting mental incapacity as the deterrent to success of some person, we have picked a focus for interference if it were possible. It need not be possible, given our technology. (6)

Thus one is not committed to the endorsement of extreme measures by a full endorsement of equality of educational opportunity. The nature of the commitment varies in accord with the conception of education being assumed, the empirical relationship that obtains, and the assumed value judgments about human dignity, the good life, freedom, etc., on one level, and taxes, bureaucracy, daily toil, economic wealth, ecological wealth, etc., on another level.

COLEMAN'S PROBLEM

In response to a request from the Congress of the United States, James Coleman organized and supervised a study that was published under the title, 'Equality of Educational Opportunity' (Coleman et al., 1966). This study has received wide notice and its data and conclusions have since been subjected to much scrutiny. In requesting the study, Congress asked 'the Commissioner of Education to assess the "lack of equality of educational opportunity" among racial and other groups in the United States' (Coleman, 1968, p.16). The problem Coleman faced, as the person appointed by the Commissioner to perform the study, was that he was given a concept, but virtually no conception.

From the many views about the aims of education, and a variety of values impinging on judgments, Coleman was in effect asked to pick a set and report about the degree of satisfaction of the resulting conception. Thus, Congress gave Coleman an insufficiently specified task. At the commencement of his study, he responded by coming up with a list of five at-least-partial operationalized conceptions of equality of educational opportunity, one of which he appears to have favored: equality of results, given the same background and ability (Coleman, 1968, p.17). In selecting which results to examine he had to bring to bear a conception of education. He picked an academic conception and argued for it (Coleman et al., 1966, p.218): 'The facts of life in modern society are that the intellectual skills, which involve reading, writing, calculation, analysis of information, are

becoming basic requirements for independence, for productive work, for political participation, for wise
consumption.' I am not meaning to quarrel with Coleman's
argument, though many people would do so - especially
since Coleman operationalized intellectual skills with
'a vocabulary test ... [as] the criterion of achievement
used throughout most of the examination of school effects'
(p.292). Rather I offer it as evidence that Coleman had
to make value judgments concerning a conception of
education (which he sought to defend) in order to conduct
his scientific study. That he felt obligated to defend
his value judgment suggests that Coleman was aware that
he was making one. And the United States Congress did not
tell this scientist which value judgment to assume.

In seeking factors that were relevant to opportunity,
Coleman received one piece of value guidance in that one
factor seemed to be suggested to him by the law (Section
402 of the Civil Rights Act of 1964), Commissioner Howe's
letter of transmittal(€oleman et al., 1966, p.iii), and
the tenor of the times: racial isolation. The implicit
judgment was that this factor, if it turned out to make
a difference, was to be deemed responsible - an appropriate focus of change.

So far as I can see, little or no other guidance was
provided for this scientist. What he apparently did was
to select factors for study, changes in which he thought
1, would not violate some set of values (at least mostly
his), and 2, might make a difference, or be thought by
someone to make a difference. He then did an empirical
study of these factors in an attempt to see which ones
did make a difference.

To the extent that Coleman operated in accord with the
operationalized conception, equality of results given the
same background and ability, he was resolved in advance
to ignore (as constitutive of opportunity) facilitators
and deterrents from a person's background (ability being
already ruled out by the concept, opportunity). To ignore
background factors is a conservative stance. Roughly
speaking, it is in effect to say that the background
factors are not recommended intervention points. Perhaps
Coleman would not really care to endorse this conception,
given his other views.

To attempt, from the point of view I have developed,
a detailed discussion here of Coleman's operationalized
conceptions of opportunity, and the details of his pursuit of the problem would make this paper too long. So
I shall leave this tempting enterprise to another time
and place, and invite others to join in, for there is
much to be learned - positively and negatively - from

Coleman's work. The point that I do want to make here is
that, as a scientist, Coleman was put in a difficult
position, having been given a concept without, save one
part, a conception.

SUMMARY

Although most people I know are in favor of equality of
educational opportunity, there is much disagreement among
them about how to implement this goal. To explain this
phenomenon I have offered an analysis of the concept
'equality of educational opportunity' which locates the
problem not in our concept of equality, but rather in our
conceptions of education and of having an opportunity.
Determination of these two conceptions requires the making
of value judgments; that this is generally so for a conception of education is fairly obvious, but that it is so
for a conception of having an opportunity is not so easy
to see. Judgments about opportunity, I suggested, are
in part responsibility judgments, which are dependent on
empirical-fact judgments about what environmental changes
would have made a difference and what the consequences of
such changes would have been, and on judgments about the
appropriate focus for change. The latter judgments, since
they are about appropriateness, incorporate value judgments.
    If the approach is correct, then we know better where
to focus our attention in the disputes about whether
equality of educational opportunity exists: on the determination of a conception of education, on the empirical
determination of what would have made a difference and
the consequences thereof, and on the determination of
appropriate foci of change. All these judgments are very
difficult to make and justify, but at least we can know
what we are about - and we can abandon fumbling efforts
to arrive at a definition of equality of educational
opportunity, efforts that in my experience have often led
to confusion and people's talking past one another.
    Second if the approach is correct, then endorsers of
equality of educational opportunity need not feel guilty
about not going all the way - for example, about not
endorsing interference with 'early upbringing, size of
families, and breeding.' They might instead judge these
factors to be inappropriate change areas, and thus not
to be deterrents to opportunity.
    Last, a legislative body (like the Congress of the
United States) that seeks from a scientist (like James
Coleman) a study of the extent of equality of educational

opportunity within its domain owes that scientist some
guidance, if the scientist is not to assume a legislative
function. It owes an indication of aims (or sets of aims)
of education, the opportunity to achieve which it is
interested in; and it owes an indication of criteria for
judging possible avenues of change. To the extent that
these are not supplied, a legislative body turns over its
legislative functions to the scientist.

For this paper I have tried to paint a broad picture
of equality of educational opportunity, and have left
many topics and problems unexamined or only mentioned.
It is the beginning rather than the end of a series of
related investigations. I invite others to join in the
effort.

NOTES

Cultivation of the thesis and argument of this paper was
helped by the comments of Darrell Cauley, Norman Care,
Hugh Chandler, Ann Diller, Helen Ennis, Robert Halstead,
Bruce Haynes, Robert Holmes, Michael Johnson, Adele
Laslie, Robert Nomk, Ralph Page, Hugh Petrie, Susan
Purcell, Martin Schiralli, Kenneth Strike, Ronald Szoke,
and Donald Tunnell.

1 In my 'Logic in Teaching' (1969) I have considered
   the problems involved in trying to settle disputes
   about definition (though in a teaching context). I
   think that the approach of the current paper constitutes a further development of the programmatic
   definition theory offered there, which had its roots
   in Scheffler's 'The Language of Education' (1960,
   pp.22-7) and Stevenson's 'Ethics and Language' (1944,
   pp.206-26).
2 Incidentally this case shows the incorrectness of the
   Komisar's and Coombs's (1964) view that in educational
   opportunity contexts 'equality' means fitting. The
   Earl of Hertford might consistently judge there to be
   a fitting inequality between Tom and Edward. C.J.B.
   Macmillan (1964-5) has discussed this problem.
3 The Biological Science Curriculum Study (BSCS) has
   captured the personal-environmental distinction in
   the title of a curriculum it has developed: Me and
   My Environment. Ralph Page has called my attention
   to the fact that this distinction is employed by,
   among others, Joel Feinberg (1973) and David A.J.
   Richards (1973). As I did in early drafts of the
   present paper, they use the language, 'internal-
   external' instead of 'personal-environmental.'

I abandoned the 'internal-external' language only
because so many people found it confusing; I think
that either pair of terms is acceptable.

Richards employs the distinction in the opportunity
context as I have, claiming that 'it is not normally
proper to speak of the internal capacities of A that
enable him to do x as being opportunities to do x'
(p.41).

4   Slightly refined since then: to say that a caused b
is to say that 1, given the other conditions, a was
sufficient for b, and 2, that a was responsible for
b; this second condition implies that the best place
(or if b was overdetermined one of the best places)
to have interfered with the production of b, if one
had wanted to and been able to, was in the functioning of a (that is, either with a or the chain between
a and b). This is not a reductive analysis, but I
feel it is enlightening.

5   Unless the non-doing of z was overdetermined. In
this paper I shall consider only results that are
not overdetermined. Adjustments could be made to
allow for overdetermined results, but for the sake
of simplicity of presentation of a matter that is
complicated anyway, I shall not make these adjustments here.

6   The recommendation implied in a responsibility
ascription, as indicated in note 5, is a qualified
one. It might simply indicate the least offensive
focus of change, and it does not guarantee that we
have the technology or resources available.

BIBLIOGRAPHY

COLEMAN, JAMES S. (1968), The Concept of Equality of
Educational Opportunity, 'Harvard Educational Review,'
vol.38, no.1, pp.7-22
COLEMAN, JAMES S. et al. (1966), 'Equality of Educational
Opportunity,' Washington DC: U.S. Government Printing
Office.
ENNIS, ROBERT H. (1969), 'Logic in Teaching,' Englewood
Cliffs, N.J: Prentice-Hall.
ENNIS, ROBERT H. (1973), The Responsibility of a Cause, in
Brian C. Crittenden (ed.), 'Philosophy of Education 1973,'
Studies in Philosophy and Education, Edwardsville,
Illinois, pp.86-93.
FEINBERG, JOEL (1973), 'Social Philosophy,' Englewood
Cliffs, NJ: Prentice-Hall.
GREEN, THOMAS F. (1971), Equal Educational Opportunity:

The Durable Injustice, in Robert D. Heslep (ed.) 'Philosophy of Education 1971,' Studies in Philosophy and Education, Edwardsville, Illinois, pp.121-43.

HEMPEL, CARL G. (1952), Fundamentals of Concept Formation in Empirical Science, 'International Encyclopedia of Unified Science,' Foundations of the Unity of Science, vol.II, no.7, University of Chicago Press.

KOMISAR, B. PAUL and JERROLD R. COOMBS (1964), The Concept of Equality in Education, 'Studies in Philosophy and Education,' vol.III, no.3, pp.223-44.

LIEBERMAN, MYRON (1961), Equality of Educational Opportunity, in B. Othane Smith and Robert H. Ennis, (eds), 'Language and Concepts in Education,' Chicago: Rand McNally, pp.127-43.

MACMILLAN, C.J.B. (1964-5), Equality and Sameness, 'Studies in Philosophy and Education,' vol.III, no.4, pp.320-32.

PETERS, R.S. (1966), 'Ethics and Education,' London: Allen & Unwin.

RAWLS, JOHN (1971), 'A Theory of Justice,' Cambridge: Belknap Press.

RICHARDS, DAVID A.J. (1973), Equal Opportunity and School Financing: Towards a Moral Theory of Constitutional Adjudication, 'The University of Chicago Law Review,' vol.XLI, no.1, pp.32-71.

SCHEFFLER, ISRAEL (1960), 'The Language of Education,' Springfield, Illinois: Charles C. Thomas.

SCRIVEN, MICHAEL (1966), Causes, Connections and Conditions in History, in William Dray (ed.), 'Philosophical Analysis and History,' New York: Harper & Row, pp.238-64.

STEVENSON, CHARLES L. (1944), 'Ethics and Language,' New Haven: Yale University Press.

Technology and work

Technology and educational values

10

H.S. Broudy

It is almost a cliché that modern technology is a plethora
of mechanical gadgets that serve as mindless, value-free
instruments for whatever ends their owners prescribe.
Yet when so regarded, the relation of technology to value
is highly and perhaps mischievously oversimplified.

For one thing, one can speak meaningfully of better
and worse technology, apart from its instrumentality.
Ingenuity, sophistication, and even a certain aesthetic
elegance can be attributed to technology. Furthermore,
the degree to which a technology is science-based,
genuinely a logos of technique, also serves an intrinsic
criterion, e.g. witch doctors use a less rationalized
technology than does modern medicine.

In the second place, technology is more than a means
to value attainment. Obviously, it can enlarge whatever
values are incidental to the production of goods and
services. What is not so obvious but nonetheless the case
is that technology can affect the domains of intellectual,
aesthetic, and moral values as well. New technology - in
microscopy, holography, carbon dating, to name a very
few - has certainly enlarged the compass of scholarship.
New technologies of photography, plastics, lighting, and
construction have expanded aesthetic possibility. Least
obvious is the change in the moral domain that technology
has or could bring about.

Insofar as technology increases control over experience
it transforms the human condition morally, for with
increase of control arises the possibility of moral
obligation to exercise or to refrain from exercising that
control. Moses or Socrates could deplore disease and
poverty, but morally about all they could do was to behave
so as not to deserve either. Technology has deprived us
of the luxury of moral indifference to these evils. Even
the common man can, and therefore perhaps should, do
something about them.

The relation of technology to educational values is
likewise complex and often ambiguous. Question of fact
are intermingled with problems of value; of efficiency
with those of propriety; of principle with issues of
practicability. Sorting out the various components of
these relationships does not of itself solve the problems
of relating the school to them. Nevertheless, educators
cannot evade the pressure to technologize instruction
nor postpone taking a stance toward it, and for them
clarification of the issues could be useful.

The relation of technology to education is not ex-
hausted by these issues. There is also the impact on
education of the effects of technology on the ethos of a
society and on the consciousness of its members. This
latter factor raises questions that are only indirectly
related to the methodology of teaching or theories about
the teaching-learning transaction. What, for example, is
the individual to study if he is to live in a society
in which making up one's own mind, earning one's own
living, developing one's own personality are made almost
impossible by the complex net of interdependence? What
would one have to know in order to exercise democratic
citizenship in such a society? What does moral integrity
mean in a society in which it is virtually impossible to
fix the responsibility for anything on an individual
agent? Technology, insofar as it imposes large-scale
mass production methods on every walk of life, deperson-
alizes and demoralizes them. Is there any sense in which
it also repersonalizes and remoralizes life? What is the
face of the human condition in a modern technological
culture? By what images is it perceived and by what
categories is it to be interpreted?

The discussion of technology and educational values,
therefore, can be directed toward the challenges to
schools and schooling and/or toward the broader impact of
a technological way of life on the tasks of education.
To a considerable extent they are separable issues, but
one is reluctant to leave out either for two reasons:
first, the methodological issue is immediate and pressing,
and no less so is the passionate resentment of many
articulate citizens against the effects of technology on
the quality of life. Second, the two areas of concern
with technology are linked by a metaphysical - or at
least a philosophical - question: Is man no more than a
machine? Is he, for that matter, a machine at all? This
paper, however, will be devoted to the impact of a technological society on the humanistic consciousness and an
education consonant with it.

THE CHALLENGE OF TECHNOLOGY TO HUMANISM

Much could be said about the accomplishments, prospects,
and danger of technology. Research, one hopes, will give
definitive answers to some of the questions about effectiveness. Economic developments, the stance of teacher
organizations, changes in the tax structure, shifts in
patterns of occupational mobility, and the increase of
dual-salary households are other factors that will determine the role of technology in instruction and the
organization of the school system. (1)
    Important as these questions are, even definitive
answers to them do not settle the more fundamental
questions that a highly developed technological society
poses to its institutions and individual citizens. Can
men live in a technological society without becoming
mechanized, manipulated by mechanisms, thingified, and
robotized? Can the aspirational, aesthetic, and moral
dimensions of experience survive under the demands for
efficient and profitable mass production? Can the belief
that these aspects of life are real be maintained? Is
education in nurturing these aspects of experience as if
they were real perpetuating a myth?
    Or to put the questions differently: Do the techniques
of mass production make it necessary to redefine virtue,
freedom, individuality, personhood, responsibility, duty,
and the other categories thought to be relevant to moral
experience? Or are the meanings these notions acquired
in a pretechnological society still valid? What, for
example, is moral responsibility to mean if interdependence makes it almost impossible to assign responsibility for anything to anybody? What is freedom to mean,
if, as B.F. Skinner argues, we ought to get 'Beyond
Freedom and Dignity'?
    There is a rich literature, including that of the
counter-culturists of recent times, that seems to argue
that technology must be limited, controlled, and perhaps
even abandoned if the human or humanistic consciousness
is to survive. (2)
    Much of this literature stresses the need to preserve
the natural environment against the depredations of
industrial pollution associated with technology. Some of
it centers upon the problem of remaining sane in what
seems to be an insane world; some, like R.D. Laing, argue
that sanity is itself a conventional attitude fostered
by those in power that defines socially sanctioned
behavior. (3)
    I shall not recount this literature, nor will I try to
show that for every cloud technology emits, it also

fashions a silver lining. The crucial point for the
relation of technology to the human enterprise is whether
it permits us to take the moral point of view at all, and
if it does, whether it entails a wholly new morality or
new view of human nature or the same morality and the same
human nature expressed in new behavioral forms.

To a participant in a modern technologically mature
society/culture, two of its salient effects on consciousness are anonymity and impotence. The first is so
familiar that only a few examples need be cited. Products
one buys are not traceable to any particular workman.
The processes are too intricate and complex, for one
thing, and the workers are interchangeable, for another.
Some items are identified by brand names, but it is no
easier to trace a particular General Motors automobile
to a particular worker than it is to trace an unmarked
box of soap powder. As a consumer and citizen, one
receives anonymous products from the factory, the press,
the legislatures, and inscrutable economic forces.
Workers see their contributions disappear in collective
products and processes. (4)   Intricacy and interchange-
ability - the outstanding characteristics of mass production - yield depersonalization as their sum. To treat
these and kindred phenomena in personal terms is regarded
as immature - an exercise in outmoded animism.

With anonymity comes a sense of impotence. Whatever
the enterprise, individuals feel powerless to affect or
evade the result. The collective is too massive for the
individual to attack, and individuals on whom an attack
might be effective cannot be identified. Impotence yields
a fear of dependence on others; one feels that nobody can
or will help anybody. The response to this may be despair,
resignation, or a defiant determination 'to care' anyhow -
witness the ideology of love in the communes of the late
1960s and early 1970s. One cannot laugh at such defiance,
but what attitude toward it is proper is hard to say.

The frustrations imposed by dependence lead to attempts
to achieve self-sufficiency by a reduction of need. But
reduction of need can also be a reduction of life.
Security is purchased at the cost of richness. When self-
sufficiency, and fullness of life are sought by erecting
wealth and status as defenses against the vagaries of
fortune and the indifference of men, one discovers that
the potentialities of misfortune and misadventure are
beyond calculation. A technological society expands the
volume of contingencies exponentially, and thus randomizes
the incidence of both good and evil.

The fear of dependence plus the randomizing of evil
(and good) induces a hostile, suspicious wariness of life.

It becomes imperative to protect oneself against want, sickness, fire, flood, wind, earthquake; against vandals, thieves, muggers; against crooks, swindlers, manipulators - and the very bureaucracy established to defend us. More and more insurance policies are bought to protect oneself from the consequences of evil as its incidence becomes more and more unpredictable.

Impotence plus depersonalization leads to demoralization or the renunciation of responsibility as relevant to life, since only efficacious agents (persons) are morally responsible. This melancholy conclusion is traumatic to those who are steeped in the ideology of the work-individual agency-responsibility ethic and who persist in interpreting their world in these terms. For succeeding generations, we are warned by George Orwell and others, the trauma will be replaced by a robotized, collectivized, rationalized, and hedonized harmony with the world of technology.

Is this the inevitable consequence of technology for human consciousness? I shall argue that it is not, first by trying to show that consciousness oscillates around certain modes or within parameters that remain constant: the characteristic virtues, the dramatic tensions of personality, and the integrity of the self. In the second place, it will be argued that these characteristics of the humanistic consciousness can be achieved, albeit only under certain conditions, in a technological society.

RESPONSIBILITY AND CAUSAL EFFICACY

The search for responsible agents in a technological society is frustrated by disclaimers of responsibility on the grounds that the cause of the action lies outside of the agent. Colloquially, this is known as passing the buck, which more often than not ends by blaming the system as a whole, thus exculpating any agent within it. If, on the other hand, we refuse to accept the disclaimers and insist that a given event was caused by a particular agent who is to be held responsible for it, then it is important that the parties agree on the boundaries of the causal sequence to be judged. Thus during the student riots in the late 1960s, the answer to the question Who started it? depended on where the starting point was to be fixed. The 'event' could have begun when the first stone was heaved through a window in the administration building or at the moment the police arrived or when bombs fell on Vietnam.

The difference in temporal segments chosen for judgment is especially prominent in controversies about the responsibility for wars, economic depressions, ecological disasters. Each party insists that, if only the segment were broadened or narrowed, the responsibility would fall elsewhere, i.e. the cause would be located outside of himself or his agency, his nation. (5)

Another aspect of the problem is illustrated by the attempt to allot responsibility to various social institutions or professions for certain functions. For example, if an engineer or the engineering profession argues that engineers are responsible only for that segment of the action that has to do with finding a suitable technology to achieve an end assigned to it, then it can refuse to take responsibility for any social damage the technology may entrain. Lawyers, physicians, architects, and all manner of businessmen and bureaucrats can and do insist that theirs is a specialized activity with responsibility limited to approved procedure, legal rules, etc. On these grounds the responsibility for the total act cannot be fixed; the individual segmental responsibilities never quite add up to it. The only recourse is to allot total responsibility to government, a responsibility that is accepted more in form than in substance.

Thus when ecological concerns were pressed upon engineers, they disclaimed responsibility for them, as did industry, contending that only the government or the people could make policy decisions that would take in all facets of the common welfare. For its part, the government, claiming the right to legislate for the common good, assumed the responsibility formally. Substantively, legislators pleaded that their decisions were determined by their particular constituencies, and these spoke with many voices. They could only weigh the relative strengths of their constituencies and arrive at some kind of tolerable compromise between the automobile culture and pollution; between energy needs and the preservation of the environment, the need to stop inflation and the need to maintain a high level of employment.

So in the last analysis it would seem as if responsibility ultimately has to be placed on the voters who make up the majority on a given issue. But in what sense can the conglomerate of judgments of thousands of voters be regarded as a moral agent? Some of them are only partially informed of the issues; some are motivated by interests other than those of the common good, and some are voting the party line without thinking about the issues at all. This hardly conforms to the image of the individual agent taking the moral point of view and making a commitment after moral reflection.

Yet the pressures of events and of new political constituencies (environmental, consumer, minority) are
stretching the boundaries of responsibility that social
institutions and the professions have drawn for themselves. Engineers are expected to calculate the environmental impact of projects, and lawyers will be forced to
take into account the social justice of legal rules when
minorities are strong enough to challenge them. But
inasmuch as a technological society lives by the division
of highly specialized labor, the expansion of responsibility will be slow. The pace will be slowed even further
by the fact that it takes a new generation of practitioners within a guild (lawyers, doctors, etc.) to
acquiesce in such expansion. This is understandable
because the more fuzzy the outlines of the guild function
become, the more difficult it is to define the rules of
entry into and exclusion from the guild, and the control
of these rules is important to the guild. (6)

The slowness with which agreement on the limits of
social and moral responsibility is achieved in a technological society points to a hard alternative, viz. that
each individual citizen must be ready to act in a double
role: as a specialist vocationally, and a generalist
civically. This means shifting judgments between small
segments of the causal stream of events and larger segments (and perhaps very large ones, e.g. the future of
the nation or the human race). Broadly speaking, the
school does try to prepare the individual for this dual
role through general and vocational education, although
elementary and secondary schooling are largely generalist
in emphasis. Post-secondary schooling, on the contrary,
is under ever-increasing pressure to become explicitly
vocational, even in colleges of liberal arts and sciences.
The centrality of occupation in a technological society
makes the generalist role seem secondary, postponable,
and even irrelevant.

About the only help technology can give to the generalist as a citizen is the computer. The computer makes it
possible to analyze complex social problems by sorting
out and calculating the effects of many variables combined in various patterns. For example, one can formulate
alternative strategies for war on the basis of the ways
in which the enemy might react to a variety of circumstances. Or one might use it to estimate the effects of
different policies for meeting the energy crisis or
spending large sums of money on the relief of the poor.
So, in a way, technology provides one of the means to
cope with the very complexity it causes or, more
accurately, to understand more clearly the alternatives

among which we are called upon to choose. In this sense
it enables the individual to choose more responsibly.

A somewhat different approach to defining the locus
of moral responsibility abandons the attempt to apportion
praise or blame by identifying who did what, to whom,
when. It contends that, regardless of the segment of the
causal flow used to define the boundaries of the action
to be judged, it will contain events not caused or
intended by the agent and perhaps by any agent. These
elements contribute to every moral situation undetermined
amounts of undeserved good and evil to be accepted with
humility, a moral virtue that modulates and moderates our
moral judgments. (7) While humility can be and often is
construed in religious terms, it need not be. Justice,
the virtue that seems to be outraged by undeserved good
and evil, can be appeased by the probability that each
of us produces about as much undeserved good and evil as
he receives.

If the quest for causes of the present situation is
tempered with humility, the significant moral situation
begins with the now. The question What is my duty now?
thus becomes partly disengaged from the question Who
was the cause of the present situation? but not from the
consideration of the consequences my decision may have,
although humility should also govern how far into the
future our responsibility will extend.

Thus the student gunman should have refrained from
shooting the policeman even though, strictly speaking,
he was not responsible for the events that led up to the
shooting, for he is causing a death, which is wrong
legally and which may be the morally wrong thing to have
done even though the action was provoked by others.
Similarly, the engineer can be expected to act in a
morally justifiable way about a possible ecological disaster, even though he did not cause the events leading
up to it and his professional guild has absolved him from
their consequences. Regardless of our responsibility for
the past, responsibility for the future and consonance
with moral principles are always relevant issues. (8)

PARAMETERS OF HUMAN CONSCIOUSNESS

The flow of human thought and feeling can follow many
paths; its flexibility is almost limitless. Nevertheless,
human consciousness generates some constraints on itself,
and these constraints correspond in one way or another
to the demands of selfhood or personhood.

It is interesting to note how one kind of thinking will

be stopped by another. The kind of thinking I have in
mind consists of imagining or expecting a certain trend
or process to continue indefinitely. For example, the
search for causes can go on indefinitely and can only be
halted by saying there must be a beginning to the series
of causes, i.e. a First Cause, or it can be halted by
fatigue. Or one can think of dividing a line into parts
and these parts into parts, ad infinitum. The same sort
of iteration is exhibited when one thinks of interdependence leading to more interdependence, and this in
turn to even more. Or we imagine that depersonalization
will produce further depersonalization until presumably
there are no persons left, or one tires of trying to
imagine smaller and smaller bits of personality.

However, the human mind can interrupt this iterative
process so that it produces not more of the same but a
trend in the opposite direction. At some point in the
growth of interdependence the demand for independence is
created or augmented; after depersonalization has been
carried to a certain point, the restoration of personhood
becomes imperative. (9)

Virtues as limits

At what points does consciousness begin to resist trends
in given directions and set countervailing trends in
motion? One such set of limits or parameters are the
virtues, especially the moral virtues. Courage, temperance, wisdom, justice, honesty, truthfulness, generosity,
loyalty - there is no fixed list - in any culture denote
dispositions to act so that the action meets certain
formal requirements. Courage, for example, to qualify as
such must be a fairly reliable willingness to face danger
when it is judged reasonable to do so. Aristotle thought
that a proper estimate as to what ought to be feared
enters into the courageous act, and that for a given
person at a given time the act will be a mean between
cowardice and rashness. Temperance is the disposition to
modulate the passions, but especially the appetites by
rational considerations - a mean between unbridled indulg-
ence and indiscriminate self-denial. These and other
moral virtues define zones of humanness. Action or ideas
that fall outside the zones set up resistances to counter-
act them.

It is not being argued here that these dispositions are
deposited in the genes. Nor is it necessary to suppose
that Aristotle or anyone else discovered and named the
one set of virtues once and for all. I would want to

claim only that being human carries with it dispositions to act in accordance with the moral point of view (the moral virtues), and that these dispositions seem to transcend differences in cultures. It may be that these virtues serve as definitional limits of what is human, and indirectly as survival values, so that in time they become species characteristics. For example, if we ever encounter Martians, the crucial test of their humanness may not be intelligence or even physiological sensitivity, but rather an awareness of norms of conduct and an obligation to conform to them. If they acknowledge norms, albeit transgressing them from time to time, we shall call these Martians human. If they have renounced their obligation to these norms we would call them inhuman; if they had neither norms nor a sense of obligation, we would call them nonhuman.

Such a definitional gyroscope might serve the same stabilizing function as heredity, for presumably the definition would be used to impose sanctions against inhuman and the nonhuman behavior. If this conjecture is at all plausible, then despite the impacts of a technological society, human consciousness will demand that the virtuous life be possible and will strive to find ways to express it. If, for example, a society decreases the opportunity for the exercise of courage, men will find or imagine forms of behavior that will conform to the requirements of that virtue, and similarly for behavior that conforms to the formal demands of temperance, wisdom, justice, truthfulness, honesty, loyalty, etc. (10)

The technological society, for example, does not provide many opportunities for expressing courage in the forms familiar to the Spartan warrior or the Christian martyr. But we do have wars and even the possibility of a final war. How is courage to be expressed in modern wars? Was the evasion of the draft during the Vietnamese War cowardice or virtue? And what is the proper mean between cowardice and rashness with respect to the countless terrors of crime, violence, accident, and divers natural catastrophes? I suggest that the question is not whether courage is good, but rather whether a given act is really courageous. To ascertain a reasoned answer is the task of moral reflection.

The dramatic imperative

A second set of limits on the tolerance of human consciousness are the requirements of dramatic tension. To be endurable, life must be interesting; suspense,

surprise, anticipation are necessary for interest. When
human events exhibit conflict, climax, and resolution,
we call them dramatic; lack of these results in boredom,
a sense of drift, and a loss of tension. When life is
not sufficiently dramatic, the temptation is strong to
make it more so by dressing up the facts. A story is
made interesting by enhancing the danger, drawing out
the suspense, sharpening the denouement. The enemy of
the interesting and the dramatic is the routine, the
uniform, the easily predictable. Soren Kierkegaard
remarked that nothing is more lacking in aesthetic potentiality than eternal blessedness. Equally lacking in
drama are the uniformity, routine, and predictability
characteristic of technology. Indeed, a technological
system is made interesting by its imperfections; by the
fortuitousness of errors - human errors - and the con-
catenation of unforeseen circumstances.

For example, air travel is still an interesting venture
because nobody has as yet been able to foresee all that
can befall a journey on these technological marvels.
Every air traveler has his own store of marvelous stories
of how the unexpected happened, and many such a traveler,
despite hundreds of trips, can hardly believe that his
flight is somewhere on time, that it has made connections
with another flight, and that he is landing without the
captain clearing his throat and announcing that weather,
mechanical trouble, traffic, a strike, or some other
event that had no business happening had in fact happened.
But the fortuitousness of the errors in a technological
system provides better material for farce than for genuine
drama. The latter requires that human striving that makes
sense be blocked by other strivings that make sense, and
that the conflict be resolved in a way that also makes
sense, although it may not always make the kind of sense
one would like. This structure makes life significant.

A moral life is the natural scenario for the drama
that makes life interesting and compelling. The hero and
the villain (moral agents) locked in conflict, the
uncertainty of the outcome, despite the inevitability of
the hero's triumph (real or symbolic), are the standard
materials of drama. If, however, a technological society
makes the very notions of the responsible moral agent and
the conflict between good and evil or between inclination
and duty or between conflicting duties nonsensical, whence
is the dramatic tension of life to come?

Of conflict there is plenty. War, battles between
corporations, struggles between political parties and
between generations have not been eliminated by technology.
The mass media do their best to present endless opportun-

ities to take part vicariously in the drama or the melo-
drama of life. Yet sooner or later each individual must
have some dramatic tension in his own life. The de-
dramatization of life can go only so far before a reaction
sets in.

So powerful is the need for dramatic validity that the
assassination of an important figure such as the late
President Kennedy continues to spawn conspiracy theories
despite the weight of empirical evidence to the contrary.
Dramatically the facts in the Kennedy slaying were simply
all 'wrong'; it would make no sense on the stage to have
such an event attributed to fortuitous or trivial causes.
Hence the effort to find a plot that would give the event
dramatic sense.

The search for dramatic tension takes a multitude of
forms. Some fortunately find it in their daily lives.
For those who do not, climbing mountains, self-imposed
tests of survival in the wilderness, risk-taking, all
create suspense and tension. Other forms are developed
in fantasy: the heroic exploits of Thurber's Walter Mitty,
identification with characters in the movies or in fiction,
and the like. The human imagination's fecundity in producing dramatic potentialities is prodigious. Needless
to say, not all of these ploys are equally successful.
Sometimes the drama ends in farce with fruitless rounds
of frustration taking the place of conflict. The amount
of illusion, sublimation, and fantasy the health of the
individual can stand is not unlimited. The virtues are
the correctives to responses to the dramatic imperative
because they are dispositions to use reason and therewith
the reality principle. The virtues, however, are dispositions of a self and, one might add, of the healthy
self.

The imperative of selfhood

There is also a limit to the amount of fragmentation,
anonymity, and impotence the human consciousness can live
with, although it can take a great deal. There is no need
to recite the innumerable ways that the self is asserted
when it is threatened. Psychiatry is kept busy straight-
ening out the circuitous ploys for self-assertion that men
invent. Sooner or later the self has to be a genuine
center of meaning and be strong enough to sustain its
integrity in the face of the impotence and anonymity that
threaten individuality in a technological society.

What are the criteria of selfhood? At the risk of
repeating some of the points already noted and some to be

discussed below, we can think of three: self-determination, self-realization, and self-integration. Self-determination clearly entails some degree of genuine freedom to initiate action and sufficient power to implement some of these choices. The problematic component of freedom is power, since the desire to be free from restraint and the desire to fulfill one's wishes can be taken for granted. In a technological society the individual's power is a minuscule fraction of the total; how then does one achieve enough power to make the claim to freedom plausible?

By self-realization is meant the process of developing one's potentialities for value realization. This is abstract, to be sure, but the failure to realize potentiality is familiar enough. The person with high scholastic potentiality who cannot go to the university; the person who could do neurosurgery who spends his life sweeping hospital corridors; the list is endless. The importance of self-realization is expressed in the belief that the self is defined by its potentialities; that the true self is what one could be as much, if not more, than what one happens to be. For selfhood, accordingly, some evidence that these potentialities are being actualized is indispensable. This is the sense, perhaps, in which the existentialists have defined the self as 'my project.'

Finally, to be a self is to be a center of meaning. This centrality calls for a unification of diverse forces, impulses, and activities. Self-determination and self-realization can result in action so fragmented, so centrifugal that one effort cancels another. The actions of such a self can become so unpredictable that it is called a self only by courtesy.

HUMANISTIC POTENTIALITIES OF TECHNOLOGICAL SOCIETY

Where in a technological society can the individual – the run of the mill individual – find the power, the freedom, the individuality to render him a morally responsible, socially significant, and aesthetically interesting individual or self?

Impotence, I would conclude, is not a necessary or inevitable consequence of a technological society, provided one realizes that to be effective in many areas of life one must collectivize the efforts of many to move the system.

The knowledge of the workings of a technological system in its industrial, commercial, and political phases constitutes one of the high priorities of schooling. Any curriculum that does not provide for such knowledge and

the rudiments of the skills of participating in collectivized power takes the palm for irrelevance. That all
people should have this knowledge, skill, or the disposition to use them seems to me to be obvious.
The problems of anonymity, facelessness, flatness, can
all be considered as problems of demoralization and depersonalization. Can one remoralize and repersonalize
experience in the face of the pressures to the contrary?
Reference has already been made to the fact that for many
generations, even the moral heroes of those generations,
poverty, slavery, disease had no moral import because
the ability to make significant choices with respect to
them were absent.
Technology changes that, but what can an individual do
about cancer, about war, about poverty and other social
evils? Again, one answer is collectivization of effort.
Research costs lots of money; only large numbers of con-
tributors make a significant difference in the research
effort, and so large numbers must be organized, and each
individual has a choice as to whether to join or not.
And if this is not a grand moral drama watched by a great
crowd, it is perhaps not unheroic for all that. The
decision to contribute a few dollars to a cause, if made
intelligently and with moral reflection, has the same
moral quality as a president making a choice that affects
millions. Indeed, the very absence of public plaudits
may purify the moral quality of the private decision.
Humility suffered anonymously differs from humility
celebrated by a mass media magazine.
As to individuality, selfhood, and dramatic tension,
these too are possible, but perhaps not in their conventional or traditional forms. If by individuality is meant
fame or a marked deviation from the average, then indeed
individuality is out of the reach of most people. For
most persons, the job is hardly conducive to individuality
in the light of what has been said about anonymity,
impotence, etc., and yet to be a distinctive individual
requires no more than to develop one's powers into a
pattern that is authentically chosen by the self. And in
a complex technological society the potential patterns
are virtually limitless in number and variety.
The potentialities of the mature technological society
for a high material standard of living release for even
the assembly-line worker time and resources for non-
vocational pursuits. They also proliferate the opportunities for experience and cultivation in every field of
value: the aesthetic, social, intellectual, recreational,
civic, moral, and religious. Can a life of self-cultivation pursued without fanfare have the dramatic tension

needed for the good life - the life interesting to live
and perhaps to behold? Here a metaphor may have to do
for an answer. A work of art is interesting by virtue of
its form, i.e. by the way it gives a unified feeling or
flavor to a complex of elements. It too sets up conflicts
and resolutions that capture the aesthetic interest.
There is a sense in which the individual by taking advantage of the potentialities of a technological society can
to a considerable extent fashion an interesting instantia-
tion of the characteristics of a work of art.

But the individual needs two ingredients to activate
the actualization of these opportunities. One is the
educational resources for self-cultivation and the other
is the will to undertake such cultivation.

As to education, despite great inequalities, there is
far more opportunity than most young or older persons
seize. The extraordinary importance attached to motivation at every level of schooling in this country - yes,
even at the collegiate level - indicates how far even the
existing opportunities for learning are being evaded.
And the learnings that are being rejected are precisely
the intellectual disciplines that traditionally have been
used for the cultivation of the individual.

It is argued by educationists that these disciplines
are abstract, artificial, academic, and remote from the
natural concerns of the young, and the young agree. They
are right, of course, but they miss the essential point,
viz. that cultivation of the human potentialities of men
has to be an intervention by disciplined thought and
feeling into the flow of untutored thought and feeling.
Commonsense science, commonsense morality, commonsense
art need no explicit, deliberate cultivation; if one
lives in a culture, he is enculturated by its informal
educative inducements. And it should be obvious that a
technological society does provide an extraordinarily
rich ambience for informal education through the opportunities it provides in travel, the mass media, museums,
the films, recordings.

But if individuality is the goal, then clearly mass-
produced ideas, like mass-produced clothes, are not the
means for achieving it. Distinctive individuality
requires the cultivation of a peculiar combination of
talent by the best that has been thought and said and
wrought - by disciplined science, humanities, and the
arts. (11) A life so cultivated will be individualized
and distinctive, but it will also be highly personalized,
moralized, and above all interesting to live and to
behold. The sensitive individual in a technological
culture is subjected to the highest tension once he

becomes aware of the possibilities of self-cultivation
and enters into the dialectic of cultivation in such
a culture.

The dialectic is set up by the fact that self-
cultivation is not mandatory for any individual and
failure to undertake it is not attended by drastic sanctions. On the contrary, if the Devil is still about
today, he is painting a vivid and persuasive picture of
the ease with which one can enjoy a pleasurable life
without self-cultivation. This is the great boon of
technology - that it builds rationality into a system
of mass-production, but it does not require a high order
of rationality to consume it. The good automobile technologically is precisely the one that the operator needs to
know very little about - it is driver proof. So it is
also with mass-produced ideas and opinions - they are
manufactured by persons with great talent, but they mini-
mize the talent and knowledge needed to use them - they
are thinker proof.

And so to be or not to be cultivated is itself a
decision of the deepest and gravest consequence; having
this choice remoralizes life and to that extent dramatizes
it. Technology is not simply and finally destructive of
the humanistic values; but one cannot be a Pollyanna
about outwitting the facelessness, the anonymity, the
depersonalization that are inherent in it. About the best
that can be promised is that freedom, individuality, and
a truly human life can be wrested from it.

NOTES

1 The literature on this aspect of the topic is extensive. For example, see 'Planning for Effective Utilization of Technology in Education', ed. L. Morphet
   and D. Jesser (New York: Citation, 1968) as well as
   many articles in 'Educational Technology.'
2 To mention a few: Kurt Baier and Nicholas Rescher
   (eds), 'Values and the Future: The Impact of Technological Change on American Values' (New York: Free
   Press, 1969); Jacques Ellul, 'The Technological
   Society' (New York: Knopf, 1967); Lewis Mumford,
   'Technics and Civilization' (New York: Harcourt Brace,
   1963); Theodore Roszak, 'Where The Waste Land Ends'
   (Garden City, New York: Doubleday, 1969).
3 R.D. Laing, 'The Politics of Experience' (Harmonds-
   worth: Penguin, 1967).
4 Industry, notably in Sweden, is trying to mitigate
   these effects. Kockum's shipyard in Malmo is offering

'work enrichment' by putting some variety and responsibility into tedious production jobs. The Volvo plant
at Kalmar has replaced the conventional assembly line
by groups of workers who assemble a whole auto rather
than repeat a single operation as an auto moves along
the production line. See Bowen Northrup, 'The Wall
Street Journal,' October 25, 1974.

5 Obviously, if a number of simultaneous causal chains
are involved, and if some items or their effects
interact, the search for responsible agents becomes
even more difficult, because we are now involved with
coincidences and unintended effects.

6 An excellent discussion of this topic is found in
Abraham Edel, Knowledge and Responsibility, a paper
presented at the Conference on The Uses of Knowledge,
Urbana, Illinois, 1974.

7 Cf. Peter A. Bertocci and Richard M. Millard,
'Personality and the Good' (New York: David McKay,
1963).

8 Judging each act separately can serve to trivialize
responsibility to the point of farce. For example,
a traveler who has been bumped from a flight on which
he had confirmed reservations rages at the ticket
counter that his mother will die before he can reach
her bedside or that he will lose an important contract.
Whereupon he is arrested for disorderly conduct.

9 This tendency to reverse itself has been called
dialectical thinking or thinking by opposites, and it
is featured in Hegel's dialectic and its economic
derivative in Karl Marx. For Hegel, thought necessarily moves from thesis to antithesis, from self to
other; for Marx, economic activity necessarily creates
conflict between the classes, so that each form of
production (slavery, capitalism, etc.) in time produces its own enemy and the seed of its own destruction. Whether these theories are true I cannot say,
but thought does change its focus and direction for
many reasons. One is that an idea is not limited to a
particular frame of meaning, and once imagination
starts running with an idea such as blood, there is
no telling where it will go. Life, war, death, fire
all have aesthetic meanings for blood. Another is
that the demands of selfhood impose limits to what
thought it will tolerate, so that, for example, we
allow ourselves to be manipulated so long as we don't
know that we are being manipulated, and then resentment against being manipulated sets in.

10 One can imagine cultures that place differential
premiums on the several virtues. Seafaring cultures,

for example, place great value on courage. A tropical
paradise places less emphasis on temperance and the
duties of work. But if one could imagine a 'society'
in which all the virtues were irrelevant, the inhabitants would, because they were human, create dis-
crepancies between inclination and duty (as did Adam
and Eve) or they would experience no such discrepancy
and therefore be reckoned among animals or the angels.

11   The standard liberal studies are disciplines in this
sense, but there may be other ways of inducting a
generation into the best that has been thought, said,
and wrought.

Career education and the pathologies of work   11

Thomas F. Green

I SOME USEFUL DISTINCTIONS

Pathology is the science of disease. It is concerned with
the causes of disorders and their effects. The concept
of pathology has no meaning except in relation to some
understanding of healthfulness, wholesomeness, and normality. To speak of the pathologies of work is, therefore,
to speak of the diseases, the disorders, or the unhealthy
conditions to which work itself is subject. And that, in
turn, presupposes that there is such a thing as the
healthiness, wholesomeness, and normality of work.

The idea that there are pathologies of work is also a
normative idea. It does not simply describe a state of
affairs. Rather, it describes someone's idea of a good
state of affairs. When we say that a certain condition
of the liver is pathological, we imply that we know that
that state is not normal, healthy, or wholesome. It is
not good. And that implies that we have some idea of what
is good, normal, healthy. Thus, anything described as a
pathology of work will have, on its other side, someone's
notion of what is healthy, normal, wholesome about work,
or what is healthy, normal, and wholesome about the role
of work in a given society.

We are unlikely to get much detailed agreement on what
constitutes a good society, nor are we likely to get much
agreement on what constitutes career education. It may
seem impossible then to develop any persuasive view of
the relation between career education and the pathologies
of work, and still less possible to explore what curative
effects we may reasonably expect from career education.

The prospect is not hopeless, however. We can take a
different approach altogether. Whenever we speak of
pathology, we must always be prepared to speak of the
pathology of something or other. And we must always be

211

able to answer what that something or other is. And so
no matter what we may identify in detail as the pathologies of work, we must be prepared to explain whether we
are referring to a pathology of jobs, of the employment
system, of the separation in some society of work from
the rest of life, and innumerable other things. It is
worth noting that there may be some things that could be
described as pathological that arise from the very nature
of the human condition itself. That is to say, there may
be some hopes, aspirations, expectations that men seek to
attain through work which by their very nature will remain
unsatisfied. In that case, it would make sense to suggest
that some of the pathologies of work are in fact pathologies of man himself. If there are such pathologies,
it is unlikely that career education, or for that matter
any kind of education, will do much to change them. I do
not suggest this possibility because I believe it is true,
but only to point out that in order to examine the relation between career education and the pathologies of work,
and in order to speak realistically of what we may expect
from career education, some elementary distinctions will
be useful.

But what kinds of distinctions? There are important
differences to be understood between (i) work and labor,
and (ii) between work, job, vocations and careers. The
mere making of these distinctions will help to separate an
and arrange a great many issues that arise from career
education and the pathologies of work.

Work and labor

The term 'work' is ambiguous in a way that the term
'labor' is not. By 'work' we may refer either to an
activity itself or to the finished 'thing' that results
from that activity. The word is either a verb or a noun.
We refer either to 'work' or to 'a work.' Indeed, what
is essential to the concept of work itself is the connection between these two elements - the activity, and the
product or result of that activity. Indeed, if you try
to imagine a world totally without work, what you will
have to imagine is a world without one or the other or
both of these two elements - the activity and some durable
result of that activity. You would have to imagine either
(a) a world in which there is an expenditure of energy but
no resulting works, or (b) a world in which all the works
of men are present, but without any expenditure of energy,
i.e. without them being the works of men.

There is no need to elaborate extensively on these

suppositions. But there are some important points in
them that need to be made explicit. The second supposition is really the idea of an immensely benign form of
nature. We are asked to imagine a world in which the
paintings, houses, tools, and utensils that are the works
of men are present, but not as a result of any human
effort. They are simply there, just as the plains, mountains, and streams are there. Food is prepared and the
table is set, but nobody prepares it or sets it. Indeed,
nobody makes the table. Under these conditions it is
doubtful that the very idea of civilization itself would
remain unchanged, for the very idea of civilization
requires not simply that there be artifacts, but that
those artifacts be the consequence of human effort. The
concept of work itself, like the concept of civilization,
requires that there be effort and that there be some
durable result that is the consequence and end of that
effort.

If the second supposition is really the conception of
a benign form of nature, then the first supposition is
the conception of a particularly self-defeating form of
nature; for in the first supposition we are asked to
imagine a world in which there is the expenditure of human
energy to produce some works, but the failure to do so.
The house dissolves, perhaps, as fast as it is constructed.
No work can endure long enough to be completed. That is a
world in which man is impotent, a world in which his
energy is expended in futility.

This idea that human energy might be spent without any
result in some durable work is the idea that defines the
concept of labor. Labor is that kind of activity that
never ends because it cannot result in any durable work
itself. There are lots of activities like that. The
table is set only in order to be undone. The ancients
accepted slavery not because they disliked work, but
because they recognized that there are certain activities
that answer to the fact that man is an animal rather than
to the fact that he might be human. Those were the
activities of labor. They were activities essentially
slavish, in the sense that they were endless, futile, and
yet necessary. They corresponded not to the fact that man
is a social, political, religious, or artistic creature,
but to the fact that he is a biological creature. Thus,
to be freed to do works, one must be freed from labor.

There is no need to accept the distinction as I have
drawn it, but there is every need to understand the
difference that the distinction is intended to illuminate.
It is the difference between human potency and human
futility. We all recognize the pathos of the life spent

in accomplishing some great work only to see it vanish in
an hour of disaster. And that pathos is easily translated
into moral offense when we see people who, through no
fault of their own, are rendered impotent. Work, it can
be said, is man's refusal to acknowledge that his life is
futile, pointless, and without effect, that one's energies
have been expended without avail.... That is a condition
against which men have always shouted in defiance. It may
almost be taken as the definition of man that he is, among
all creatures, the one who demands most to escape from
labor into work.

The first and most serious pathologies of work, therefore, are all those that stem from the tendency to transform work into labor. There are many of them. I shall
discuss some in more detail later. But the principle can
be seen in the following points. When it happens that
things that were made to be used are now made only to be
used up, then it also happens that, in some degree, energy
that was expended to produce a work is now expended without that result. That is the transformation of work into
labor. The object of the work is converted from a use
object to a consumer object with all the transitoriness
and tentativeness that that implies. The result phenomen-
ologically can be the difference between work and labor.
Or again, it sometimes happens in the excessive rationalization of work-tasks that the expenditure of energy in
the task is so far removed from any resultant object that
it can be understood only as an act of labor. We often
overlook this fact because when we describe a work-task,
we usually make the connection between the effort and its
object. Instead of describing the task as 'Plugging this
thing into this device and reading the dial,' we describe
the task as 'testing circuit components.' Or instead of
saying, 'I want you to push pieces of paper like this into
this slot,' we say, 'I would like you to sort the mail to
each of the different departments.' But clearly the
principle involved in this kind of description of work-
tasks is our acknowledgment that in many contexts the
tasks to be performed have no clear or visible relation to
their purpose or aim in some stable or durable result.
That is to say, the tasks resemble labor more than they do
work. We find it necessary to give the activity some
connection to its object in order to describe it as work.
Without that connection many activities required in the
job structure of the society would be recognized for what
they are, namely absurd activities for anyone to perform
when considered simply by themselves. Finally, we might
observe that work gets transformed into labor when the
specific tasks required in a particular work position do

not require the exercise of any human capacities such as
intelligence, judgment, or a sense of craft.

Work, job, vocation and career

There are two fundamentally contrasting ways to understand
the idea of a career; and there is an enormous difference
between them. But no matter which view you wish to take,
these days, the idea that everyone, or even most people,
should have a career, is likely to strike many people as
an excessively grandiose, and unnecessarily serious and
heroic, view of life. But in order to understand such a
point of view, it is useful to have some appreciation as
to how the ideas of jobs, careers, and vocations have
developed historically.
    A detailed exposition of the tortuous change of these
ideas is unnecessary. Essentially, what happened was
something like this. Originally - that is to say, before
the Protestant Reformation - the idea of vocation meant
simply 'calling.' And there was essentially only one
kind of calling, the religious calling of the clergy and
especially the regular clergy. There was no question of
one being 'called' to be a shoemaker, a tavern-keeper, or
even to the lofty post of jurist. The ordinary jobs of
the 'common life' or even the lofty positions of leader-
ship could not be described as 'callings' or 'vocations.'
They were simply jobs. They were the ways - and there
were many ways - that people tried to make a living.
    Luther, however, began to bring these ideas together,
in a way that wrought a social revolution. We are still
living with the consequences of that revolution. Our
conceptions of career education are strongly shaped by it.
What Luther did was to extend the idea of 'calling' or
'vocation' to include the ordinary jobs or roles that
ordinary people filled in the fabric of society. Thus,
it became possible to speak of the roles of tavern-keeper,
maid, housewife, teacher, lawyer, and so forth, as vocations. That is to say, they became callings. The idea
was still that the central vocation of every Christian
was to be the 'bearer of love and of service to neighbor.'
But the way in which one was to do that was through his
particular job or position. One was not to discharge his
vocation as a Christian by escaping from the world in
monastic retreat, nor by long pilgrimages, but in the
particular station where he found himself.
    The Christian should 'carry out his "calling" within
the "calling" wherein he was "called."' That is a fair
rendering of what St Paul wrote. The word he used was

klēsis, which is the Greek term for God's calling of men
to fellowship with him and to love and service of neighbor.
It had nothing to do with jobs or with the way people
make their living. But I imagine that when Luther read
St Paul and came to the second rendering of the word
'calling,' in this passage, he probably read the word that
means religious calling, thought the Latin word 'status'
and wrote the German word 'Stand.' Thus, he came to the
idea that, 'The Christian should carry out his calling
within the job (or position or role) within which he
received his calling.' From the idea that one's job is
the place where one carries out his calling, it is only a
small step to the view that carrying out one's job is his
calling. Thus, the idea of a job came to be transformed
from merely a way of making a living and came to be
infused with all the power of a religious duty. It came
to have almost cosmic significance. In fact, it came to
be the way that a person identifies who he is.

So jobs got transformed from the idea of a mere economic role into the context for the performance of some
useful religious service to neighbor, and they came to
bear the heavy psychological freight of having to be the
expression of one's self-identity. The usual account of
Luther's contribution to our ideas on work and vocation is
to say that he transformed the status of an ordinary job
by infusing it with the religious idea of vocation. That
is correct. But the more important part of his thought
was that, for the first time, Luther tended to identify
the idea of a man's work with his job. He transformed the
idea of making a living into a religious work.

This identification of work and job has been enormously
powerful and beneficial in many societies. The association of jobs with the performance of a religious duty has
done much to raise the standards of craftsmanship and to
increase the social expectation that jobs performed will
be performed well. But this association of work and job
has also been the source of a great deal of intellectual
and practical mischief. Indeed, it is from the association of these two ideas that the second great class of
pathologies can be seen to flow.

I shall mention only three of them by way of illustration. It is often suggested that by extending the idea
of 'vocation' to the 'callings of the common life,' work
received a kind of dignity that it had never had before,
and that is an important asset in the development of
modern industrial societies. But with that asset comes a
liability. The fact is that it is never work itself that
has dignity. It is always the worker. To confuse the
two is what makes it possible for a society to insist that

however demeaning a man's job may be, nonetheless, he
should somehow manage to find great dignity in its performance. And that result leads immediately to a second
kind of pathology.

The idea that there is dignity in work itself, together
with the idea that a man should find his work in his job,
leads inevitably to the notion that the worker should find
his dignity in his job. It leads to the notion that somehow one's own self-identity is to be displayed, discovered,
and made public to others in the performance of his job.
This is the association of ideas and dispositions that
leads us to identify who a person is with what kind of
job he holds. For example, in the contemporary practices
of education we ask a youngster, in effect, 'What do you
intend to be when you grow up?' rather than 'How do you
expect to make your living?' This educational approach is
not only dysfunctional but positively cruel in a society
where many jobs that need doing cannot possibly provide a
sense of self-identity or a central life interest. There
is abundant evidence that in the USA today many jobs -
perhaps most jobs, including even some professional positions - do not provide people either with an adequate
sense of self-identity or any satisfactory central life
interest. The result is often described as a kind of
'alienation from work.' It would be more adequately described as alienation from jobs or from the institutions
of employment. What is clearly happening is that people
are finding it increasingly necessary to separate their
job life from the rest of their lives. They are tending
to find their work - if they have one - but certainly
their life interests and their sense of self-identity in
some arena of activity away from their place of employment
or their jobs.

The psychological and moral 'fall-out' from this
historic association of work and job has also lead to some
distressing educational conceptions and practices. In a
world where a man's job is the vehicle for self-identity
and self-expression, it follows that jobs will have to
receive some social and moral justification. That is to
say, we shall have to find a way - to take an extreme
example - of demonstrating that the real justification for
the job of installing telephones is that it is an important way of 'connecting people.' It is not enough merely
to say that it is a decent way to make a living. One has
to say that it is a socially and morally needed activity.
If the personal justification of the man is to be found in
the justification of the job, then that job must be justifiable by its social and moral significance and not merely
as a way of earning a living. It becomes unacceptable for

a person to justify taking a certain job simply on the grounds that he is good at it and that it returns enough income to do other things away from the job. Instead, he has to find some rationalization for taking the job on the grounds that it is good in itself. Under these conditions, part of the educational task necessarily is to teach people how to give acceptable moral and social justifications for pursuing quite self-seeking ends.

What may well be needed in the modern world of work, and therefore in modern education, is the observance in thought and practice of a clear distinction between work and job. It is true that in the modern world increasing numbers of people are not able to find any kind of central life interest or life work in their jobs. But if we begin to recognize this fact, and to observe it in educational practice, we will also begin to see the difference between asking a child 'What do you expect to be your life work?' and 'How do you expect to earn a living?' The first question is really the basic issue in education for work. The second is the fundamental question in education for entry into the employment system. They are not the same questions. They do not require the same educational strategies or the same educational programs. Their differences are reflected in the contrast between the questions 'What are you going to be?' and 'What are you going to do for income?'

This last point leads immediately to a third distinction, the contrast not between vocations and jobs or between work and jobs, but between careers and jobs. We must recognize that having a life work is a very different thing from having a particular job. There is an enormous difference between the man who sees his life in prospect as involved in the accomplishment of some work, and the man who sees his life in retrospect as a mere succession of jobs that he has held. Only the first, in the strict sense, has what can be called a career. The difference is between the man who sees his career defined by the jobs he has held, as opposed to the man who engages in a succession of jobs because they contribute to his career. having a career is a very different thing from having employment, even steady employment, or even steady employment over a lifetime. Indeed, there is no necessary reason why anyone should find his career in or through his mode of employment at all. Career education should never be confused with vocational education insofar as that kind of education is directed toward training for jobs or for employment. Careers, most certainly, will not develop without employment; but neither should education for careers ever be confused with education for

employment. They are, therefore, two educational tasks
that need to be distinguished - education for work or
careers, and education for jobs or employment.

II   CAREER EDUCATION AND THE PATHOLOGIES OF WORK

The pathologies identified so far are not, in fact, pathologies of work. Nor are they pathologies of career
education. They are the pathologies that are likely to
arise in a changing society in which the place or work-
life is no longer clear, and the traditional ideologies
used to explain the place of jobs and employment no longer
command belief. These are the pathologies of the employment structure and of the institutions of employment in
modern societies. If we ask to what extent the development of career education can reasonably be expected to
change the conditions that lead to such pathological
states, the answer must be that we cannot expect very
much.
    The reasons for this judgment can be enumerated simply.
In the first place, education has never proved to be a very
useful policy instrument for the transformation of basic
social institutions. One reason is that its effects are
too indirect and too long in appearing for it to be a very
effective force in changing basic institutions over the
short- and middle-range periods within which educational
policy is likely to be framed and sustained. Second, that
the structure of the employment system will influence the
ways that work and jobs are presented in the process of
education, is always more likely than that the educational
system will influence the behavior of the employment
system. Thus, if the significant pathologies of work have
their roots in the employment system itself, we ought not
to expect renewed focus on career education to make very
significant differences in the basic employment.
    There is a final precaution. Much of the current
literature on career education appears to stress the need
to combat widespread alienation from work. I suspect
that this emphasis is fundamentally misplaced. As far as
I know, there is little evidence of any basic alienation
from work in American society. On the other hand, as I
tried to explain earlier in this paper there is strong
evidence of growth in alienation from the institutions of
work, or from the ways that jobs are structured and organized. There is alienation from the employment system.
Furthermore, I have tried to explain why that alienation
is often justified and why it is not likely to be reduced,
let alone reversed, by anything that the educational
system does in the way of career education.

My own judgment is that the movement of career education is an important one. It is potentially of enormous
benefit both to American education and its capacity to
equip people to lead wholesome and happy lives, if not
actually useful lives. But unless those engaged in the
enterprise learn to make some distinctions of the kinds
that I have tried to outline, they will promise too much.
But more importantly, unless they learn to do so, the
literature on the subject as well as the practice, I fear,
will continue to sound like a pleading to make the educational system a special department of the United States
Chamber of Commerce. (See, for example, Hoyt, Evans,
Mackin and Mangin, 'Career Education: What It Is and How
To Do It', Olympus Publishing, 1972.) That is a movement
which, besides being unlikely, is undesirable.

The point can be pressed. One of the developments in
contemporary education is the expansion of what has been
called 'mastery learning.' Mastery learning is based
upon the assumption that anyone can learn what anybody
else can learn, only it may take some a longer time to do
it. Thus, what should become the variable in instruction
is not the level of mastery attained by anyone, but the
amount of time it takes to reach a satisfactory level of
mastery. All programmed learning and all forms of individualization of instruction are based upon the principles of mastery learning. It is easy to see also that
nearly all employment settings involve the same principles. But imagine what it would be like to work in a
situation in which one has mastered the lesson to be
learned and the lesson leads to no subsequent lesson. One
is simply asked to learn the same thing over and over and
over. The result would have to be a sustained, seething,
feirce, anger. Yet, the fact is that an enormous number
of blue-collar positions, and even positions within the
service occupations, are of precisely that sort. They
lead to no subsequent lesson. They are dead-end jobs.
Under such circumstances, the alienation from work is
really alienation from the job, and it is justified.

There are only two possible answers to such a problem.
On the one hand, one might quit trying to overcome the
alienation from such jobs, and quit trying to give them
some moral and social justification, and begin trying to
assemble the social resources to help people find creative
ways (which usually means inefficient ways) of using their
abilities away from the job. The other way is to attend
to the hidden curriculum of the job structure itself in
an effort to see that there are no jobs that have the
character of a total mastery setting leading to no subsequent lesson. This would mean, of course, that the

structure of employment institutions would then have to
be examined in the light of their educational potential
as a setting for human learning and development.
Neither of these attacks on the pathologies of work is
likely to be carried out by the schools. The latter
especially means that the greatest arena for career
education is not in the schools but in the employment
offices and executive planning offices of major employer
institutions. There are some recent developments that
point in the direction of both tactics at once. In
Germany, and more recently in the USA, employers have been
experimenting with different versions of the work calendar.
In Germany especially, one of the more interesting developments is the re-introduction of the time clock for all
classes of employees, asking only that they complete a
total of forty hours of work in a week in any sequence
they wish between seven in the morning and seven at night
provided that they are all present during the 'core hours'
of ten in the morning to two in the afternoon. The experiment has been remarkably successful. The amount of
sick leave has dropped, productivity and job satisfaction
have increased. People can now arrange their time as they
wish, and they have learned to do so. They can work early
in the morning or late at night, which permits them to
arrange the employment of their creative powers in other
ways away from the job. Job alienation thus has decreased
because it does not need to take the 'prime' hours of the
day, and the sense of dignity is enhanced because it encourages the use of human capacities for judgment and
decision. Some real pathologies of work are being confronted in this experiment.
     Many observers have attributed the so-called Japanese
'economic miracle' to the intense (almost familial) cor-
porate loyalty that the major employers have instilled.
The result is that transfer between companies in the past
was regarded as a signal sign of disloyalty and a definite
bar to promotion. Moreover, the amount of overtime in
Japanese concerns has been among the highest in the world.
Both of these features are now changing dramatically. The
number of transfers between companies is increasing so
rapidly that it is no longer seen as a bar to promotion,
but as an instrument of education. Thus, the hierarchical
structure of the employment system is being severely
tested. Second, it is increasingly the case that when
Japanese workers are confronted with the choice of more
overtime or more time away from the job to 'do their own
thing,' they choose the latter. They now choose it so
often, in fact, that some companies have had to place
limits on the amount of overtime that any employee can
accumulate.

These are evidences that in perhaps the two most 'work-oriented' societies of the world many of the pathologies of work are being met in ways compatible with the set of distinctions outlined in the beginning of this paper. They constitute new approaches to defining the place of work in modern life, and in significant aspects they constitute a departure from the 'work ethic' that has produced those pathologies of work. In neither case, however, are these attempts to deal with the pathologies of work carried on in, by, or through the system of education. In each case, they implicitly acknowledge, however, the educational components that are discoverable within the ways that the employment system is structured. They constitute the most direct and effective attack on the pathologies of work that I know of.

No scheme for education in any society can be regarded as successful if it fails to prepare the young to take authentic and responsible roles within adult society. It might be argued then that preparation for work must receive central attention in any satisfactory arrangements for education in any society. Thus, in a society in which work is a predominant aspect of most adult roles, it follows that the process of education must pay serious attention to preparation for work. Indeed, it would seem a shaky conclusion to suggest that that essential educational task should not be carried out in some central way by the system of schools itself. But how should this be done to pay some serious attention to the pathologies of work?

The Yugoslavian experience suggests that the central issue is how to organize the schools themselves so that no matter what content they convey they do it through a process and a system of social organization that simulates the ways that work roles are organized. That should be an old idea to Americans whose schools have been modeled, timed, evaluated, and manned in the way that we man the industrial enterprise. But for career education in the new day, it means a vastly more flexible schedule of school operation, the teaching of management skills in reaching educational objectives, a stress of cooperative rather than competitive activities, the presentation of a greater variety of occupational roles for emulation, and a quicker and easier access to enter employment and return to the educational system. These it seems to me are the essential demands that career education places on the organization and conduct of schools. But I see very little of them being expressed either in the plans, policies, or programs of the movement.

Index

223